"Schweitzer presents a unique perspective on the recent history and future prospects of the ISTC and the reasons for its decline as far as the Russian Federation is concerned. He has had unparalleled access to decision makers and administrators who impacted the ISTC throughout its history. I recommend this book to serious students of nonproliferation and to those who closely follow all aspects of U.S.-Russian relations."

—STEVEN GITOMER, *Senior Science Advisor to the U.S. Department of State for Science Centers in Russia and Ukraine*

STUDIES IN SECURITY AND INTERNATIONAL AFFAIRS

CONTAINING RUSSIA'S NUCLEAR FIREBIRDS

Harmony and Change at the

International Science and

Technology Center

Glenn E. Schweitzer

The University of Georgia Press
Athens and London

© 2013 by the University of Georgia Press
Athens, Georgia 30602
www.ugapress.org
All rights reserved
Set in 10/14 Minion Pro by Graphic Composition, Inc.
Manufactured by Thomson-Shore
The paper in this book meets the guidelines for
permanence and durability of the Committee on
Production Guidelines for Book Longevity of the
Council on Library Resources.

Printed in the United States of America

16 15 14 13 12   P   5 4 3 2 1

Library of Congress Cataloging-in-Publication Data
Schweitzer, Glenn E., 1930–
    Containing Russia's nuclear firebirds : harmony and change at the
International Science and Technology Center / Glenn E. Schweitzer.
        p. cm. — (Studies in security and international affairs)
        Includes bibliographical references and index.
    ISBN-13: 978-0-8203-3869-9 (hardback)
    ISBN-10: 0-8203-3869-9 (hardcover)
    ISBN-13: 978-0-8203-4434-8 (paperback)
    1. Nuclear nonproliferation—International cooperation.
    2. Nuclear nonproliferation—Former Soviet republics.
    3. International Science and Technology Center.   I. Title.
JZ5675.S42 2013
327.1'7470947—dc23   2012022222

British Library Cataloging-in-Publication Data available

CONTENTS

PREFACE

Every night there came flying into the garden a bird that shone like the moon, with feathers like gold and its eyes like crystal which perched on the apple tree, plucked a golden apple, and flew away.
—"Tsarevitch Ivan, the Firebird, and the Gray Wolf"

"The Russian Government informs you of its intention to terminate the provisional application of the agreement on the International Science and Technology Center and withdraw from the associated protocol."

So read part of a diplomatic note addressed to the executive director of the International Science and Technology Center (ISTC) announcing Russia's withdrawal from the center. A Russian colleague forwarded the note to me in mid-July 2011. I had spent twenty-seven months in Moscow in the early 1990s leading the on-the-ground effort of the governments of the United States, the then European Economic Community, Japan, and Russia to establish a center that would help curtail a brain drain of Russian weapons expertise. Thus, I had some difficulty witnessing the demise of the institution we had created from scratch—an institution that would help save the world from a nuclear catastrophe, so we thought.

In 1994 I became the first executive director of the ISTC and took pride in the early stage of its development. Now the sixth executive director has the less glamorous, but equally important, task of dismantling the headquarters in central Moscow and arranging for the exodus of the Russian government from the organization. The center's activities will continue in other member states that emerged after the splintering of the Soviet Union. But the ISTC will never be the same without participation of the country that has been the primary focus of attention throughout the center's history.

The news came as no surprise. One year earlier, President Dimitry Medvedev had signed a decree announcing Russia's intention to withdraw, but it did not specify the withdrawal date. Several years earlier during my trips to

Moscow, I had heard rumblings about such a forthcoming development. Russian officials contended that the ISTC had accomplished its mission and the country no longer needed "foreign assistance programs" that penetrated the country's national security establishment. The center had devoted about one billion dollars to support redirection of underemployed weapon scientists to civilian tasks in Russia during difficult economic days; but Russia had recovered, and the period of redirection was over, they underscored.

Nevertheless, I could not help but think that Russia's withdrawal from the ISTC would reawaken dormant concerns in Washington and other capitals over potential leakage to irresponsible governments and hostile groups of Russia's nuclear secrets and of the insights of its scientists concerning the fabric of other closely guarded technological achievements. Surely, Russia's departure would disappoint thousands of Russian scientists who longed for a continuing association with the center. Also, Russia's separation from the international scientific networks that the ISTC had established would have a negative impact on the nation's science capabilities that were just beginning to rebound after decades of isolation and stagnation.

Russia's withdrawal will signal the end of the first phase of an amazing experiment. This international effort has helped avoid a massive brain drain of nuclear scientists, chemists, aerospace engineers, and biotechnology pioneers while increasing the difficulty of illicit access by desperate individuals and foreign agents to bomb-making expertise and materials that abound in the world's largest country. Let us hope that a second equally promising experiment with similar goals will soon begin.

ECHOING A RUSSIAN LEGEND

When I received the copy of the formal notification of Russia's forthcoming withdrawal, I was reminded of a popular Russian legend, *The Firebird*. As the story goes, a clever firebird escapes its cage and in the dark of night slips into the grounds of a wealthy prince to steal precious golden apples. In a story rife with intrigue, mistaken identities, and a touch of magic, the firebird is ultimately returned to its cage, and the thefts of valuable treasures come to an end.

After seventeen years of witnessing ISTC projects in action, I am convinced that we have held at bay many potential nuclear firebirds nesting throughout Russia that could collect and sell weapons expertise in the dark of night. We surrounded Russian scientists not with cages but with incentives—money, respect, and new opportunities in their laboratories. In exchange, they focused on scientific and economic advancement of their country.

Thus, the rewards that these cash-strapped scientists received from participating in the new program trumped temptations to trade secrets for cash with unsavory characters. The scientists had new opportunities to enjoy success in the laboratory that benefited the people, while supplementing their own declining paychecks.

A UNIQUE SOLUTION EMERGES

My earlier book, *Moscow DMZ: The Story of the International Effort to Convert Russian Weapons Science to Peaceful Purposes* (M. E. Sharpe, 1996), discusses in detail the events leading up to the establishment of the ISTC. It describes the legal and technical foundations for launching the unique institution in 1994. And it sets the scene for reviewing operations of the center.

This new book assesses the most important activities of the ISTC from that time forward. By 2011 the center had become the mechanism for facilitating foreign investments of more than $1.3 billion in activities involving scientists of seven new independent states. The center had supported more than 2,740 projects. Nearly one hundred thousand scientists from these seven new states and from the ISTC's other member countries participated in these projects and related activities. A large percentage of participants have been former weapons scientists living in Russia. Substantial political will and personal commitments have characterized the collaborative efforts of the thirty-nine governments that have become part of the ISTC family—including the twenty-seven member governments of the European Union and the governments of Russia, the United States, Japan, Norway, Canada, Korea, Georgia, Belarus, Armenia, Kazakhstan, Kyrgyzstan, and Tajikistan.

How good an investment in Russia has this been? What lessons might be applied to future challenges in Russia and in other countries in the future? These questions are the central issues addressed in this book.

DOCUMENTING OUTCOMES

After finishing my tenure as the ISTC executive director in 1994, I avoided second-guessing the policies or operational activities of the center. At the same time, however, I maintained an interest in the outcomes of the center's programs that were often reflected in reports from Moscow that found their way to my desk in Washington. I occasionally visited the headquarters of the ISTC during my travel to Russia, as I became involved in many nonproliferation and scientific exchange projects related to the activities of the center. In short, I became an interested but not a meddling observer.

In the summer of 2010 when I initially heard the news about the winding down of the center's activities in Russia, I decided to document the history of the ISTC, lest the lessons learned simply be buried in long-term storage bins. I traveled to Moscow not only to review past achievements of the center but also to discuss the impending Russian withdrawal that would close the doors on all activities based in Russia, including operations of the ISTC Secretariat in Moscow. At the same time, the ISTC parties were discussing new diplomatic arrangements to continue support of the center's programs in the six other states in the region that had been accorded membership in the ISTC.

During this visit, a number of Russian and international specialists who had been deeply involved with the ISTC for many years were eager to discuss its record. Each had a somewhat different view of the basis for the Russian decision for withdrawal. At the same time, all my Russian colleagues, even those who had not been involved in projects financed through the ISTC, were complimentary of the center's accomplishments. A recurring theme was that the center gave highly talented Russian scientists a second chance in the laboratories. This opportunity was particularly important for those scientists who were ready to abandon their research careers for more profitable business endeavors, including deal making involving the international diffusion of dual-use technologies.

Many scientists were heralding ISTC's accomplishments in the scientific realm as a justification for continuing the activities of the center in Russia. They claimed that only minor modifications of the existing international agreement were necessary for continuation in a manner that would satisfy concerns of the Russian government. But the ISTC's primary mission from the outset was to reduce the likelihood of weapons proliferation and only secondarily to contribute to international efforts that address global issues such as energy, environmental, and health problems. It simply was too much of a stretch from the original intent and from the specific provisions of the ISTC Agreement to persuasively advocate scientific achievements as the primary reason to sustain the center's operations.

This book expands on the debate on this subject. But the bottom line is that the ISTC will close its doors in Russia in 2015. By capturing details of events up to the final years of the Moscow science center—making the book a matching bookend to *Moscow DMZ*—I present facts, analyses, and conclusions that should be useful for the international community in containing future firebirds, whether they be in the form of nuclear darts or other worldwide threats.

INSIGHTFUL INPUTS FROM COLLEAGUES

The ISTC has been a successful and effective venture. Of course there have been missed opportunities, questionable policies, and many bumps in the road. These shortcomings are noted throughout the book.

Most important, the objective of the center has often been misinterpreted as "prevention" of proliferation. Preventing proliferation involves establishing regulations, enforcing security requirements, and policing the activities of individuals with access to classified information. Such activities have not been part of the center's mandate, which has been directed to reducing incentives for scientists to engage in illicit activities. Only the concerned government, and with regard to this book the Russian government, has the capability to focus on the entire range of factors that impinge on prevention of proliferation. Despite the limited mandate of the center, the consensus of both insiders and observers is that the ISTC experiment has returned good value for the investment. It has significantly reduced the likelihood of proliferation by redirecting underemployed weapon scientists to civilian tasks.

I am fortunate in having an opportunity to tell a portion of the story of this success. I am profoundly grateful to colleagues from many countries who have shared with me their perspectives as to the accomplishments of the ISTC and why they have been proud to have contributed to its activities. They can rightly claim personal ownership of achievements of the center in reducing the threat of proliferation of dangerous weapons expertise during a time of chaos and recovery in the region—the period from 1992 to 2011. They are the ones who have made this book possible.

I owe a special debt of appreciation to the members of the ISTC staff who were in place during 2010 and 2011, and particularly to Executive Director Adriaan van der Meer. They were helpful to me in many ways as I pieced together this manuscript. They unhesitatingly responded to my requests for documents and for their personal views concerning the activities of the center since its earliest days. Also, they directed me to other knowledgeable specialists, both to obtain additional views and to continue my fact-checking of the information that has been incorporated into this text.

When the University of Georgia Press agreed to publish the book, I knew I had an important partner in this undertaking. For many years, specialists at the university have followed closely the developments in the new independent states. In recent years, they have extended their interests in nonproliferation to other continents. Their insights have improved a manuscript that covers a wide range of topics. And Jane Curran added a skilled copy editor's polish to the manuscript.

In response to my request, my daughter Diane Leigh Schweitzer took time off from her successful career as a business consultant to point out inconsistencies, confusion, and redundancy in the original manuscript. She sharpened the focus of each chapter. She forced me to be straightforward in my personal views on the courses followed by the center over the years. "No time for weasel words," she argued.

Finally, as has been the case with my previous books, my wife, Carole Dorsch Schweitzer, continued to devote her energy and extend her patience to a spouse totally consumed with book writing for more than a year. Again, she used the magic pencil of a professional substantive editor to help transform a muddled draft manuscript into a readable document. Having shared many of my personal experiences involving Russia, she greatly improved the bottom lines that permeate the entire book.

Wintergreen, Virginia, January 2012

SIGNIFICANT EVENTS IN THE HISTORY OF THE ISTC

1992

- January: Tripartite statement by Andrei Kozyrev (Russia), Hans-Dietrich Genscher (Germany), and James Baker (United States) calling for establishment of ISTC; initiation of negotiation of ISTC Agreement.
- July: Arrival of international planning group for ISTC at facilities on Luganskaya Street, Moscow.
- November: Initialing of ISTC Agreement by United States, Russia, European Atomic Energy Community/European Economic Community, and Japan.

1993

- January: Establishment of Preparatory Committee for ISTC.
- December: Acceptance by four parties of Protocol on Provisional Application of ISTC Agreement.

1994

- January: Completion of internal procedures by United States, Russia, European Atomic Energy Community/European Economic Community, and Japan for entry into force of protocol.
- March: Establishment of ISTC; first meeting of ISTC Governing Board; adoption of ISTC Statute; approval of initial research projects; announcement of initial budget commitments.
- Initiation of Travel Support Program and Seminar Program.
- Finland, Sweden, Georgia, Armenia, and Belarus become members of ISTC. (Finland and Sweden subsequently withdraw when they enter European Union, which then represents their interests.)

1995

- Kazakhstan and Kyrgyzstan become members of ISTC.
- First of many projects with CERN.

1996
- First two-year review by Governing Board.
- Establishment of Partner Program.

1997
- Review of ISTC programs by U.S. National Research Council.
- Establishment of Japanese Workshop Program, Technologies Data Base Program, Valorization Support Program, and Patent Support Program.
- Beginning of Business Management Training activities.
- ISTC branch offices in place in five member countries, eventually increasing to six.
- Norway becomes ISTC member.

1998
- Second two-year review by Governing Board.
- Republic of Korea becomes ISTC member.

1999
- Y2K program with emphasis on nuclear safety.

2000
- Establishment of EU, U.S., and Russian Workshop Programs and Communications Support Program.
- Major assessment of overall program (ISTC 2012).
- Third two-year review by Governing Board.

2001
- Confirmation by Russian Ministry of Foreign Affairs that ISTC headquarters has status comparable to status of diplomatic missions.
- Support of U.S. government-initiated survey of 620 participants in ISTC projects concerning willingness to live in rogue countries.
- Award by President Putin to VNIIEF (Sarov) of the First State Prize of Russia for achievements in investigating super-strong magnetic fields with ISTC support.
- Review of science centers by U.S. General Accountability Office.

2002
- Survey of five hundred managers of ISTC projects concerning their commercialization activities.
- Governing Board establishes Complex Evaluation Program for Institutes.

2003
- Initiation of structured ISTC program for commercialization.
- Beginning of decline in funding available for projects in Russia.
- Canada and Tajikistan become ISTC members.

2004
- EU member states increase from fifteen to twenty-five (eventually to twenty-seven).
- Tenth anniversary celebration.
- Beginning of decline in resources available to support projects in Russia.

2005
- Staff level peaks at 253 persons.

2006
- Preparation of new version of Project Management Manual.
- G8 Global Partnership Program embraces ISTC activities.
- Announcement at G8 meeting by Russian representative of completion of process of redirection of Russian weapon scientists to civilian careers.
- Move of ISTC Secretariat to Krasnoproletarskaya Street, Moscow.

2007
- Completion of evaluation of ISTC commissioned by European Commission.
- Merger of ISTC programs on commercialization and innovation.
- New Vision Statement for ISTC developed but not adopted due to Russian resistance.
- Rosatom, official Russian representative for ISTC matters, is reorganized with new emphasis on commercial activities concerning nuclear power.

2008

- Signing of Memorandum of Cooperation with IAEA (supplemented in 2009).
- First sustainability plans for selected institutes adopted.

2009

- Fifteenth-anniversary celebration.
- Initiation of program on management of responsible science.
- ISTC Secretariat solicits views of Russian scientists on value of ISTC.
- Recognition of large contribution of science centers by G-8 working group on knowledge proliferation.

2010

- Presidential decree announcing Russia's intention to withdraw from ISTC.
- Interim report on new organization for multilateral scientific and technological cooperation adopted by Governing Board.
- Kazakhstan proposal to accept administrative responsibility for establishing and supporting new headquarters for ISTC in Almaty.
- Reactions of Russian scientists to announcement of Russia withdrawal from ISTC posted on Kremlin blog.

2011

- Extensive ISTC staff reductions, leading to staff of 118 by end of year.
- Diplomatic note notifying ISTC Governing Board that Russia will withdraw from ISTC Agreement and associated protocol in 2015.
- Development of plans to address financial, archival, personnel, and program issues as activities in Moscow wind down.
- Review of impacts of nuclear and energy projects, as prototype for assessing ISTC's contributions in selected areas of interest to the Governing Board.
- Initial secretariat contacts with leaderships of Skolkovo project and Rusnano.
- Initiative to transfer know-how developed in Russia with ISTC support to Japan in view of the Fukushima nuclear incident.

CHAPTER ONE

A Unique Experiment for Security and Prosperity

The objective of the International Science and Technology Center shall be to give weapons scientists and engineers opportunities to redirect talents to peaceful activities.
   —International agreement for establishment of the International Science and Technology Center, 1992

The ISTC was among the organizations that were nominated for the Nobel Peace Prize.
   —Authoritative report circulating in Moscow, 2010

ECONOMIC CHAOS PREVAILED as the Soviet Union disintegrated into fifteen independent states in 1991. Once-secret research and development organizations throughout the new Russian Federation began to open their doors to foreign visitors, who indicated that they might finance advanced technology activities directed to peaceful purposes. Initially, the Russian government tried to orchestrate the efforts of a handful of well-controlled Russian institutions to attract foreign customers. But soon scores of other institutes and enterprises within the country joined the hunt for new revenue sources.

In short order, these institutions began exercising an increasing amount of autonomy from central control. Their representatives exhibited considerable flexibility in accommodating the interests of well-heeled "businessmen" from abroad. Economic hard times had engulfed the entire population, including scientists and engineers with weapons-related skills who suddenly had entered the ranks of the underemployed and often the unemployed. Many Russian institutions were in a desperate economic state and were reaching out in all directions for relief.

The corridors of government departments and the unbridled press in the United States and Europe were awash with stories about Russia's potentially dangerous loss of control over its nuclear assets. In January 1992 the *New York Times*, for example, reported the following conditions in the ten formerly secret nuclear cities of Russia: "Their disintegration is now seen as threatening to send scientists and materials flying into foreign hands in a new kind of international peril. Foment is real. Russian nuclear experts have received job offers from Iraq and Libya. . . . Bomb-makers in the secret cities are trying to invent new ways of making money at home. Some of the initiatives would hinder atomic leakage. Others would encourage it."[1]

By the spring of 1992 such reports had triggered diplomatic efforts in Europe and the United States to prevent the possibility of a nuclear Armageddon. International negotiations were under way concerning practical steps to shore up Russia's uncertain security systems and to dissuade nuclear scientists from looking abroad for sustenance from unsavory sources. In Washington and Brussels, government officials set aside tens of millions of dollars for multilateral and bilateral efforts to engage Russia's high-tech scientists in peaceful endeavors.

In Moscow, high-level Western officials with nuclear credentials and security clearances became regular visitors under instructions from their governments to work with Russian counterparts in reining in scientists with special know-how about the design and development of weapons of mass destruction. Russian authorities were convinced that the country's financial shortfalls would be temporary. Then the problem would be under control. In the meantime, they were searching for pots of money at home and abroad to enable the government to supplement the dwindling financial support being allocated to Russian scientists. At the same time, these officials were interested in increasing their own paychecks, which also were in jeopardy.

ESTABLISHMENT OF A NONPROLIFERATION CENTER IN MOSCOW

Amid this chaos, the U.S. Department of State recruited me during the spring of 1992 and then dispatched me to Russia in June to lead the on-the-ground activities of a new multilateral effort to help address the dangers of weapons scientists on the loose. We were to focus on underemployed nuclear, biological, chemical, and aerospace specialists who had skills that might be of interest to rogue states and other dangerous opponents of the United States and its allies. The creation in Moscow of a nonproliferation institution—the International Science and Technology Center (ISTC)—was the goal.

A freshly negotiated nonproliferation agreement, developed by representatives of Russia, the United States, the European Economic Community/European Atomic Energy Community (hereinafter referred to as the European Community), and Japan, provided the basis for establishing the ISTC as soon as the four parties initialed and then signed the international agreement. For many months, U.S., German, and Russian officials had already played active roles, independently and collectively through a variety of diplomatic channels, in promoting new concepts that they developed for inclusion in the agreement. The European Community and the Japanese government had also joined the effort.

The principles embedded in the agreement were designed to reduce the likelihood of illicit flows of dangerous weapons expertise out of Russia and other new independent states that emerged on the territory of the former Soviet Union. Like millions of other citizens of these nations, the scientists possessing special knowledge about weapons were caught in the downward economic spirals of their countries. They needed financial supplements—and quickly.

The new institution would increase paltry paychecks by providing financial support for civilian-oriented projects. Impoverished weapons scientists in Russia and other interested states in the region could then afford to remain at their home institutions, but they would redirect their talents from military to peaceful endeavors. This program was designed to help them resist temptations to sell their services to high bidders of unknown reliability.

Initial financial commitments from Washington, Brussels, and Tokyo totaled $67 million for the first year of anticipated program activities to be carried out through the ISTC. The Western and Asian parties supporting this initiative promised to provide additional resources as the center's activities expanded. Of particular importance, the projects would include funds for salary supplements for the participating scientists from the region, since paychecks were not only small but often delayed for six months or more. In Russia, when salary payments by the government did arrive, they usually reached only $150 to $200 per month for senior scientists and sometimes declined to as low as $25 per month, even for scientific leaders. The new international funds would also cover the costs of needed research equipment and supplies for laboratory experiments. As to the administrative costs of the ISTC, the participating governments committed to providing still other funds.

The parties that prepared the ISTC Agreement had selected me to be the first executive director of the center. I optimistically thought that the ISTC would become operational shortly after my arrival in Russia, and I would then deserve my new title. Within several months, additional specialists from Russia, the United States, Germany, and Japan joined me in Moscow as members of the planning group for the center. The parties soon transformed our group into the ISTC Preparatory Committee (Prep Com). This elevated status gave us confidence that the governments were making good progress in completing diplomatic formalities.

Our team's first priority was to develop documentation clarifying the ISTC's purpose, scope, operational procedures, financial operations, and ethical business practices. We were to help convince a wide range of political leaders in many countries that the new institution could become an important and responsible mechanism for preventing a major weapons brain drain to organizations with hostile intentions. We were particularly concerned about organizations lurking in the shadows beyond the borders of Russia.

To this end, an important task was to ensure that ISTC programs were configured in such a way that finances provided through the center helped in stabilizing important high-tech segments of the defense-oriented workforce of Russia. Of special importance was the development of widespread confidence within Russia and abroad that the ISTC approach was to be immune from corruption. This malady plagued efforts of many other international organizations in Moscow that were involved in fund transfers.

Also, we needed communication and outreach strategies to acquaint interested Russian scientists—who soon numbered many thousands—with the procedures for applying for support for redirection projects. They would have to shift their efforts from what had once been well-subsidized, mostly weapons-related research programs to new and less familiar civilian activities. There was to be a heavy emphasis on overcoming the difficulties of moving results of scientific research into commercial markets. We quickly recognized the need for a long educational process as to how a market economy works.

While the parties to the agreement concluded their diplomatic discussions, we turned our attention to practical implementation issues. Of course, the mechanism for dispersing money was of key interest to both the providers and the potential recipients of research funds. We placed at the top of our proposed action agenda the process for rapid disbursement of funds without loss of control as to how the funds were used. Only after the conclusion of this ground-work could the ISTC begin to move into fast forward.

A particular challenge for the Prep Com was to help persuade leaders of the Russian Supreme Soviet (the parliamentary body existing in 1992 and 1993 that was subsequently reconstituted as the Duma and the Federation Council) that the defection of Russian scientists onto the payrolls of a new wave of nuclear weapons states was a real possibility. These leaders saw little evidence of such a trend. Many were skeptical that foreign intervention in Russia through the ISTC was essential to protect Russia's secrets.

At the same time, the Russian Ministry of Foreign Affairs was very aware of both the international concern over nuclear proliferation and the dire economic conditions throughout the country. With the support of the Ministry of Atomic Energy and the endorsement, or at least the acquiescence, of the other power ministries, the Ministry of Foreign Affairs recommended to President Boris Yeltsin that the ISTC be promptly established. To this end, the interested ministries urged that he seek ratification of the agreement by the legislative branch of the government.

According to Russian legal experts, parliamentary ratification was needed since the agreement provided for exceptions to the Russian tax code, which was jealously guarded by both the Ministry of Finance and the legislative branch. Tax exemptions were to help guarantee that (a) the scientists, and not the tax inspectors, would be the principal recipients of the influx of foreign funds, and (b) international experts who joined the ISTC staff would not be subjected to harassment by the tax authorities. After several administrative delays, by the summer of 1993 President Yeltsin was in the process of obtaining ratification of the agreement by the Supreme Soviet.

However, some Russian parliamentarians were very suspicious about the overall approach. In their view, Western governments had designed the contours of the ISTC to suit their own needs, without adequate Russian input. The skeptics asked the following questions, for example: "Would the diplomatic status within Russia, which was to be conferred on foreign members of the ISTC staff, give them licenses to spy throughout the country, without fear of punishment if they were caught? Would the ISTC have special money exchange privileges, which could lead to large-scale currency operations beyond the reach of Russian financial authorities, including inspectors who were accustomed to sharing the proceeds from such transactions? Would Western partners have unlimited rights to use intellectual property created in Russia? Would Western auditors have unbridled access to sensitive financial and personnel information within Russian files that Soviet authorities had closely guarded for decades?"

Also, despite warnings by Russian international security experts of potential proliferation problems linked to Russian institutions, the legislators did not seem overly concerned about agents of third-world nations or of terrorist organizations penetrating their country. They asked, "How could primitive scientific organizations in Middle East countries—organizations that were on the watch lists of all responsible governments—secretly design and construct weapons that could destroy large cities and eventually the world, with or without foreign advisers?" As to Western concerns that local undercover collaborators being paid by such countries might quietly knock on the closed doors that shielded Russian expertise, the skeptics in the legislature argued that the Soviet security system had been impenetrable in the past. They dismissed the dangers of temporary security lapses during the economic crisis that had spread throughout the country. In their view, Russian weapons scientists—including underemployed scientists—were simply too loyal to their motherland to sell secrets.

In parallel with my meetings in Moscow with both ISTC advocates and Supreme Soviet skeptics, a Russian colleague was collecting many troublesome documents circulating in Moscow. A particularly foreboding advertisement came from the Far East. The Sun Shine Industrial Company, an established Hong Kong trading company that thrived by serving customers who carried out off-the-books arms deals, was on the prowl for business in Russia, as well as in third-world states. The recruitment of Russian scientists had indeed become a serious concern. The advertisement read as follows: "We have detailed files of hundreds of former Soviet Union experts in the fields of rockets, missiles, and nuclear weapons. These weapons experts are willing to work in a country that needs their skills and can offer reasonable pay."[2]

One month later, a second incident further confirmed my view that the skeptical parliamentarians were wrong in believing that money from nefarious sources could not be seductive for poorly paid scientists when family survival was at stake. Several Russian rocket experts from a research complex in the southern Urals came to my office in search of projects that could be supported by the ISTC after the center was established. For decades, their complex had specialized in designing guidance systems for missiles, including submarine-launched missiles. They informed us that they were members of a group of twenty-five Russian scientists who had tried to go to North Korea in 1992, only to be apprehended at the Moscow airport by Russian authorities and sent back to the Urals.

They had planned to work for thousands of dollars per year in a rapidly expanding technology center in North Korea, which reportedly was developing communication satellite systems. The director of a research institute at the Urals complex and officials of several Russian government agencies had approved their trip, perhaps with promises of receiving a share of the earnings. But at the last minute, a Russian security agency became concerned over the transfer of rocket know-how to North Korea. This security watchdog canceled the visit as the scientists waited at the Moscow airport to board their international flight to Pyongyang.[3]

At the same time, we were receiving other reports of a variety of illicit activities originating in Russia. For example, in 1993 as we attempted to interest chemical weapons experts working in several Russian institutions in participating in ISTC activities, we received disturbing reports about Russian exports of dangerous chemicals in several directions, exports that were not approved by the Russian government. In particular, several documents came to our attention about Russian shipments of VX precursors for nerve gas to Syria. While we had few details, there was little doubt that retired Russian military leaders with extensive chemical backgrounds were deriving profit from such dangerous trade arrangements.[4]

Then much later, in 2011, I, and indeed the world, learned about another highly questionable activity that was underway in 1993. Russian scientists at one of the country's two nuclear weapons design centers had established a small firm, with headquarters in Ukraine, to provide advisory services concerning nuclear developments. The Russian firm established relationships with the Iranian Institute of Physics, allegedly to perfect a process for producing artificial diamonds. At least one Russian scientist became a frequent visitor to the Institute of Physics, where he gave a series of lectures about nuclear developments.

According to a report of the International Atomic Energy Agency in 2011, the lectures covered highly sensitive topics, with relevance to the design of initiators needed to ignite a nuclear explosion. The Russian physicist immediately took issue with the report, stating that he was not a technically skilled weapons scientist but simply gave lectures about basic physics with little relevance to weapons. In the aftermath of his association with activities in Iran, he had applied for an ISTC grant in the mid-1990s. His project proposal was favorably approved, but it was not considered to be of high enough priority for financial support by any of the ISTC parties.[5]

Despite such developments, ratification of the ISTC Agreement by the Supreme Soviet was not possible. In September 1993 President Yeltsin disbanded that body in the wake of gunfire exchanges on the main thoroughfares of Moscow. Armed discontents, allied with the legislators who were strong opponents of many policies of the Yeltsin government, had taken their revolt into the streets, initially clashing with the police and then with government troops. Finally, military tank brigades rumbled onto the streets as arsonists set large bonfires in the city center. With point-blank shelling, the tanks severely damaged the White House, which at that time was the home of the Supreme Soviet and a bastion for the discontents. As the legislative branch of the country disbanded activities, order was restored in Moscow.

Evidence kept mounting that a growing number of foreign buyers with suspicious credentials were seeking Russian weapons technologies. Potential Russian sellers of their expert technical knowledge—the weapons scientists—were becoming increasingly desperate in the wait for overdue paychecks. Would the ISTC be in place in time to help reduce the likelihood of an outflow of dangerous technologies? Or in our anxiety to launch the center, were we being overly melodramatic about an unlikely development? Were we exaggerating the significance of our personal observations of events unfolding in Moscow and other cities of Russia?

With no parliament in place, the Russian authorities developed without delay a procedure to establish the ISTC on an interim basis. The government prepared an international provisional protocol to immediately activate the center, while awaiting eventual approval of the ISTC Agreement by the four parties to the agreement, and particularly ratification by a new Russian legislature. The Russian government sent the proposed protocol to Washington, Brussels, and Tokyo, and within several months all four parties approved the document. This internationally agreed-upon provisional protocol did not require legislative ratification in Moscow, and each of the other parties was able to sign after following its own internal approval procedures.[6]

This legal maneuver activated the provisions of the ISTC Agreement on a temporary basis until formal ratification could be achieved—with no specified deadline for ratification. According to Russia's experts responsible for tax issues, the procedure avoided the need for ratification in Moscow, since exemptions from tax payments were only temporary. Thus, throughout its lifetime, the ISTC has operated in a manner consistent with an old adage—"Nothing is as permanent as that which is temporary." (See Appendixes A and B for the texts of the agreement and the protocol.)

For many years, the ISTC moved smartly along the newly blazed path. From 1994 to the end of the century, almost all observers hailed the center's programs as highly successful, particularly in supplementing salaries of Russian scientists with unique skills and encouraging redirection of weapons-relevant talent into new civilian careers. But then skepticism began to increase about the economic payoff from investments in scientific research that Western economists often heralded as an essential ingredient in lifting Russia into the ranks of economic powerhouses. Caught in a wave of misguided pronouncements as to the simplicity of taking technologies that were honed though ISTC projects to market, the technology commercialization activities of the center simply were not living up to expectations. At the same time, Russia's security services had been revitalized. In the eyes of important Russian leaders, the possibility of proliferation of weapons technologies rooted in Russia had been brought under control. In their view, the arguments of the early 1990s for establishing the ISTC were fast vanishing.

Thus, during the early 2000s, Russian officials began to raise questions as to the need for further ISTC operations in Russia. At that time, assessments of the early record of the center and of future possibilities became quite important. The ISTC Governing Board routinely carried out snapshot reviews of ISTC programs at its frequent meetings, and the parties to the ISTC Agreement also enlisted external organizations in order to bring fresh insights and perhaps greater objectivity to the evaluation process. Both internal and external reviews provided warning signals that the center needed to evolve in new directions as Russia entered an era of increased oil revenues with aspirations to regain recognition as a leader in international security affairs.[7] These assessments have provided many important points of departure for my commentary later as to the basis of the Russian decision to withdraw from an out-of-date center.

A FOCUS ON SCIENTISTS

Prevention of proliferation of dangerous weaponry has for decades been high on the agendas of the U.S. government, governments of many other countries, and a number of international organizations. During the negotiations for the establishment of the United Nations following World War II, anxieties over the spread of nuclear expertise were paramount. The Biological and Toxin Weapons Convention, which entered into force almost forty years ago, reflected growing concerns over opaque laboratory experiments. More recent international agreements to limit the spread of missile technologies and to rid the world of chemical weapons also have roots that date back many years.

In these and other areas, a number of international organizations promote constraints on sensitive exports that governments then impose in order to prevent dangerous trafficking. Also, many less formalized arrangements are in place to limit cross-boundary smuggling, both globally and in specific geographic regions. International regulatory agreements are essential, but national authorities play a critical role every day in reducing the likelihood of technological disasters triggered by malevolent organizations or individuals within their countries or abroad.

Given all this activity, why was it necessary to establish yet another international bureaucracy to corral potentially wayward scientists with Soviet pedigrees? A number of nonproliferation programs that spanned the globe were already in place at the time of the splintering of the Soviet Union, and several programs focused on Western cooperation with Moscow authorities. Had the existing programs that were directed to limiting flows of dangerous technologies embedded in cross-border movements of materials and equipment not taken into account the roles and interests of the scientists involved in developing and deploying the technologies?

In fact, most of the international attention given to constraining the spread of dangerous technologies had focused on securing tangible items—materials such as highly enriched uranium, potent biological pathogens, toxic chemicals, and gyroscopes; equipment required to produce such items; and physical components that could be assembled into workable weapons. While technical expertise is of course essential at every step of the weaponization process, the international community simply had not taken on as an explicit priority the task of harnessing expertise. In contrast, the central goal of the ISTC from its inception has been to influence the activities and careers of technical experts—a process that has been referred to as addressing the expertise dimension of the spread of weapons of mass destruction.

Also, the ISTC has had a clear geographic focus on developments of concern—the territory of the former Soviet Union, primarily Russia. In recent years, however, the ISTC leadership has repeatedly underscored that the center should not be about geography but about global dangers from irresponsible diffusion of technical expertise. Nevertheless, at the outset, the founders of the center firmly established geographical limits of its activities, and the parties have kept core activities within these boundaries ever since.

This laser-like focus on an international hot spot—the former Soviet Union—quickly attracted the interests of the U.S., European, and Japanese governments in establishing the organization. Never before had such a large reservoir of dangerous technologies embodied in materials, equipment, components, and expertise been threatened by external thievery. At the same time, the Cold War legacy of mistrust of the USSR was strong. The ISTC was to motivate redirection of scientists who had worked behind long-locked doors to a new world of transparency, and this exposure of their capabilities was of great interest to the outside world.

That is not to say that there have not been overlaps between the mission of the ISTC and the objectives of other efforts throughout the world. In some ways, the new center was to reinforce long-standing policies to reduce dangerous confrontations. For example, the Japanese government has for many years been infuriated by Russian occupation of several islands off the Japanese coast near Hokkaido. Tokyo expected that assistance provided to Russia through the ISTC, as well as through other routes, would help influence Russian policies toward the occupation. The Europeans have monitored nuclear-laden Russian submarines transiting their northern coasts for decades. Perhaps the new center could encourage greater transparency in these activities. The U.S. government had warehouses of satellite imagery of unexplained Russian activities in the Arctic perilously close to the Alaskan frontier, and the new center might help illuminate some of the activities. In short, as a byproduct in establishing the ISTC, collaboration between scientists would reduce in a limited way suspicions about Russian intentions in many areas of concern.

The achievements of the ISTC should be judged within the context of a broad array of interrelated activities devoted to global security including, but not limited to, programs designed to address brain drain and directly related issues. The experience of other organizations has clearly benefited the center, particularly since many key officials of these organizations have worn second hats in their liaison roles with the center. At the same time, the ISTC frequently demonstrated that Russian scientists could contribute in new ways to addressing technical issues of interest to the international scientific community.

Joint efforts involving the ISTC and other organizations have often underscored the significance of coordination in a field increasingly crowded with international programs. As concepts and programs pioneered by the center attract new champions, such coordination will surely grow in importance.

There are pluses and minuses in advocating strong multilateral approaches to prevent proliferation of expertise rather than placing greater emphasis on bilateral programs. In a sense, the ISTC has embraced both multilateral and bilateral efforts. The key to this hybrid model has been the process for deciding which projects would be supported.

This decision process requires that all governments represented on the ISTC Governing Board agree that a proposed project is appropriate for support by the center. If there is a single voice in opposition, the proposed project is considered inappropriate. In most but not all instances, project proposals that have made their way through the center's reviews and have been approved by the Russian government for implementation in Russia have then been judged by the governing board to be of sufficient interest and quality for funding consideration. A few well-developed proposals have failed to pass muster during deliberations of the governing board, but they have been exceptions. Hesitancy in the approval process has usually been linked to concerns over diffusion of dual-use technologies.

After approval of a project, one or more of the center's funding parties are then required to provide funding if the project is to be implemented. Many approved projects have not been financed simply because they did not coincide with the funding priorities of any of the parties. In short, it has been easier for an applicant to obtain from the ISTC Governing Board a multilateral endorsement of a project than it has been for the applicant to obtain project funding from individual member states, which have long lists of funding priorities but only limited financial resources.

NEED FOR A ROBUST RUSSIAN SCIENCE INFRASTRUCTURE

At the core of the ISTC mission have been career changes to sustainable civilian jobs within the advanced technology sectors of the Russian economy. The redirected weapons scientists, while grateful for the temporary respite provided by three-year projects, have obviously been concerned as to whether they will continue to have professional employment opportunities when their ISTC projects come to completion. Such opportunities have been directly linked to the success of the Russian government in invigorating, but not taking over, the Russian industrial sector as a viable economic machine. However, in the words of the Russian minister for education and science in June 2010: "Implementation of innovation is still not a bright picture. Russia is using knowledge developed elsewhere. In the processing and technology industries, innovation is virtually absent. The government needs to play a role in promotion of innovation but also needs to get out of the process at the right time. The state should create the conditions for business; but if it acts like a business, the economy will suffer."[8]

Only with the emergence of a knowledge-based economy, resting in large measure on technological innovation, can there be a large growth of new career opportunities for highly skilled specialists. At the same time, Russia simply cannot afford to support a bloated scientific research establishment primarily for the purpose of advancing science, which might generate wealth, but only many years in the future. Favorable conditions for near-term economic payoffs from research are essential. Then political leaders can be persuaded to commit higher levels of resources to sustain activities of hundreds of thousands of researchers in a manner different from, but still reminiscent of, the support they received in past decades when science propelled the USSR to the status of a special type of superpower.

Increasing the number of science-related jobs linked to economic requirements has been a daunting challenge in the new Russia for more than two decades. In the early 1990s, Russia had a depressed economic base characterized by a large stock of rapidly depreciating and obsolete industrial capital. A legacy of institutional rigidities further inhibits technology-driven progress. All the while, many of the country's sophisticated scientific research facilities, a well-trained technical workforce, and impressive technical universities that had underpinned military-related achievements have remained in place. Still, Russia's exports are primarily raw materials, while the country's share of the world's advanced technology market is hardly measurable. How were newly minted civilian scientists with impressive technical credentials to find an economically important niche?

Indeed, the scientific infrastructure of the country has not become a strong platform for development of a market economy. Industrial firms have had little interest in using their limited resources to support leading-edge research and innovation activities with highly uncertain prospects for creating competitive new products and processes. While a few Russian firms have adopted import-substitution strategies in selecting market opportunities, usually it is easier for them simply to buy the needed technological production assets abroad than to pay the price of developing them locally. At the same time, only infrequently have Russian research groups been able to find foreign customers for their products, even though such market outlets for Russian achievements were a priority interest of many foreign businessmen who have searched through Russia's widely dispersed technological treasure chests. In sum, researchers have found few opportunities to transform the outdated centrally controlled economy to a competition-oriented knowledge-based economy.[9]

In 2011 Russia was still having difficulty in fostering private sector development; improving industrial productivity and increasing competitiveness, even with guaranteed government purchases; and stimulating emergence of profitable high-tech firms. Presumably, successful steps in these areas could lead to an influx of underutilized high-quality talent of the type engaged through ISTC projects into the value streams of manufactured products. But the synchronization of the approaches and activities of externally financed Russian research organizations with the demands and technological interests of the major industries of the country has not been achieved. It simply is not realistic for Russian enterprises to expect to sell products in major markets abroad if they cannot sell them in Russia.

Russian officials have recognized for many years that moving research results from the bench to the marketplace in Russia is a difficult challenge and can take many routes. Learning from the experiences of Finland, Israel, and other countries, the government has established technoparks and incubators, invested in capital venture networks, and provided risk capital for new industrial endeavors. It has tried to address the importance of mobility from the science cities of previously isolated researchers who are potential champions of specific technologies. The government has emphasized the need for improved linkages between small and medium firms and the large enterprises, but such networks have not been easy to achieve.[10]

In Soviet times there were highly stylized processes to accomplish technology transfer, with few questions as to who was responsible for various steps along the way. State subsidies were available to cover costs when necessary. But the world of today is dramatically different, and the good and bad experiences of the ISTC in attempting to blaze new trails for specialists who are ready and able to contribute to increased prosperity of the nation are extensive. A clear lesson learned is that Russia, like almost every country, has its own legacies and its own characteristics. The many Western textbooks on innovating for profit must undergo fine tuning before such approaches will have major impacts in the country.

In summary, a healthy science and technology sector cannot emerge in the midst of an unhealthy industrial environment. At the same time, the revival of science and technology will not occur without a demand by domestically oriented Russian companies for innovation that results in marketable products that will eventually be attractive to international markets. Graduates of many ISTC projects will have new careers that generate wealth only when these conditions are met.

STRUCTURING THE ANALYSIS

The book is organized in four sections following this introductory chapter as follows:

- Three chapters organized chronologically present operational highlights of the ISTC from spring 1994 through 2011. The discussion pays special attention to (a) policies adopted by the center that have guided its programs, (b) programs and projects that have had particularly significant impacts, and (c) trends in the interests of member governments of the center.
- Three chapters are then devoted to topics that have provided an important context for the operations of the center. These topics are (a) the internal and external brain drain of Russian scientists with weapons-relevant skills, (b) the commitment of the Russian government to upgrade its innovation capabilities and thereby increase the international competitiveness of its firms, and (c) the kaleidoscope of bilateral nonproliferation programs, particularly those of the United States, that have intersected with programs of the ISTC.
- Three project-oriented chapters describe the center's nuclear, biosecurity, and aerospace portfolios. Each chapter identifies a number of projects that illustrate the breadth of topics supported by the center and the ingredients required for successful applications of advanced technologies.
- The final three chapters look to the future and the opportunities for building on the life and legacy of the ISTC in addressing both proliferation and scientific problems that will never fade from the scene. They address (a) metrics to gauge the impact and effectiveness of the center, (b) diffusion of components of the ISTC nonproliferation model to areas of the world

beyond the borders of Russia, and (c) suggestions regarding the way forward in Russia as the ISTC closes its doors in Moscow.

Throughout the book, I underscore the opportunities for the international community to draw on the ISTC legacy in addressing important aspects of the global spread of advanced technologies. In the early 1990s the United States and Canada copied the ISTC model with few modifications in leading the international effort to establish a similar center in Ukraine. During the early 1990s a few lessons learned from the ISTC experience were exported to Iraq in a limited effort to help revive its scientific workforce. While the center's approach has been considered for application in North Korea by some U.S. officials, intervening in internal security affairs of this rogue state has not yet become a viable option. Less ambitious efforts, sometimes championed by ISTC alumni including myself, often draw on ISTC experience in opening doors to institutes and scientists of concern in many countries. Overarching such activities, the governments that comprise the G20 multilateral approach to global stability have repeatedly endorsed the center as a model institution for addressing the diffusion of expertise.

The book encompasses past and future international engagement activities involving scientists and institutions in Russia. I add only a few comments on ISTC activities carried out in other newly independent states that became members of the center. Having spent many weeks in Georgia and Kazakhstan during the past decade, I am particularly regretful that observations from those vantage points have not been included in this book. Unfortunately, time and space limitations prevent discussions of the security and scientific situations beyond Russia.

In brief, the book highlights many of the most important policy and program decisions that have determined the ISTC's course in its two-decade journey in Russia, from inception to the end of 2011. I have also cited a number of significant events related to implementation of these policies and programs. My emphasis is on activities that I have witnessed firsthand.

To assist the reader in tracing the development of the programs of the center, a chronology of significant events from 1992 to 2011 is presented after the preface. This timeline highlights a few milestones in the history of the center. A more complete chronology of the activities of the center is set forth in the annual reports of the ISTC, which are readily available at www.istc.ru.

Appendix E presents the annual program budgets of the ISTC from 1994 to 2010. The budget trend is generally consistent with the rise and decline of the enthusiasm of the members of the ISTC community concerning the center's success in fulfilling its role primarily as a nonproliferation organization and secondarily as a supporter of science that can assist in Russia's transition to a market economy.

CHAPTER TWO

Off to a Fast Start (1994–2000)

Nuclear scientists of all friendly countries unite. The International Science
and Technology Center will soon be established in Moscow.
  —*Red Star* newspaper, 1992

We will pay salaries as usual: little and rarely.
  —Russian Ministry of Finance, 1999

THE POLITICAL TURMOIL IN MOSCOW in the fall of 1993 led President
Boris Yeltsin to abolish the Russian Parliament (then called the Supreme Soviet) that was created when the Soviet Union splintered into fifteen separate
countries. My Russian colleagues anticipated that in the wake of this political
clash, the Duma, which was established soon thereafter as Russia's key legislative body, would spend many months and perhaps years wrangling over a host
of issues affecting both the nation's role in a rapidly changing world order and
the internal governance of the country. Only then, they predicted, would the
legislators turn their attention to the plight of Russian scientists and the ratification of the ISTC Agreement.

However, as discussed in chapter 1, clever Russian diplomats quickly developed a provisional international protocol designed to establish the ISTC on a
temporary basis without the need for ratification by the Russian legislature. The
other interested governments agreed that an imperfect arrangement without
ratification by Russia was better than no arrangement when it came to stem-
ming proliferation of weapons expertise. Thus, by early 1994, the protocol had
been signed by all parties, the ISTC was in place, and operations began. With
the establishment of the ISTC came needed sources of money from abroad,
which would flow through new pipelines to Russian scientists.

This interim status continued for many years. Ratification by the Duma actually was never achieved, although ISTC representatives and senior Russian

officials held frequent discussions with Duma leaders over this possibility. At times, the likelihood of negative reactions among key legislators to proposed ISTC policies influenced in a minor way the shaping of some policies, with particular attention focused on the role of the center in supporting commercially oriented research activities. In this area of concern, several Duma members were adamant that the ISTC remain at a distance from commercial transactions. Still, while taking into account these views, the ISTC Secretariat provided advice and travel support to Russian researchers who were trying to make commercial deals for the products of their research. Somewhat amazingly, reluctance within the Duma to ratify the ISTC Agreement and occasional expressions by Duma members of opposition to approaches of the ISTC did not thwart the operations of the center in a significant way over many years.

Early successes and shortcomings in addressing significant policy issues, initiation of different types of programs, and development of mechanisms to increase the effectiveness and the impacts of ISTC projects are the focal points of this chapter. The lack of international experience of some previously isolated Russian scientists and their questionable readiness to participate in international projects were early concerns. But in short order, even some of the most reclusive specialists learned how to compete for research funding in contrast to their previous experience of simple reliance on funds earmarked by central planners in Moscow for their use.

I highlight in this chapter early assessments of the effectiveness of the center by the ISTC Governing Board and recommendations set forth by several external evaluation teams that provided important insights as to new opportunities for enhancing the effectiveness of the center. My observations are directed primarily to developments through the year 2000. However, many administrative challenges and barriers to effective interactions of Western scientists with colleagues at previously closed facilities during this period remained important issues well into the following decade.

LAUNCHING THE ISTC

Throughout 1994 the four original proponents of the ISTC Agreement inaugurated the center with the launch of nearly a hundred projects approved during four meetings of the ISTC Governing Board. Almost all of these projects were carried out in Russia. They addressed a wide variety of advanced technology topics.

Soon the ISTC membership expanded. In 1994 Finland and Sweden became funding parties. In later years they withdrew their memberships so that they could participate through their new affiliations within the European Union. Other countries that had once been components of the former Soviet Union also joined and became recipients of international funds for projects located within their boundaries. These new recipient states were Georgia, Belarus, Kazakhstan, and Armenia. Later, Norway, the Republic of Korea, and Canada became funding parties. The Kyrgyz Republic and Tajikistan also joined the center and became additional countries where projects were carried out. The governing board established procedures to ensure that new members had a voice during board deliberations.

Within a few months after its establishment, the ISTC had become a highly visible flagship in Moscow of international efforts to prevent leakage of Soviet weapons expertise to rogue states and terrorist organizations. The focus was containment of know-how in Russia that could contribute to the development of weapons of mass destruction in distant lands.

Realistically, the ISTC leadership knew that the center's program could not prevent proliferation, although it could reduce the incentives for scientists to earn desperately needed funds through illicit means. After all, nations of concern could continue to acquire equipment and components that would facilitate development of weapons through a variety of legal trade arrangements and through shadowy illegal cross-border mechanisms. Some weapons components might well come directly or indirectly from Russia, and technical advice usually accompanied trade transactions. Within Russia, many scientists continued to be involved on a full-time basis in defense efforts that were outside the reach of the ISTC. The Russian security services had the responsibility to ensure that their scientific research activities comported with regulations that helped prevent unacceptable proliferation practices. Of most concern to the center were the financial difficulties of thousands of underemployed Soviet-trained weapons scientists who were unknown outside Russia and had begun searching for new income streams at home and, at times, abroad.

Recognizing the uncertain mix of responsibilities and motivations of Russian scientists and questionable activities of unsavory forces abroad, many governments nevertheless were convinced that the ISTC could reduce the likelihood of proliferation. The center's grants could moderate the financial incentives for underemployed former weapons scientists to consider orders from abroad for purchase of their secrets. In short order, Russian managers at a number of sensitive defense facilities reported that the ISTC was more effective in funding research designed to support the civilian economy than they had anticipated.

The ISTC energized scientists throughout the country to pursue new career challenges. Even for some former weapons scientists who did not receive salary supplements from the ISTC, the success of their colleagues in redirecting their careers gave hope to all that the nation's science infrastructure would be strengthened. Scientific research would be revived on a broad basis, so they believed; and a large number of civilian-oriented workplaces would become more secure.

The Russian government strongly supported the ISTC at its inception for several reasons. At the top of the list of benefits to be derived from the center were new income streams for supporting highly talented and important Russian scientific teams that had fallen on hard times. During negotiation of the ISTC Agreement, Russia had made a number of concessions to gain access to foreign funds that would be available through the center. For example, difficult internal negotiations were undertaken between the Ministry of Finance, which opposed any form of legalized tax "evasion," and the science-oriented ministries, which wanted the available international money to be used to the greatest extent possible for program activities—a position strongly supported by the international partners. A particularly contentious issue within the Russian government was the exemption from personal income taxes by Russian scientists who were to receive salary supplements for their participation in projects. Also of importance was the controversial exemption from customs fees of Russian institutes that received foreign equipment for ISTC-funded projects. In the end, ISTC project agreements provided tax and customs exemptions for projects financed through the center.

Second, the Foreign Ministry recognized that the ISTC's programs provided considerable credibility for Russian pronouncements in many international forums over the need to combat the dangers of weapons proliferation. The on-the-ground activities financed through the center were particularly important for facilitating programs of nonproliferation agencies in the United States and Europe, which also were developing bilateral programs with Russia. The parties to the ISTC Agreement soon witnessed how such bilateral efforts could benefit from the pathfinding efforts of the ISTC, particularly from the center's efforts in reducing barriers to contacts with newly identified colleagues at sensitive Russian facilities.

In addition, the Russian government was painfully aware of the difficulties faced by its scientific community in adjusting to Western approaches for supporting research and international cooperation. The ISTC experience was to be a good introduction to the details of international administrative, management, and business practices in developing and carrying out technology-oriented projects of international interest. Russia was trying to adjust to the demands of a new market economy that required economic as well as scientific justifications for requests for research support.

Thus, Western approaches in linking research to economic development were of considerable interest, both in theory and in practice. Russian officials correctly reasoned that this increased familiarity with international approaches would be particularly helpful. As Russian leaders sought widespread recognition of the country as a constructive participant in a wide range of global technology endeavors, they often highlighted the government's role in the establishment and operation of the ISTC.

The euphoria among the ISTC member states over the success of their investments continued to grow as Russian scientists repeatedly demonstrated their expertise. For example, in 1995 U.S. secretary of defense William Perry characterized the capabilities of Russian specialists as follows: "Russian scientists and engineers are an amazingly competent, diverse, broad group of talented technical people; and so the opportunity to use them in an effective way for the good of not only their country but of our country as well is very, very real."[1]

Success was initially defined as having in place projects on important topics that enabled former weapons scientists to begin the process of redirecting their talents from defense to civilian activities. The first metric for gauging this success was the number of weapons scientists participating in projects. But in short order, the concept of long-term sustainability of projects shared center stage. The chairman of the governing board underscored the importance of this metric in a pronouncement in 1997. "The ultimate objective of the ISTC should be to develop projects which will sustain themselves when other organizations, either private or institutional, can exploit the project results. Only then will the ISTC's objective of long-term career opportunities for weapons of mass destruction scientists be fully achieved."[2]

ISTC staff gave considerable attention to (a) acquisition of patents that could lead to long-term income streams for Russian institutions, (b) commercial activities with immediate payoffs that resulted from projects, and (c) associated sustainable jobs that were created. However, often-predicted financial success in these areas was less than anticipated throughout the early years of the ISTC. The leap of technologies from the laboratory to the world of business was a challenge that eluded most scientists.

LINGERING ISSUES

During the initiation of ISTC activities from 1994 through the end of the century, many controversial issues that were presumably resolved during the negotiation of the ISTC Agreement in 1992 and in subsequent intergovernmental debates during the crafting of the ISTC Statute emerged again. Elaboration and interpretation of initial compromises on taxes, customs payments, ownership of newly acquired laboratory equipment, patents, foreign access to sensitive facilities, auditing of project records, and overhead charges returned to the table. This revival of differing viewpoints was not surprising. During the negotiation of the ISTC Agreement and Statute, the parties carried out many discussions within the framework of hypothetical settings, with disagreements resolved by adoption of very general diplomatic language.

As the approval and implementation of projects began in 1994 and continued for many years, the political landscape changed again and again. Incoming Russian officials who had not participated in the early negotiations were suddenly involved. Russian institute directors became personally responsible for ensuring appropriate uses of project funds. Foreign partners were going through a continuing education process. Most important, detailed statements that would clarify the general provisions of previous political compromises were required within a number of operational documents.

In 1993 the Russian legislators in the original Supreme Soviet had considered many of the policy ramifications of the establishment of the ISTC. Still, the new breed of legislators in the reconstituted Duma that followed raised additional questions as to the interface of the new organization with the national security responsibilities and policy approaches of the evolving Russian government. Although the Duma leaders recognized the importance of preventing proliferation of weapons expertise, they were intent on preserving the integrity and leadership of Russia in combating its own internal proliferation issues.

Following are a few questions that the parliamentarians originally raised in 1993 and that officials who were new to the scene revisited many times. We paid close attention to the concerns at the outset, since we were hopeful that ratification was close at hand. My responses set forth below indicate the ways in which important issues were addressed as the ISTC moved forward.[3]

1. *May the center monitor work of a military nature? Won't Western scientists use the knowledge that they receive from Russian scientists for their own military development?* Many ISTC research projects addressed dual-use issues, frequently through development of enabling technologies, which were important in both the military and civilian arenas. On a case-by-case basis, the Russian authorities usually decided that the benefits of working openly and sharing results in such areas outweighed the dangers of technology diffusion to other countries with military programs that might threaten Russia. Since the Russian side selected the participants in the projects, surprises were unlikely. Occasionally, for unexplained security reasons, the Russian government did not approve project proposals en route to the ISTC. However, in general, Moscow's hard-line, Cold War mentality to protect all Russian research that could conceivably contribute to enhancement of military capabilities changed, as all of the ISTC parties recognized that dual-use technologies, wherever developed, were spreading throughout the world in support of civilian activities.

2. *Won't the reorientation of weapons scientists to civilian-oriented research topics weaken the military readiness of the nation?* There has not been any publicized evidence that the quality of Russian military programs declined as the result of leading scientists spending their time working on ISTC projects. The economic slumps in Russia during the 1990s undoubtedly were a significant factor, if not the major factor, in erosion of important military capabilities. Many weapons scientists have participated in ISTC projects on a part-time basis, thereby retaining their readiness to continue military activities as required. This practice of part-time employment led to early criticisms in the West that the ISTC was supporting active rather than former weapons scientists. Nevertheless, the Western parties repeatedly made the judgment that it was an acceptable trend to have such key weapons scientists devote portions of their time to peaceful activities that could strengthen the civilian science infrastructure, as well as encourage at least some participants to eventually become full-time civilian scientists in later life.

3. *Won't the Russian scientists, the enterprises, and the nation as a whole suffer because of the loss of legal entitlement of Russian scientists to the intellectual property that they created?* The protection of intellectual property devel-

oped in Russia was an issue being debated throughout Russia during the early years of the ISTC, and it is still being debated. While the ISTC Statute addressed equitable distribution of intellectual property generated through the center, a funding party could insist on having the sole claim to intellectual property as a condition for providing financial resources for a particular project. Russian participants in ISTC projects repeatedly raised the unfairness of this approach. The concerns were usually addressed on an ad hoc basis, sometimes after much Russian complaining as to a process that gives the funders all the negotiating chips. Overall, intellectual property rights were an irritant but not a major barrier during project implementation. Often the Russian partner had unrealistic expectations as to the marketable value of the intellectual property involved.

4. *Isn't the procedure for initiating projects too long?* Despite the heroic efforts of key ISTC specialists to move internal paperwork forward once a project was approved for funding, the delays in project initiation became longer and longer. Initially, projects were usually launched within a few months after approval. But in time, the start-up procedures extended to many months and even years, particularly if Russian recipient organizations were involved with the ISTC for the first time. When governments are in transition, funding delays are a common problem, particularly for sensitive international research projects that must be protected from corrupt practices by complicated regulations.

5. *Isn't it simpler to create direct bilateral connections (without the center) between Russian and foreign organizations?* In addition to projects implemented through the ISTC, many projects with nonproliferation objectives have been carried out on a bilateral basis (see chapter 7). While bilateral projects are often simpler to develop and implement, the ISTC has offered a variety of unique safeguards for both the funding party and the recipient organization—particularly with regard to clarity as to the ways funding would be handled, access to sensitive facilities assured, and project results either sheltered or disseminated.

6. *Won't the center attract the best scientists of the country for future work abroad?* While some Russian participants in ISTC projects have eventually emigrated to the West, Russian regulations have limited emigration for five to seven years by specialists with histories of security clearances. In time, some important weapons scientists did move to the West and to other countries (e.g., Israel). But the Russian government's scrutiny of the

security backgrounds of participants in ISTC projects has probably been a significant deterrent to emigration of alumni of projects of the center.

7. *Will the financing of the center reduce humanitarian aid for Russia and other former Soviet states?* The levels of foreign assistance to Russia were large during the 1990s. For example, during a number of years the annual U.S. commitment was in the hundreds of millions of dollars. Most countries provide funding for ISTC projects through ministries of foreign affairs rather than through foreign assistance agencies with different budget objectives and constraints; the two streams of funding are considered independently. At the same time, however, nonproliferation funds are sometimes aggregated with humanitarian aid funds when governments report their expenditures for assistance through the Development Assistance Committee of the Organization for Economic Cooperation and Development in Paris. Thus, there may have been some erosion of levels of humanitarian assistance due to funding commitments to ISTC that took pressure off the U.S. government, or other governments, not to lag behind in their foreign assistance commitments; but the amount of erosion probably has been small.

8. *Doesn't organizing the ISTC on the material base of the most advanced Russian scientific centers create a one-way street of disseminating leading technologies abroad with nothing in return?* Well before the establishment of the ISTC, Western countries were repeatedly accused of cherry-picking Russian technologies for their own commercial benefit; and within the ISTC at the outset, there was clear recognition that Russia was providing "brain power" for projects as its matching contribution to foreign financial contributions. However, international collaborators have usually been involved in high-tech ISTC projects—not only as monitors but also as contributors of their know-how to the success of the projects. Thus, two-way streets for the flow of technology are common, although the technology exiting Russia has usually been larger than the inflow.

9. *If there is no change in the international bans on imports of advanced Western technologies into Russia, there should be bans on exports of technologies from Russia.* In parallel with ISTC activities during the 1990s, the U.S. and other governments were working with the Russian government and Russian enterprises to strengthen the Russian export control system, which deteriorated after the collapse of the USSR. Also, Western countries were revising the entire international system for controlling the diffusion of

high-tech exports that had military applications. Progress was rapid in both of these areas. However, the ISTC did not give adequate attention to these international developments, and some Russian authorities were repeatedly upset with the failure of Western states to recognize Russia as an equal partner in the global effort to control exports to unreliable states. In particular, some Western partners refused to comply with the international practice of providing assurances to Russia that Russian technologies acquired by foreign partners would not be re-exported to third parties without Russian concurrence.

APPROACHES EMBRACED BY THE ISTC

Financial support of regular research projects has been the core activity of the ISTC since its inception.[4] In 1994, for example, the level of support for such projects was impressive—more than fifty million dollars annually. In the years that followed, many achievements within the Russian scientific community were linked to regular research projects. The following two testimonials illustrate the broad scope of the work funded by the ISTC:

- "The Japan Aircraft Development Center and Boeing have been deeply impressed during their ISTC projects not only by the worldwide significance of the facilities of the Central Aviation Research Institute but also by the institute's scientific capabilities." General Manager, Aerodynamics Division, Japan Aircraft Development Corporation, 1994[5]
- "Thanks to the ISTC, we have become well-established figures in scientific circles concerned with ecological issues in the Arctic and Far East oceans; and we have gained valuable knowledge in computer technology and scientific research technologies meeting international standards." Deputy Director, Lazurit Design Bureau, 1998[6]

From 1994 to 2000, funding of ISTC projects that supported research activities exceeded $314 million, with more than 90 percent of the expenditures devoted to increasing salaries, upgrading equipment, and providing travel for Russian participants. The average size of a three-year project was about $400,000. In 2000, for example, the ISTC compensated over 21,000 project participants for a total of more than 1.2 million person-days of effort. Also in that year, ISTC fund allocations in Russia for research projects and for related activities reached a record high of $78 million.[7]

In addition to support of regular research projects, the ISTC formalized many other activities during its initial years. Some of the most important programs and their objectives were the following:

- The *seminar program* heightens international awareness of the scientific potential of Russia and other former Soviet states and thereby attracts foreign collaborators to participate in strengthening ISTC project proposals through early consultations.
- The *business management training program* assists managers of ISTC projects at the recipient institutes in developing business skills, polishing presentation capabilities, and understanding intellectual property rights.
- The *patent support program* provides funds to cover costs related to initial stages of the process of obtaining patents for new technologies.
- The *project development grants program* supports international travel for scientists of several recipient states and their foreign partners to continue technical consultations on proposals submitted to the ISTC while awaiting decisions.
- The *U.S. biotechnology travel grants program* covers costs of international travel by Russian and other scientists to attend international meetings of particular relevance to their specialties.
- The *promising research abstracts program* features a data base of abstracts intended to generate interest in projects that are under development.
- The *Japanese workshop program*, which soon included participation by the European Union and the United States, supports international workshops on topics of global significance that could lead to development of proposals for submission to the ISTC.[8]

The *partner program*, established in 1996, has been highly popular within the governments of the United States, Canada, the European Union, and Japan. It has provided opportunities for private companies, government agencies, scientific organizations, and other interested institutions to finance research and related projects in the former Soviet Union using the ISTC as the mechanism for transferring funds provided by the partners to research organizations of interest in Russia and other recipient states. Of course the research activities should be consistent with ISTC objectives in order to receive ISTC support.

This program has several advantages for the foreign partners. For example, the projects enjoy tax exemptions on payments to Russian partners for their services and custom duty exemptions on imports of equipment and material.

The center conveys payments directly to project scientists and institutions, with audit requirements ensuring appropriate use of the funds. The ISTC obtains host government approval for each partner project. This approval enables the foreign partner to use well-established ISTC fund-transfer mechanisms, which have reduced the likelihood of corrupt practices and helped enforce protection of confidential business information.

As of 2000, a total of 98 partner organizations had joined the ISTC network. More than 150 partner projects had been approved. Funding for these projects exceeded forty-one million dollars.[9] In subsequent years, the number increased several fold.

Throughout the lifetime of the ISTC, the Russian government has officially welcomed partner projects financed by foreign governmental and intergovernmental agencies and by nonprofit institutions. However, from the outset of the program, some Russian officials have raised concerns about the involvement of private international companies that, in their view, could use the ISTC mechanism simply to avoid taxes. Such a practice would give these companies an advantage over Russian companies operating in similar fields but unable to obtain comparable tax exemptions. Nevertheless, the Russian government has never formally objected to the influx of new partners. In some cases, Russian authorities have pointed to the successes of companies in raising the technological capabilities of Russian partner organizations, particularly applied research institutions.

Against this background, in 2001 the chairman of the ISTC Governing Board summed up the early accomplishments of the center as follows:

> The ISTC was created in full recognition of the fact that technology can be used for war or for peace. In this age, in which weapons of mass destruction were invented, the ISTC is a unique organization committed to nonproliferation of such weapons through cooperative science. In the short period of its existence, the ISTC has created a number of tools to achieve its objectives. In some cases it funds scientists directly to assist them in applying to civilian use skills originally developed for the military. In other cases, the ISTC provides travel and training to facilitate the advance of basic science. In yet further cases, especially through the partner program, the ISTC creates opportunities for the development of products that can be commercialized. The ISTC even funds research in support of arms control monitoring and verification. The ISTC continues to create new tools and to increase its efforts as

support has expanded. All of this is possible because the ISTC serves the interests of all of its members.[10]

This type of praise would be expected from leaders of most organizations. But the support throughout Russia and the international community for the ISTC quickly became widespread, even though many issues needed to be more fully addressed.

One of the most important questions that remains today is how to measure the ISTC's contribution to reducing the threat of proliferation. The world is clearly safer due to the ISTC. But how much safer? And has the investment been commensurate with reduction of the threat? Each of these issues is addressed in later chapters.

ASSESSMENTS OF INITIAL ACTIVITIES

During the ISTC's first few years, most observers had very positive comments on the activities of the new organization. The importance of reducing the likelihood of an exodus of scientists and engineers from the former Soviet Union seemed clear to all. But addressing the leakage of weapons-relevant information by means other than migration of scientists was also important. As links between scientists in Russia and colleagues in North America, Europe, and Asia increased, the hope was that use of these other channels for surreptitious activities in the Middle East and elsewhere would be tempered, as the Russian specialists concentrated on gaining respect within the international scientific community.

At the same time, Russia had long-standing commercial and scientific contacts with many countries and was developing new ties with still other countries, with scientific cooperation being a central feature in some relationships (e.g., China and India). Of course, the Internet provided new opportunities for information exchange with few limitations. Indirectly, through its global networks, the ISTC was able to encourage transparency for important elements of this outreach.

The ISTC Governing Board has been the primary mechanism for assessing the effectiveness of the ISTC. The parties represented on the board commit their financial and in-kind resources to ISTC activities. The process of allocating funds from limited budgets in Washington, Brussels, Tokyo, and other capitals has encouraged the individual parties to maintain careful scrutiny of ISTC activities before they determined the specific projects that would be supported through the center with their national funds. This approach to financing was a strong feature in forcing the parties to focus on ISTC impacts as they justified at home their budget requests for activities of the center.

The international Scientific Advisory Committee (SAC), established pursuant to the ISTC Agreement, also has provided oversight of ISTC programs. Its focus has been both on (a) the scientific integrity of individual projects and clusters of projects and (b) emerging opportunities to expand activities to additional topical areas. With scientists designated by the parties serving on SAC, the parties have paid attention from the outset to the views of the committee.

In addition, there have been a number of reviews of ISTC program and administrative operations. Auditing organizations from the United States and the European Union, in particular, have frequently reviewed the financial and related administrative aspects of the ISTC program. From time to time the parties have also initiated their own assessments of the ISTC activities. Several particularly significant assessments were carried out during the early years of the ISTC's operations.

The first formal assessment was undertaken in 1996 by a special committee established by the ISTC Governing Board. The assessment was generally positive as indicated below.

> The agreement provides a solid framework for the center and is sufficiently flexible to allow the center to operate efficiently. In a very short period of time, the ISTC has developed into a stable and effective organization capable of performing its basic functions of developing, approving, funding, and monitoring scientific projects for peaceful purposes. The center is a very useful vehicle for working on technologies in support of nonproliferation. Projects could also support the transition to market economies.[11]

Shortly thereafter, the U.S. National Research Council (NRC) issued a report on the activities of the ISTC, which was prepared at the request of the U.S. government. This report also rendered a positive assessment of ISTC activities. The principal conclusion was as follows: "The proliferation risk remains high, and the ISTC continues to have a role in mitigating this risk. Based on the ISTC's success to date, the other benefits of its activities to national security objectives, and the continuing threat of proliferation, the committee recommends that the U.S. Government sustain annual core funding for the ISTC at least until, and probably beyond, 2003."[12]

The NRC report noted, however, that efforts for achieving the ISTC's objective of reinforcing the transition of Russia to a market-driven economy had shown only limited success. According to the report, the connection between research activities and user needs that was prominent under the Soviet system was absent and was only beginning to develop in the new Russia. Traditional Russian industry was in very poor condition, except perhaps in the oil and gas sectors. High-tech industry, with the exception of aerospace, was undertaking almost no research and did not have the capital to exploit new developments. The private sector simply was not strong enough to give rise to a substantial domestic demand for innovation.

Finally, the report pointed out that the conversion of the weapons activities of institutes to civilian efforts is often an extremely difficult—at times, some would say impossible—task. The effort was particularly pronounced in Russia, where many weapons scientists and engineers had lived under greater isolation than in the West, and the market system was not yet in place.[13] Of course the relevance of many weapons-related skills to civilian work has long been in question as some U.S. experts have repeatedly contended that, in general, defense activities have little in common with civilian work. These two areas demand different skills and marketing techniques and have different cultures and organizations, according to some specialists.[14] But in some ways, the ISTC was beginning to show that Western defense conversion experts were not always correct when focusing on Russia, where skills could be adapted to new tasks.

To help remedy some barriers to success, the NRC report offered the following three recommendations to which comments on the status of the proposals have been added.

- *The ISTC should consider organizing an industrial advisory council.* The ISTC did not follow up on this recommendation since the center was already overburdened with a variety of organizational requirements, including advisory committees.
- *The ISTC should expand the scope of Western collaborators, including collaborators from industrial laboratories, and require more active participation by collaborators.* The ISTC steadily gave increasing emphasis to the role of collaborators from both academia and industry.
- *The ISTC should provide grants for communications equipment to facilitate interactions with both research and industrial partners at home and abroad.*

The ISTC adopted a major initiative in this area, financed by the Japanese government.[15]

In short, while the report commended the strides of the ISTC in addressing immediate nonproliferation objectives, it gave considerable weight to the secondary objective of contributing to the longer-term development of a viable market economy.

A third report in 2001 by the U.S. General Accountability Office (GAO) was less complimentary. It reflected the difficulty for external evaluators to quickly grasp both the essence and the details of the ISTC approach. After describing a few of the characteristics and operations of the ISTC, which it generally endorsed, the report offered several observations that were of a critical nature. The first criticism was as follows: "There are no reliable estimates of the total population of senior weapons scientists in Russia. Four biological weapons institutes under the Russian Ministry of Defense have not submitted project proposals to the science center in Russia. This effectively denies the State Department access to the senior scientists at these institutes, an issue of potential concern, since Russian intentions regarding inherited biological weapons capacity remain unclear."[16]

The ISTC did not have a comprehensive overview of the totality of Russia's defense-oriented workforce. This was not surprising, given the secrecy constraints of the time. Of course, such information would have assisted in targeting activities to achieve early payoffs. Even today, fifteen years later, Western governments do not have access to complete information about the weapons-oriented component of the overall Russian workforce. But what country does release such information?

The GAO report included other criticisms. For example, the report pointed out that the ISTC supported part-time redirection of weapons expertise, thereby enabling weapons scientists to continue working in parallel on defense projects as well. However, Russian scientists were reluctant to give up completely their permanent jobs if they were not reasonably certain that their short-term support by the ISTC would lead to new careers with support from other sources. Now, thanks to the center's flexibility, many part-time defense researchers have become full-time civilian researchers.

The GAO underscored that Russian staff members of the ISTC rather than international experts carried out most of the monitoring of research activities supported by the ISTC. The Department of State strongly defended this practice. It argued that the practice reflected six years of observations of the diligence and competence of these Russian staff members and that there were substantial difficulties in recruiting adequate numbers of well-qualified international experts for service at the center.[17]

In summary, in short order the ISTC had convinced most skeptics that its novel approaches were working, that consequently the world was safer, and that revival of Russian civilian science had been stimulated by an influx of talent from the defense sector. Of course, many issues of both political and technical concern arose every day as the ISTC Secretariat and Governing Board grappled with sensitive concerns involving former adversaries. But in general, the redirection goals and the technical achievements exceeded expectations of the ISTC founders. Remarkably, there were no significant financial scandals nor serious breaches of security, which had often been predicted when the center was in its formative stage.

Five years after the ISTC began operations, a highly respected European scientific leader—the director of the European Organization for Nuclear Research (CERN) in Geneva—gave the following ringing endorsement of the progress of the ISTC, which was shared by many others: "Clearly the ISTC has come of age. The confidence of governments, the analysis of experts, and the reviews of independent politicians have documented the effective operation of the center. We are looking forward to state-of-the-art contributions from our Russian and other former Soviet colleagues in the years to come with the effective mediation and support of the ISTC."[18]

By the turn of the century the quality of ISTC proposals and projects had improved dramatically. The competition for funding had increased, and the Russian scientific community had adjusted accordingly. Thousands of Russian weapons scientists were on promising courses to new careers.

On the negative side, however, Russia's governmental bureaucracy had lowered the priority of the center's activities, often resulting in long delays in approving project proposals. At times, more than one year transpired before the ideas of researchers were transformed into proposals that reached the ISTC Secretariat. The secretariat, in turn, also was transformed into a more rigid bureaucracy that slowed progress.

Nevertheless, the ISTC was truly off to a fast start. But Russia was changing. Would the ISTC adapt to the changing political and economic realities?

CHAPTER THREE

An Era of Euphoria (2001–2006)

In the early 1990s, ISTC support was crucial for the institute's survival. Now the ISTC is important for select groups of researchers. The center's programs help advance their science in terms of commercial activities.
  —Vice Director, Ioffe Institute of Physics, St. Petersburg, 2002

One can hardly overestimate the center's contribution to strengthening of the international scientific community and preparing specialists to work under new market conditions.
  —Head of Russia's Federal Atomic Energy Agency, 2004

THE ISTC ENTERED THE FIRST DECADE of the twenty-first century on a high note. Praises for its work were coming from all directions. Governments in North America, Europe, and Asia were pleased with their financial investments as both nonproliferation and scientific returns seemed obvious to all. Funding of the ISTC was on a steady course. By the early 2000s, the annual funding level for projects involving Russian scientists was averaging between sixty-eight and seventy-eight million dollars, although beginning to decline.[1]

The Russian government had significantly reduced a number of bureaucratic difficulties. For example, the process for obtaining Russian government approvals for projects of interest to the other parties, while still lengthy, had somewhat improved. The paranoia of the Russian security services over any type of foreign access to sensitive facilities had receded, as they adjusted entry procedures in accordance with the legal obligations of the government, pursuant to the ISTC Agreement. Officials in Moscow and in other capitals had accepted the center as a significant player, both in helping to reduce incentives for proliferation and in strengthening the science infrastructure of Russia.

Important international political and scientific leaders considered the administrative procedures of the center quite good, even by Western standards.

Of course, the procedures became more sluggish as the size of the program enlarged. At the same time, no significant security or financial scandals were reported.

The ISTC successfully survived the scrutiny of a steady stream of international auditors and policy officials sent to Russia by the participating governments. They looked into file cabinets, visited sites where projects were under way, and prepared recommendations on future activities. After each visit, they gave the center high marks for both its program accomplishments and its administrative integrity.

The ISTC was providing a selected group of Russian scientists with support at a critical time, which was fraught with economic uncertainties and growing concerns over future activities of rogue regimes and international terrorist groups. The scientists were becoming enthusiastic about their long-term professional opportunities. They had successfully weathered the economic turmoil and the missing Russian paychecks in the wake of the disintegration of the USSR. Then they had withstood the economic slump that encompassed the country in 1998. Many had quickly become addicted to foreign grants, and they anticipated a continuing relationship with the center.

Most Russian scientists were well aware that their country was still a long way from political stability and that a shadow economy was benefiting a handful of rich Russians at the expense of others. But all in all, thousands of scientists seemed confident that the ISTC would continue to help them in avoiding the depths of poverty. Some were already finding new opportunities to showcase their research achievements internationally, and new contacts with foreign colleagues were occasionally leading to new income streams.

In early 2001, I visited ISTC headquarters and discussed with the secretariat the impacts of the many programs that were in place. In retrospect, my two most important questions, which neither I nor the staff adequately pursued at that time, were these:

- How effectively does the ISTC currently support the national goals of Russia—in the security, economic, and scientific arenas?
- Should there be a well-planned transition to Russian funding of the types of activities that had been supported by the ISTC, and who should organize the planning for such a transition?

Nine years later, when the Russian government was beginning the formal process of terminating its involvement with the center, it was simply too late to adjust programs in response to these and related questions concerning the integration of ISTC and Russian interests. Perhaps early adjustments could have diminished the growing Russian uneasiness about continuation of the center and could have sparked an alternative approach to the complete closing of the door in Moscow. More likely, the Russian power structure had its eyes on other technology-oriented activities, far more ambitious than the ISTC's modest efforts and controlled by Russia, not international interlopers with questionable agendas. Some Russian leaders undoubtedly reasoned that these other mechanisms were better suited to combine the country's dual-use know-how with international technological achievements, while generating wealth for the Russian elite.

When the ISTC budget for projects in Russia started to decline in 2003, a few key Russian officials raised questions about the effectiveness of the ISTC. They probably considered that their time could be better spent on other initiatives from which they and their colleagues could benefit to a greater extent in the near term. At the same time, promoting their own initiatives through new channels was always more interesting than simply maintaining momentum in the organizational innovations of others.

Still, the early 2000s can best be described as a time of euphoria at the ISTC headquarters. The telephones were constantly ringing. The governing board members were regularly basking in their successes. And many Russian scientists were expanding contacts well beyond the confines of their laboratories.

SECURITY AND ECONOMIC INSTABILITY IN RUSSIA

All the while, the possibility of proliferation of Russian weapons expertise that led to establishment of the ISTC remained a concern in capitals in the West and in Asia as nonproliferation programs expanded in many areas of the world. The Russian government entered into a number of bilateral and multilateral agreements designed to shrink the size and reorient the focus of some of its weapons enterprises. With Western support increasing beyond investments in the work of the ISTC, Russia was enhancing security procedures and modifying activities at defense-oriented facilities. It was carrying out defense conversion activities, despite high cost/benefit ratios, throughout the industrial sector.

Clearly, Russian authorities did not consider the ISTC a muscular defense conversion program. It was a "redirection" program that benefited a limited number of Russian scientists. Within a few years, the growing interest in larger conversion programs began to dim the brightness of the spotlight that had been focused on the ISTC. But its supporters were not hesitant to voice their praise for its operations.

Occasional reports continued to emerge about weapons, weapons components, and weapons-related material being unaccounted for at Russian stockpiles. Of particular concern were possible breaches of security procedures at sensitive facilities that had not embraced export control regulations. Russia was trying to move away from centralized command and control of its huge industrial complex. But confusion often reigned as to who was in charge of workforces and activities at facilities that had produced both military and civilian goods in years past but were suddenly tasked to become important components of a strange new market economy.

Despite these and other problems, particularly corruption in the financial and industrial sectors and the lack of market-oriented entrepreneurial skills within the workforce, Russia was slowly becoming a more stable country with a greater sense of purpose. The population's expectations for the future were on the rise. Incomes and disposable wealth were growing, at least for a few, while foreign debt receded and the Russian population became skilled at "coping." Most important, oil export revenues began to increase. This trend meant a tax-generated boost for the state treasury, slowly rising salaries for government employees to keep pace with inflation, huge windfalls for a growing class of oligarchs, and a slow trickle-down impact throughout the economy.

While the overall economy continued its heavy dependence on oil, gas, and mineral-based exports, progress in strengthening the technological underpinnings of the manufacturing sector was slow. Given the small pools of domestic investment capital, many Russian companies continued to rely on obsolete equipment in their facilities. Foreign direct investment was largely stagnant. Hundreds of international companies retained a presence in Moscow, but only to be at the ready should the business environment improve. Thus, with little demand for locally produced items, the number of small and medium enterprises in the economy remained few in number. As for the future workforce, the demographics had become alarming. Life-expectancy ages tumbled, birth rates declined, and the population began to shrink. In this environment, a science and technology infrastructure was surviving, but with little cushion to withstand additional shocks.[2]

In the early 2000s the government repeatedly called on Minister for Education and Science Andrey Fursenko to increase the payoff from Russian research. In 2003 he bluntly described the situation for innovation, which was at the core of Russia's aspirations for emergence of a knowledge-based economy, as follows:

> Russia is relying on knowledge developed elsewhere. In the processing and technology industries, there is low efficiency; and innovation is virtually absent. The parties that are producing the innovation that does occur in Russia are not adequately compensated. Russia is part of the world economy, but the two main segments of its own economy—the government sector, including many research centers, and the private sector—are not properly linked. The government needs to act as if there is one economy and that it is well diversified.[3]

Fursenko underscored that the state should reduce its direct involvement in the management of business activities. Instead, he urged that it create a more favorable environment for business. As positive steps, he pointed out government attempts to stimulate establishment of a venture capital industry and contributions to technoparks, technology transfer centers, and communication networks. He emphasized that the government should support risky innovation projects to help the private sector gain toe holds in new areas of the economy, perhaps following the models of Israel and Finland.[4] But when would there be discernible results from such efforts?

The Russian government would surely be required to provide much of the support for the nation's science and technology infrastructure in the years ahead. The lack of innovation in the private sector combined with the paucity of market-worthy Russian products raised issues about the long-term value of ISTC programs, which were to eventually attract Russian as well as international support. Better integration of these programs with Russia's own efforts to strengthen the nation's science and technology base was clearly needed.

Of continuing concern throughout ISTC's network of collaborating science institutions was the readiness, or too often a lack of interest, of the Russian government to sustain activities initiated with ISTC funding at specific facilities after this funding came to an end. Both the common view and the reality were that only in rare instances would foreign or domestic companies be sufficiently enticed by the novelty of Russian research efforts supported by the center to pick up the financial-support mantle. In short, some Western supporters of the ISTC were simply overly optimistic as to likely Russian interests in following in the wake of the center. Throughout the early 2000s the center repeatedly addressed the issue of sustainability of projects and the role of the private sector over the long term but paid less attention to how Russia could assume greater responsibility for sustaining specific project activities.

KEY ROLE OF ISTC'S SENIOR PROJECT MANAGERS

Turning to implementation of project activities of the ISTC, beginning in 1992 the Russian government began to assign senior Russian scientists with strong technical credentials to work with the planning group for the center. The center's executive directors eventually designated most of them as senior project managers. In this capacity, they had direct responsibility for facilitating the processing of project proposals and for monitoring implementation of approved projects.

Initially, this meant that each senior project manager who was recruited during the 1990s had responsibility for five to ten projects in various stages of development and implementation. The number of senior project managers eventually increased to about twenty, with each of their portfolios expanded to include ten to twenty projects. Soon each one was handling thirty to forty projects, and even as many as fifty projects.

Other member governments also designated a few international specialists who became senior project managers. Often they handled projects of special interest to their governments. On occasion, the governments would assign additional specialists from their countries to the ISTC staff, specifically to oversee clusters of partner projects of priority interest.

Without question, the senior project managers provided a critical day-to-day interface between the ISTC and the scientists in the Russian institutions carrying out the projects sponsored by the center. They were the on-the-ground "face" of the ISTC. Fortunately, the parties took considerable care in developing instructions for preparing proposals, which clearly set forth the details of the responsibilities that were expected of the project leaders at the participating institutes or research centers. At the same time, these instructions have served as important guidelines for focusing the efforts of the senior project managers as well.[5] Also, the templates for project agreements were standardized with few ambiguities, and the senior project managers quickly became familiar with each of the requirements.

Why has each senior project manager been responsible for so many projects? Part of the answer is the limitation imposed by the governing board on the total staff of the ISTC. Another reason is the trend among the parties to fund smaller and smaller projects rather than large projects, which were emphasized during the center's early years. The smaller the projects, the greater the workloads for managing comparable levels of expenditures.

In short, the senior project managers have been the core of the ISTC staff concerned about the substantive aspects of projects. They make many visits to the institutes and centers where their projects are under way. Some have become the best-informed experts in the country in specific areas of interest. They have not only been knowledgeable about what was going on in their fields of interest throughout many institutions of Russia, but they also have been very sensitive to the interests of the funding parties and the importance of establishing international networks of specialists working in common fields.

Occasionally, visitors to the ISTC have commented that while the senior project managers have been well-respected scientists, they have not been adequately trained to provide guidance to project recipients on steps that were necessary to transform research activities into marketable products. The senior project managers themselves have long been aware of the importance of familiarity not only with the scientific aspects of projects but also with the commercialization aspects—insofar as the research offered promise of marketability. Many of these managers have taken special steps to improve their expertise in this field through consultations with outside experts. While the strengths of the senior project managers have varied, depending on their backgrounds and years of experience at the ISTC, in general they have learned quickly about international approaches and have provided important assistance to project recipients.

In short, the senior project managers deserve high marks for their contributions to the center's successes. The positive attitude of a particularly effective senior project manager was as follows: "There are always new technologies as well as new methodologies concerning project management, personnel management, and resource management. ISTC staff should be made aware of these opportunities and be trained in those developments that are most useful to their work, and they should also address recent scientific achievements."[6]

Three types of project activities that were at the core of ISTC operations during the early 2000s are discussed below. First, the North American, European, and Japanese governments gave high marks to partner projects that were financed to a large extent by foreign end users of the research results (market-pull approach). Second, many officials were less enthusiastic about regular research projects that did not involve end users financially but were nevertheless intended to lead to commercial products (technology-push approach). Third, a wide variety of regular projects directed to basic science and to issues of global concern received mixed reviews. Unfortunately, in-depth evaluations of the long-term payoffs from specific projects, and particularly basic science projects and projects that addressed global concerns, along with dissemination of the details of success stories, have not been a strong aspect of the operations of the center.

GROWTH OF THE PARTNER PROGRAM

As noted in chapter 2, the ISTC established its partner program in 1996. The program flourished during the late 1990s and into the 2000s. As funding for ISTC's regular program of grants to research institutions declined, the partner program brought a second life into the center's activities. Russian officials talked incessantly in many forums about the need to link researchers with implementers of research results, and the partner program became a model as to how this could be accomplished.

Under the partner program, private and public organizations—particularly government departments—with headquarters in the countries that were funding parties of the ISTC were encouraged to use the center's services. The center could then facilitate development and implementation of joint projects involving institutions in Russia and other states that emerged from the former Soviet Union. The framers of the ISTC Agreement wisely foresaw the possibility of allowing partners to develop and fund projects, and Article 3 provided the legal basis for such a program.

The U.S. government became a strong advocate for the partner program, which was particularly effective in assisting U.S. organizations to use the established credibility and financial transfer mechanisms of the center to engage Russian research groups. This approach enabled U.S. government agencies as well as the U.S. corporate sector to invest with minimum difficulties in sensitive areas, such as biotechnology. Other ISTC member countries recognized these opportunities and in time followed the U.S. lead.

The partner program grew rapidly. Eventually more than 450 public and private sector organizations, which had been proposed by the ISTC parties, received the status of partners, although some of these organizations were partners only in name, with no involvement in projects. There were funding partners and nonfunding partners. The latter provided expertise but not funds for projects.

As expected, most attention in Russia focused on the funding partners. By 2006 hundreds of partner projects involving the transfer of more than two hundred million dollars to scientists and institutions in Russia and other countries in the region had been carried out. Public sector entities provided more than 80 percent of the funds, with the U.S. government contributing most of the funding. As with almost all ISTC activities, the vast majority of the partner projects were concentrated in Russia, with only a few carried out in neighboring states.[7]

The enthusiasm for the partner program was quite high. Several commentaries in 2004 on the program from different perspectives follow.

- "The ISTC has been central to including leading Russian scientists in CERN's progress." Director General of CERN (Geneva)
- "Bayer's experience with the ISTC has been very positive. We feel that this type of cooperation is not only remarkable regarding the achieved results, but also important because of guaranteeing necessary security on investments in research projects and intellectual property rights." Senior official of Bayer AG (Leverkusen, Germany)
- "The ISTC has played a major role in the development and implementation of the biochip project. Truly, this is exciting work that has exceptional potential benefits for Russia and the world." Senior official of U.S. Department of Health and Human Services[8]

However, a few international partners made less favorable comments after becoming discouraged in working through the bureaucratic requirements of the ISTC, which they considered unnecessarily burdensome. Their complaints related largely to (a) delays in obtaining concurrence of the Russian government for specific projects; (b) further delays within the ISTC Secretariat in processing applications approved by the Russian authorities together with a lack of information about the status of applications; (c) a requirement that the funding partner provide all project funds to the ISTC at the outset of project activity, with funds transferred to the research institution at later dates; and (d) lack of clarity as to the responsibility for avoiding delays in project development and implementation. Nevertheless, some complaining companies continued their participation in the program.

Those aspects of the ISTC approach that seemed to engender the most interest among partners were as follows:

- The ISTC provided tax-free payments directly to those scientists who participated in the projects, although only for the time that they actually devoted to the projects.
- Imports of equipment and materials were exempt from customs duties.
- Financial control and auditing through the center helped ensure appropriate use of funds.
- Allocation of intellectual property rights was specified in advance in the trilateral project agreements involving the partner, the scientific institute, and the ISTC.
- Experienced ISTC staff members were available to facilitate the projects.
- Overhead costs were low.[9]

The approach of the Schlumberger oil exploration company, for example, was a highly successful international effort to engage talented Russian scientists in addressing global challenges around the world. The company's view of the partner program was reflected in the following statement in 2002 by the manager of operations in Russia. "We believe it is important to support Russian scientists. To do this ourselves and to work with the Russian banks would be very difficult. At the same time, we make certain that we do the technology oversight. Yes, I think we will have more projects with the ISTC."[10]

From the viewpoint of the ISTC members in North America, Europe, and Asia, the partner program has been a solid success. It has opened previously closed doors for many companies and government agencies. It has avoided taxation. It has given legitimacy to activities that might otherwise have been carried out under cloudy legal circumstances.

A few skeptical Russian observers have interpreted these very strengths as flaws in the program. These critics believed that the ISTC was exposing sensitive facilities and achievements to foreigners with aspirations inimical to the interests of Russia. At the same time, tax breaks gave foreign companies an unfair advantage when competing with Russian companies. And the critics argued that Russian sovereignty was threatened by intrusions into the Russian industrial complex in a manner that was not anticipated when the ISTC Agreement was negotiated. Russian sensitivities became an increasingly important factor as rumors about Russian intentions to close ISTC operations in Russia began circulating as early as 2004.

COMMERCIALIZATION OF TECHNOLOGIES DEVELOPED
THROUGH ISTC PROJECTS

In parallel with efforts through the partner program to involve international companies in ISTC activities, for many years the ISTC devoted considerable attention to commercialization of technologies that were developed through ISTC-funded research projects—using a technology-push approach. From the beginning of the center, the legacy of the Soviet approach of central control in introducing into practice newly developed technologies remained a brake on commercialization activities. That approach had been for the government to issue directives for enterprises to introduce seemingly relevant technologies into their operational activities, whatever the costs. This history is further discussed in chapter 6. But in a market economy, the private sector—not the government—dictates which technologies are of sufficient interest to reach the marketplace.

Throughout the 1990s Russian researchers remembered that in the old days, after they had developed a new technical innovation, their job was finished. Such fragmentation of steps in the research and development chain was contrary to the experience of profit-oriented companies in a market economy. Thus, the ISTC recognized that transformational efforts were essential if research results were to eventually return profits and not simply become unusable products that bedecked typical showcase museums of many Russian institutes.

By 2002 senior ISTC staff members concerned with commercialization repeatedly reported the word on the street. The widely held view was that the ISTC was doing a good job in redirecting defense skills to civilian-oriented endeavors, but it had not contributed to significant commercial developments through its research-support activities other than through partner projects. Some observers attributed the scarcity of successful high-tech entrepreneurship in Russia to the lack of liquid financial markets that could provide outlets for venture capital. But several key staff members of the ISTC repeatedly argued that both technology and money were available. They asked, "What exactly was missing?"

To find the answer, the staff commissioned a survey of managers at Russian institutions who collectively had guided more than five hundred ISTC-funded projects. One-third of the respondents contended they were involved in some type of commercialization activities. For them, the primary mechanism was the entrepreneurship of small enterprises that had been established at their research institutes. These entities were either marketing on a small scale a few of the research successes or offering consultancy services based on research experiences.

While such activities were important at the local level, they did not lead to the mega-economic impacts that economists wanted to witness. The fields of environment and biotechnology offered the largest number of limited successes. Breakthroughs in information technologies had been anticipated, but no major successes could be attributed to ISTC projects.

The most significant finding was that the project managers at the institutes considered themselves scientists first and businessmen only a distant second. Project managers at the institutes repeated a common refrain: "We are not good organizers. Business could really take off if we had someone to lead us. Knowledge of the needs and identities of potential buyers—not access to investment money—is the significant issue."[11]

In time, ISTC developed a highly structured program devoted to commercialization of technologies—at least on paper. It included four components:

1. Advanced matchmaking workshops devoted to specific categories of technologies, travel support for researchers to interact with potential collaborators, and consultations on intellectual property rights (IPR)
2. Analyses of IPR activities at the institutes
3. Pre-commercialization: market surveys, business consulting, travel support to develop project designs, partner searches, and industrial certification of new technologies
4. Innovation initiatives: equipment purchases, marketing expenses, infrastructure upgrades, and business-oriented introductions and follow-up services[12]

However, there is little evidence that this program and related efforts had a major impact on moving research results into the market place in the short term. While the program was probably important in focusing attention on the marketing dimension of innovation, the opportunities to demonstrate how it could transform stagnant Russian approaches to commercialization were limited. Russian officials, rightly or wrongly, considered this commercialization program far from a success.

An astute Western observer of the economic realities of Russia has underscored the stifling effect of rampant corruption, lack of transparency, and a cumbersome Russian bureaucracy on the efforts of small entrepreneurs to penetrate significantly into the Russian market, whatever the potential of their products. He has emphasized that the ISTC has been only a very small island of integrity within Russia—an island that has played by internationally accepted rules—and could not be expected to immediately gain acceptance of its mode of operation within the reality of the Russian market.[13] My observations over many years support this view and suggest that a number of international experts have simply been on the wrong track in advocating immediate adoption of Western approaches for business success in Russia. The Western models may offer the best approach in the long term, but most entrepreneurs are interested in the near term, with little staying power to experience the benefits of the long term.

WIDE DIVERSITY OF SCIENCE PROJECTS

By the end of 2006 the ISTC had supported 1,867 civilian-oriented research and related projects valued at more than $600 million in Russia. About one-third of the projects were partner projects, and the others were regular research projects. During 2006 a total of 67 partner projects were funded at $19.8 million, and 72 regular projects were funded at $20.9 million. While these funding levels were quite strong, they still represented a slow decline in the budgetary commitments of the funding parties. In addition, special activities were supported during 2006 (e.g., training in managing projects, familiarization with intellectual property issues, support of applications for patents, funding of travel to conferences at home and abroad, organization of topical workshops, and database development).[14]

As noted, the foregoing statistics embrace partner projects and commercially oriented regular projects along with other projects that were intended to advance science, survey and evaluate important scientific developments, and contribute to fulfillment of global research agendas. From the beginning through 2006, the projects had been focused in the following areas, in descending order of the financial commitments to each area:

- Biotechnology and Life Sciences
- Physics
- Environment
- Fission Reactors
- Instrumentation

- Materials
- Chemistry
- Information and Communications
- Space, Aircraft, and Surface Transportation
- Manufacturing Technology
- Nonnuclear Energy
- Fusion
- Other Basic Sciences
- Other[15]

This categorization of projects is a reasonable reflection of the types of civilian-oriented capabilities that existed throughout the Soviet defense complex. The large number of environmental projects reflected widespread, pent-up desires among the scientific community to address damage to the ecology that had often been ignored by the industrial complex. Recognition by the general population that redirected scientists were addressing societal issues—such as food production and environmental pollution—drew widespread public attention to the ISTC's contributions.

In some project areas, linkages between the experiences of military and civilian scientific leaders were obvious. In other cases, former Soviet weapons specialists who were not accustomed to stringent financial constraints on their activities undoubtedly faced a learning period to become familiar with the realities of responding in a cost-effective manner to civilian needs. Lightweight titanium shovels had many advantages, but who could afford them?

Following is a list of ten institutions (all in Russia) that the ISTC had selected as recipients of the largest numbers of projects as of the end of 2006:

- Institute for Experimental Physics, Sarov
- Institute for Technical Physics, Snezhinsk
- Center for Virology and Biotechnology, Vector, Koltsovo
- Institute for Physics and Power Engineering, Obnisnk
- Plant for Techno-Chemical Products, Bogoroditsk
- Khlopin Radium Institute, St. Petersburg
- Center for Applied Microbiology and Biotechnology, Obolensk
- Institute of Organic Chemistry and Technology, Moscow
- Phytopathology Research Institute, Bolshiye Vyazemy
- Moscow Engineering and Physics Institute, Moscow[16]

For many years, all of these institutions have been high on the priority engagement lists of the Western and Asian parties to the ISTC Agreement. The institutes were well known throughout the world, at least by reputation. Initial impressions left most first-time visitors to these institutions wanting to see more.

Only one higher education institution is on this list, the Moscow Engineering and Physics Institute (MEPHI). The focus on the institutes that had been closest to applications of dangerous technologies is understandable, given the interests of the member states in quickly preventing leakage of sensitive information. But for the longer term, a greater emphasis on helping direct the next generation of high-technology specialists down the paths of peaceful applications of dual-use technologies has also been of some concern, and a number of higher education institutions had been deeply involved in supporting Soviet military efforts. Of course, the resources of the ISTC were limited; balancing near-term and long-term concerns led to an emphasis on the more immediate dangers of proliferation.

As a practical matter, the Russian ministries involved with the ISTC were much more interested in the financial stability within their applied institutions than within the universities. As an exception, MEPHI had long been close to the center of the Soviet nuclear program, with extensive personal and organizational contacts throughout the nuclear community. Therefore, it received strong ministerial encouragement to become an important recipient of ISTC funds that could attract talent from many institutions affiliated with the Ministry for Atomic Energy (Minatom) and its successor organization, the State Atomic Energy Corporation (Rosatom), who would work on civilian-oriented projects. Thus, many of the nuclear-oriented projects sited at MEPHI have involved participants from other institutions as well.

The outcomes of several projects, as highlighted by the ISTC from 2005 to 2007, provide some initial insights both as to the breadth of activities and as to the ways that ISTC characterized project success. Some representative examples are listed below (see also chapters 8, 9, and 10):

- A cost-saving technique for increasing the accuracy of data obtained during aircraft wind-tunnel testing
- New alloys for use in the transportation and mechanical engineering industries

- Demonstration of the productivity and environmental advantages of dry-drilling with aluminum alloys using cemented carbon drills
- Test kits for rapid characterization of common human resistance to the four most commonly used antibiotics to treat tuberculosis
- Internet tools for computational genetic mapping to assist in the searches for drug therapies, bioremediation techniques, industrial enzymes, and biosolar cells
- Technology to examine in detail the eye's retina for early warning of eye-related diseases
- High-quality nanoclusters for use in catalysis and optoelectronic devices[17]

Also by the beginning of 2007, several projects stood out for their potential for job creation. These research projects were designed to support the decommissioning of nuclear power stations and submarines, production of ultra-high-purity ammonia for the electronic industry, manufacture of new water filters and purification systems, and production of radiation-modified polymer samples as the basis for new industrial activities to capitalize on an expanding market for heat-shrinking tubes and tapes. However, the number of jobs that would be created by these highly publicized activities was to be measured only in the dozens, a very small impact on the totality of the employment problem.[18]

SUSTAINABILITY OF ISTC-SUPPORTED ACTIVITIES

The ISTC concept of sustainability, a term that was repeatedly used throughout the history of the organization, seemed to change from time to time. The definition is somewhat different than the currently popular use of the term *sustainability*, which the public often links to environmental concerns. There are at least four overlapping aspects of sustainability as used by the ISTC. All of these are linked to the long-term impacts of ISTC projects after the center concludes its funding.

- The opportunities for *individual scientists* to continue to work on civilian-oriented projects, initially undertaken with ISTC support. In most cases, the individual scientists hope that their projects will continue indefinitely in some form. Such continuity may or may not involve participation of the same international collaborators. If not, the research scientists will surely require access to new financial streams of support—from the Russian government, from the Russian private sector, or from foreign sources, including international companies. In addition, project sustainability may require Russian government or institutional approval and also continuing access to laboratories, including equipment, supplies, and maintenance services.

- The opportunities for *research groups*, with or without their original key members, to continue to work on civilian-oriented projects. This requires an institutional decision to continue to devote a group's effort to the topic of interest to the ISTC, even if the activities do not coincide with the changing priorities of the host institution.

- The readiness of the *host institution* to continue to pursue the civilian activity that was originally funded by ISTC, with involvement of the original or other research groups. Again, this type of sustainability requires the institution to embrace the ISTC-supported topic or closely related topics as being of priority interest, in competition with other priorities that may emerge. Also, funders at home or abroad that are interested in providing support are usually essential.

- The willingness of the *Russian government* and other funding sources in Russia to continue to support ISTC-initiated activities. This important objective has often been given short shrift by ISTC watchers, as the competition for funds within Russia outpaces the growth in the availability of government and private sector funds to support the science and technology infrastructure of the country. In the long run, consistent support at the national level of high-tech activities, including activities involving former weapons scientists, is the most important aspect of sustainability.

In short, the ISTC has played an important role in supporting on a temporary basis a part of the overall Russian innovation system, which would have had trouble perpetuating itself with declining funding by the Russian government—a system that has long needed restructuring. Despite the passion of many Russian researchers to focus on basic research and let others focus on using the results of that research, the ISTC has repeatedly pressed project managers for a greater focus on the economic payoff from its projects—payoff that in many cases could be realized only well after the completion of the projects. At the same time, it has often been easier, but far less effective, for the ISTC to conform with the legacy of the Soviet research system whereby those who are responsible for research pass on to others the responsibility for its applications.

Innovation champions who are capable of becoming shepherds of new ideas from inception to the marketplace have been in scarce supply. The needs in

Russia were succinctly summed up by an innovation expert in 2004 as follows: "ISTC projects, in the years to come, should gradually develop from science and technology in search of societal needs and commercial markets into societal and commercial needs in search of science and technology."[19]

Several years earlier, a report commissioned by the ISTC highlighted the importance of strengthening the science and technology infrastructure of Russia as a critical step for sustaining and effectively using the results of ISTC projects. This report advocated focusing on seven pillars of such an infrastructure, pointing out how the various ISTC activities could and should contribute to the development of these pillars:

- International openness and mobility involving increased internationalization of research institutes
- Research excellence and contributions to new knowledge, including selectivity of research activities based on excellence
- Economic valuation of research to improve international competitiveness, particularly through the involvement of corporate entities
- Diversification of funding, since multiple funding sources are vital to sustainability
- Attraction of young talent to ensure a vigorous and dynamic system
- National purpose and public interest, which encompass environment and health concerns; water, energy, transport, and communications capabilities; and capabilities to reduce damage from natural disasters
- Societal value, and particularly public recognition of the role of science and technology for the well-being of the nation[20]

These characteristics are obviously important and are further discussed in chapter 11. However, this list tends to oversimplify the challenges of competing within the international market on a significant scale. Other factors include conceptualizing innovations that can be produced at reasonable costs, moving technologies into the commercial sector, stimulating a venture capital industry, developing broad-scale electronic networking capabilities, and creating a modern educational system.

In short, we all have expected too much from the ISTC in bringing products to market. The task of transforming Russia's innovation system into a coherent approach that is embedded within a broadly based market economy has clearly been a massive task that is still only in its earliest days of evolution. While the

ISTC has made contributions, they are only small inputs in addressing the large task facing Russia. Not surprisingly, the ISTC parties from North America, Europe, and Asia have been less concerned about integrating ISTC activities with the economic interests of Russia than with achieving their own nonproliferation and scientific objectives.

The seven pillars described above were helpful, and at the time the ISTC staff paid close attention to them. The staff identified specific steps the ISTC could take to bridge gaps, beginning with the selection of projects that had promise of being sustained over the long term. The challenge was to engrain within Russian officials and scientists a sense of the importance of economic and public sector payoffs from research, along with expected scientific benefits. These payoffs take time to realize, even in the best of circumstances.

Despite the problems in sustaining individuals, research teams, research institutes, and indeed a viable and effective science and technology infrastructure of the country, the praise for the achievements of the ISTC in its early days could not have been stronger than the following words in 2004 by a renowned European specialist:

> ISTC's uniqueness is based on its excellent knowledge of and controlled access to many hundreds of research institutes, safety and security in the operations involved in projects of a sensitive and confidential nature, exemptions from tax and customs duties, privileged import and export procedures, and access to top Russian authorities. In addition, ISTC has a competent staff in Moscow of more than 200 people from 19 nations and is strongly linked into global research networks. All of these elements made ISTC a pearl in the Russian innovation system in the early years of the 21st century, considered by many spokesmen as the most effective instrument for foreign collaboration within the Russian science and technology sector.[21]

THE ISTC'S VISION AND STRATEGIC PLANNING

An updated vision for the future was under development during 2006 and was unveiled in 2007. Although similar to the vision set forth in the ISTC Agreement when it was drafted fifteen years earlier, the revision directed additional attention to (a) relevance to proliferation of not only scientific expertise but of technologies and materials as well and (b) more serious engagement with the leaders of Russian institutions as well as with individual scientists. The vision included the following mandate:

> The ISTC will continue to be at the forefront of international efforts to engage former weapons of mass destruction (WMD) scientists and their institutions in preventing the spread of WMD expertise, technologies, and materials and will also be more pro-active in areas that are linked to nonproliferation, such as counterterrorism, nuclear safety, and biosecurity, through focused development of science and technology projects, programmatic activities, and pursuit of regional as well as international objectives.[22]

The linkage of this vision statement to the increasing interests of the G8 countries in knowledge proliferation and scientist engagement was clear. Beginning in 2002 the nations that comprised the G8 launched the Global Partnership against the Spread of Weapons of Mass Destruction and quickly focused on scientist engagement as a key component of this strategy. The ISTC was perfectly positioned to play an important role in this global effort. Not surprisingly, the governing board wanted to have an up-to-date basis for being active in the international swell for expanded global cooperation, and the Global Partnership became an excellent venue.

At the same time, several ISTC members were interested in development of a new strategic plan. The priority areas that were then set forth in the plan were sustainable redirection, support of international nonproliferation activities, and operational efficiency and administrative reform. The specified tasks in each of these areas were as follows:

1. Sustainable redirection:
   - Reinforce regular projects with support for a limited number of activities that have potential for collaboration and co-funding
   - Facilitate development of sustainability plans for identified institutes
   - Identify viable external funding sources and joint funding mechanisms
   - Expand the partner program
   - Develop the commercialization support programs
2. Support of international nonproliferation activities:
   - Develop targeted initiatives to match relevant international priorities
   - Establish new partnerships with nonproliferation organizations and international programs

- Undertake activities to support other initiatives addressing WMD proliferation

3. Operational efficiency and administrative reform:
   - Adjust the center's staff structure, organization, and focus
   - Implement best practices recommended in external reviews
   - Adjust the role of the Scientific Advisory Committee
   - Improve synergies with other international organizations[23]

In the end, the plan was never formally adopted, due in large measure to the intransigence of the Russian government not to support such an ambitious agenda. Still the discussions of these issues by the governing board stimulated limited actions by the secretariat in moving forward.

AN ISLAND UNTO ITSELF

Thus, until 2007 it appeared that the ISTC was rolling along a high-speed track that led to many success stories. The returns on investments by the funding parties seemed high. Future prospects for continued success were considered bright.

But all was not well. Budgetary support for ISTC projects was declining. Interest in the center by the Russian government was waning to the extent that representatives of the center had increasing difficulty even meeting with key Russian officials. Meanwhile, these officials were speaking publicly about the conclusion of the need for further scientist redirection efforts, as underscored in chapter 4.

The governing board and the senior staff of the center had done an excellent job in keeping the center on track, but they did not fully appreciate that the track was turning around new corners. Political leadership in the country was changing, and the ISTC leadership did not give the need for interactions with the new leaders sufficient priority. Why rock the boat when mini-success stories were being recorded on a weekly basis? As previously mentioned, by 2007 significant meetings by representatives of the ISTC with political leaders of Russia to discuss the future role of the center simply did not appear on personal calendars. As a consequence, while the country was changing rapidly, the ISTC was not keeping up.

CHAPTER FOUR

Unraveling of the Moscow Science Center (2007–2011)

ISTC represents exceptional nonproliferation and scientific research-coordination assets that should be preserved but adapted to new international and regional contexts.

—European Commission Evaluation Team, November 2007

For years, we have been hearing about obsolescence of the ISTC's scientific redirection mission from the Russian Government. We reached the "read-my-lips" stage of this issue some time ago. But the ISTC was so convenient.

—Official of U.S. Embassy in Moscow, August 2010

WITH STRONG WORDS OF PRAISE from the funding parties and accolades from scientists throughout Russia and other member states, in 2007 the ISTC seemed poised to continue blazing new pathways for coordinating international interests in many fields of science. The following ISTC-sponsored workshops and seminars in cities of Russia during 2007, plus a comparable number of events in other member states as well, illustrated the broad reach of the center across scientific areas of international interest:

- Astrophysical research: Berdsk
- Nano and giga challenges in electronics and photonics: Sarov
- Stem cell research: Moscow
- Anticancer drug discovery: Moscow
- Aerospace technologies: Moscow
- Cleaning up sites contaminated with radioactive material: Moscow
- Laser applications in life sciences: Moscow
- Muon-catalyzed fusion: Dubna

- Nonproliferation summer school: Moscow
- Interactions of hydrogen isotopes with structural materials: St. Petersburg
- Nano-structured materials: Ufa
- Responses to chemical emergencies, including terrorist attacks and accidents: St. Petersburg
- Advanced nuclear fuel cycle: Nizhny Novgorod
- Mechatronics and robotics: St. Petersburg
- Biological threats: Moscow
- Tuberculosis: Moscow
- Alternative energy sources: Moscow[1]

But the steady decline for almost five years in the funds available for supporting activities in Russia was increasingly obvious as the funding parties, particularly the United States, decided to significantly reduce their contributions for new project starts. While Washington's argument that the center was too slow in exhausting the funds in its pipeline had merit, the public impression was that the United States simply was curtailing its commitment to the center. Second, the Russian warning during 2006 at a G8 Global Partnership meeting in Berlin that the period of scientist redirection was over repeatedly entered into discussions concerning future activities of the center.

As noted in chapter 3, the ISTC Secretariat had increasing difficulties in arranging meetings with key Russian officials to resolve minor problems that kept interrupting the flow of activity of the center. Of particular concern, officials at Rosatom, the designated Russian representative for ISTC activities, were preoccupied with the change in status of Rosatom, which was becoming a commercially oriented agency. The Ministry of Foreign Affairs had many other more pressing issues on its plate. All the while, the ISTC staff was shrinking as departing staff members were not always replaced.

Against this background of high-intensity schedules and growing anxiety within the Moscow science center, this chapter addresses two overlapping streams of activity that preoccupied the center's leadership, its staff, and its broad network of collaborating scientists in Russia and in other countries from 2007 through 2011. First, I present descriptions of some of the important program activities that were underway. Then I turn to a discussion of the withdrawal of Russia from the center. A good starting point for the discussion is sustainability of ISTC-initiated activities, a critical issue that for many years has remained a constant theme within the center.

LONG-TERM SCIENCE BUSINESS PLANS

From its earliest days, the ISTC leadership recognized the importance of sustainability of the research activities of groups of scientists that were being supported on a temporary basis by the center. The center extended the length of a number of projects up to several years to help in the transition to sustainability. In 2007 the center initiated a focused program to encourage a few important institutes, primarily in Russia, to assume more assertive responsibilities for planning sustainability of key activities that had been nurtured through grants from the ISTC.

The concept called for the institutes, relevant Russian ministries, funding parties, and other interested partners to agree on sustainability targets and on the contributions by the ISTC and others to help achieve those targets. Institute activities would move away from support by the center in a planned fashion. However, the institutes would not be immediately categorized as ISTC graduates. They would continue to work with the center and other interested organizations within the framework of their own strategic plans (sometimes referred to as science business plans) as appropriate in the years ahead.

This approach was to help break down the perception and the existing reality of a funder-beneficiary relationship. To this end, the ISTC would act as an invited adviser and, when necessary, would consider supporting specific technical needs on a limited basis. But the choices as to the ISTC's role would be up to the institutes in the first instance.

In principle, this approach sounded like a good idea. But would the research institutes take such plans seriously? Or would they simply agree to develop plans because they considered such a step to be essential in order to qualify for additional ISTC funding?

In any event, by 2010 the ISTC had identified seven Russian institutes to participate in this process. At two institutes, sustainability plans were soon in place and implementation was underway, within the context of the institutes' own strategic plans. Specifically, the Khlopin Radium Institute in St. Petersburg installed equipment to upgrade its radiopharmaceutical facility. This enhancement would increase the quantity and quality of medical isotopes and radiopharmaceuticals used in clinics and hospitals in Russia. The ISTC provided $200,000 for this activity. At the Institute for Physics and Power Engineering in Obninsk, a plan for expanded production of high-quality radioisotopes was also initiated, with $580,000 allocated for this effort. In addition, a third plan was moving forward. At the Institute for Pulse Technologies, the ISTC had begun to provide $700,000 to upgrade the production lines of arc protection devices and to develop a device for protection of electrical equipment from arc short circuits.[2] The status of sustainability plans for four other institutions in Russia in 2010 was as follows:

- Siberian Chemical Combine, Seversk: Awaiting institution and government approvals to move forward
- Institute of Catalysis, Novosibirsk: Plan approved, but funding not available
- Institute of Immunological Engineering, Lyubchany: Plan approved, but funding not available
- Institute for Organic Chemistry and Technology: Institute apparently no longer interested[3]

Given the limitations on funding, some institutes that participated in the planning in good faith strongly criticized the failure of the center to provide the resources for the institutes to move forward. In hindsight, the center should not have embarked on such a broad-ranging program, given the uncertainty of the availability of financial resources that would be available for a very expensive undertaking. While the grants that were awarded seemed important, the significance of the effort was too often exaggerated.

OTHER PROGRAM ACTIVITIES

In 2010 the announced withdrawal by the Russian government from the ISTC led to a decision by the European Union (EU) in the same year to suspend funding of new ISTC projects in all seven countries that emerged from the former Soviet Union. The decision was based on concerns over the legal basis in Brussels for such activities when Russia withdraws and on doubts as to the future of the center. By the end of 2011 the EU had also decided to suspend funding for the supplemental programs of the center such as training and partner projects. At that time, Canada decided on a similar approach. Thus, no new funds were to be made available from the EU or Canada for projects or supplemental activities, pending the outcome of discussions on the future organization of scientific cooperation in all seven member states of the ISTC that had been components of the Soviet Union.

Against this background, in 2010 and 2011 EU activities continued in Russia at a lower financial level, but no new projects were funded. Attention concerning programs shifted to the six other member states where activities were underway, such as implementation of ISTC's targeted initiatives.

During 2010 and 2011 some activities were directed to strengthening Russian institutional capabilities for promoting a widespread nonproliferation consciousness (the Programs on Responsible Science and on Outreach), which were financed through funds already in the pipeline for approved projects. Other projects were in midcourse, with the recipients of the funding obviously interested in taking projects to completion.

Also of interest was the governing board's approval in 2010 of various initiatives to move ISTC into the twenty-first century, as the global spread of dual-use capabilities became of greater concern. From the center's outset, the parties had emphasized two directions for projects, namely, (a) preventing proliferation activities by redirection of former weapons scientists who were participating in the projects, and (b) advancing science that could contribute to economic development of Russia and other countries where projects were sited. The initiatives were to address both issues. Also in 2010 the governing board adopted an interim report containing a blueprint for future international scientific cooperation.

In mid-2011 the pipeline funding that was assigned to approved projects in Russia was as follows, with the number of projects that would be active during each of the cited milestone dates indicated:

- March 2011: 325 projects totaling $153 million
- January 2012: 184 projects totaling $89 million
- January 2013: 89 projects totaling $47 million
- January 2014: 36 projects totaling $21 million
- January 2015: 11 projects totaling $4 million
- July 2015: 10 projects totaling $3.6 million[4]

Beginning in the mid-1990s and continuing through 2011, the ISTC leadership recognized that the clustering of research projects to address in depth various aspects of important technical problems could increase the bang for the buck of the center's investments. This recognition eventually led to the Program of Targeted Initiatives. The approach encouraged specialists from different Russian institutions to work more closely together, focusing on well-defined problems of mutual interest. For example, early attention was given to

(a) development of biochips for detecting the presence of dangerous pathogens, (b) use of biological and chemical methods for reducing the toxicity of chemical wastes, and (c) improvement of techniques for measuring the nuclear cross-sections of radionuclides, which contributed to planning and implementation of scientific experiments.

Turning to an energy initiative, in 2004 Gazprom had co-financed with the ISTC a laboratory prototype of an electrochemical generator with a capability to generate six kilowatts of electricity. Having successfully tested this fuel cell in 2009, a team of specialists from a number of Russian institutions completed the design and preliminary testing of a pilot power plant based on technology available in 2010. Working in cooperation with the Institute for Experimental Physics in Sarov, Gazprom then made the decision to begin small-scale manufacturing. Also in 2010 ISTC funding supported a separate task to help develop an alternative high-temperature, low-capacity fuel cell.[5]

In the same year the ISTC expanded work under the targeted-initiative rubric of drug design. The initial idea was to enlist a core of selected Russian institutions and then to sponsor consultations with other Russian and international organizations interested in this topic. A particularly important meeting in Moscow in 2010 on multidrug-resistant tuberculosis involved more than 130 international specialists. The parties identified future activities to address prevention, control, and treatment of tuberculosis.[6] While such efforts had conceptual roots dating back more than a decade, the new focus was striking.

Also in the field of biological research, in 2010 the ISTC adopted probiotics as a targeted initiative, with enthusiastic support by Japan. As of 2011 this activity was in the early stages of development, with contacts being made with researchers throughout the world. Efforts to combat life-threatening infections was a topic that gained particular resonance in Russia and in other countries.[7]

The ISTC conducted a series of international meetings in 2010 that helped launch a targeted initiative on ultra-high-intensity light technologies. Russian specialists from a dozen institutes were interested in demonstrating the feasibility of laser-driven thermonuclear fusion as a future energy source. Linkages with activities in England, the United States, and other countries quickly became important components of this initiative.[8] Other programs initially emphasized by the ISTC in 2010 were, as previously indicated, the Responsible Science Program and the Outreach Program. They were designed to promote a culture of nonproliferation of sensitive knowledge when dealing with technology or materials that could be used in dangerous dual-use applications.

The four pillars of the Responsible Science Program are (a) education and training; (b) research and tutorials; (c) control systems for instrumentation (for safeguards and safety); and (d) international collaboration that emphasizes transparency through information exchange, web-based information systems, and international harmonization of activities. Five Russian institutions developed pilot education and training programs during 2010–11, with particular attention given to the roles of nuclear specialists. Among the anticipated outputs are education guidance documents, multimedia presentations, reference materials, and, of course, the program's graduates, who should lead future activities in the rapidly developing field.[9] The International Atomic Energy Agency (IAEA) made important contributions to this effort, based on a Memorandum of Understanding between the agency and the center, which was linked to the agency's Educational Program in Nuclear Security.

The Outreach Program was designed to promote responsible management of dual-use know-how, particularly in states beyond the ISTC members. The program helped establish new linkages between Russian and counterpart organizations in other countries. For example, a major nonproliferation conference in Moscow in March 2010 attracted specialists from twenty countries. Participants included specialists from China, India, Brazil, Iran, and North Korea. In each of these countries, questions about appropriate use of dual-use technologies have long been of considerable concern to the international community.

Another example of the scope of this ISTC outreach initiative was an evolving relationship between the ISTC and the Organization for the Prohibition of Chemical Weapons. This activity was linked with a program sponsored by the World Bank to destroy outdated pesticides. The ISTC also envisaged engagement with Balkan countries on chemical security.[10]

In underscoring its latest achievements, in the spring of 2011 the ISTC Secretariat highlighted the following project results:

1. Countering terrorism
   - A robotic arm
   - Small suitcases for detection of concealed explosives
2. Commercialization of research results
   - Gas/fire detector
   - Water purification system
   - Dental implants using titanium

- Hand-held detector for precise measurement of beta and gamma radiation
3. Hydrogen energy technologies
   - Water boiler prototype
   - Car equipped with Hydrogen-Rich Gas Generator[11]

All of these activities addressed scientific and nonproliferation issues in a manner that gave priority to a high level of international transparency. As the ISTC closes its doors in Russia and the foreign and local staff dwindles, it seems likely that some of the seeds that have been well planted will be nurtured by other organizations and individuals. Of course, much of this responsibility can only be picked up by Russian institutions. Let us hope that Russia's responsibilities to the international scientific community are clear, and that the international agencies and Russian institutions will build on the pioneering efforts of the ISTC.

In another area of continued activity, in 2011 the secretariat was quick to remind visitors that 450 partners had sponsored ISTC projects. U.S. partner projects alone still had fifty-nine million dollars in the pipeline.[12] Over the years, particularly strong industrial partners have included, for example, the following organizations:

1. European Union: Airbus, CERN, Bayer, Philips, BASF
2. United States: Boeing, 3M, General Atomics, General Electric
3. Asia: Samsung, Komatsu, Nissan, Toshiba, Hitachi[13]

A final initiative of considerable political importance during 2011 was the announcement by the United States that it was prepared to commit two million dollars through the ISTC to support activities related to the Fukushima nuclear disaster in Japan. The governing board promptly established a new supplemental program to facilitate exchanges involving all interested parties. The title of this activity is Cooperation and Support for Nuclear Safety, Emergency Preparedness, Response, Rehabilitation, Remediation, and Monitoring.[14]

SETTING SUN OF RUSSIA'S INVOLVEMENT IN THE ISTC

Meanwhile, in early 2009 I attended the celebration in Moscow of the fifteenth anniversary of the establishment of the ISTC. I had prepared a written commentary on the early days of the ISTC, which was included in the brochure prepared for the celebration. I then made a few remarks at the festivities on the center's future directions.

I had also participated in the tenth anniversary gala in Moscow, which was characterized by ringing endorsements of past achievements and optimistic predictions of future successes. I anticipated that the fifteenth anniversary would be yet another celebratory gathering to revel in further accomplishments of the center. Significant changes in the global security and scientific situation had been evolving since the inception of the concept of the ISTC, but the growing role of Russia in international security deliberations should have become a change agent in Western thinking about the structure or operation of the center. Unfortunately, the ISTC was too small an operation to expend political energies to change what was widely viewed as a success story.

Before heading for Moscow, I learned that there had been much discussion within the governing board and within the member governments about the evolving security context that surrounded the ISTC. According to those who were close to day-to-day activities, the parties had concluded that the best strategy for the ISTC was to stay the course. Programs could be adjusted, but the overall approach—and particularly the political framework for activities—would not be modified.

During preparation of my comments for the celebration, I quickly learned from long-time colleagues in Moscow of strong rumblings emanating from the Russian government about the future of the ISTC, signaling that the center might be in trouble. As previously noted, at a meeting in Berlin in 2006 a Russian government official had announced that the redirection of Russian weapons scientists to civilian endeavors had been completed. This statement raised eyebrows but did not stir significant reactions in Washington or Brussels. And I also discovered how badly communications between the Russian government and the ISTC Secretariat had atrophied.

The Russian government had apparently concluded that the basic mission of the ISTC had lost its relevance. Why was there further need for the center to be operating in Moscow? If scientific cooperation was the rationale for the continued existence of the center, why couldn't the organization be located in Brussels or some other capital rather than continuing to be a burden on the Russian government? These were important questions but not yet urgent ones for busy officials in any of the capitals other than Moscow.

It was quite clear to many representatives of the Western and Asian parties to the ISTC Agreement that redirection was only partially completed in Russia. Why else would hundreds of Russian weapons scientists continue to apply to the ISTC for their first-ever redirection grants? Why were Russian scientists in the outlying regions of the country loudly complaining that Moscow did not understand that ISTC support continued to be essential to sustain redirection? Support from the Russian government or from other sources for their projects was simply not available, regardless of the merits of their ideas. And well-respected leaders of the Russian scientific community were intensively searching for greater financial assistance from abroad, strongly suggesting that while redirection was well underway, newly organized civilian research teams were not on solid footing.

Thus, I arrived in Moscow aware that I would surely encounter crosscurrents concerning the ISTC's future. On arrival, I amended my planned remarks to include recommendations for significant modifications of the ISTC governing structure. I planned to call for a new orientation for addressing global issues — issues that were increasingly linked to worldwide proliferation concerns, as even some poor countries were being confronted with home-grown and imported technologies that could cause considerable destruction. My comments, however, contained no mention of the possible shuttering of the Moscow headquarters of the center.

My first awakening in Moscow in that regard was the absence of senior Russian officials at the anniversary celebration. The other ISTC members were well represented, but Russia sent only several midlevel officials who sat silently in the background. At the tenth anniversary, the scene had been quite different. It was the U.S. government, not the Russian government, that had decided that midlevel representation was appropriate. In 2004 the center seemed on course, and apparently there were many other high-visibility activities in other venues that commanded political support from the Russian leadership.

Despite my trepidation throughout the fifteenth anniversary events, the parties praised the work of the ISTC while at the same time emphasizing the need to support a transformation of objectives and priorities. Indeed, the governing board issued an optimistic report on the outcome of its meeting held the day before the celebration. As already mentioned, the governing board called for a change in direction in its programs. It established a working group to sort out what this meant in practice. But rumors were circulating, particularly during

coffee breaks at the festivities, that the Russian government would soon announce its withdrawal from the ISTC Agreement; and such a move would close
the doors on ISTC operations in Moscow.

I sensed little enthusiasm for continuing ISTC activities in Moscow in the absence of strong Russian government support. Nor was there much enthusiasm
to inaugurate the working group on the future of the center that the ISTC Governing Board had established, if it was to be faced with a done-deal within the
Russian government.

Sensing the push for dramatic changes in the ISTC's future ranging from closure of the ISTC to its replacement by an organization that focused on science
cooperation rather than nonproliferation, I further modified my prepared presentation to the assemblage. I proposed several significant adjustments in the
political and policy framework of the ISTC, but I did not call for a rewriting of
the ISTC Agreement, which others were advocating. In my view, opening up
the agreement would surely mean losing tax exemptions and probably privileges for access to sensitive facilities. These were core concerns of the Western
and Asian parties to the agreement. My proposals included the following suggestions:

- Appoint a Russian cochair of the governing board
- Invite Brazil, China, and India to become nonvoting members of the governing board
- Invite selected international organizations to become nonvoting members
  of the governing board
- Give increased attention to countering terrorism involving dual-use technologies
- Adopt better metrics for assessing ISTC's impacts in preventing proliferation (see chapter 11)
- Modify provisions of the ISTC Statute that had given funding parties the
  option of claiming exclusive rights to intellectual property developed
  through ISTC projects being carried out in Russia or in other recipient
  states

I regret that none of these global suggestions were seriously considered.
They simply were offered too late in the lifetime of the ISTC.

All of us finally realized that the governments supporting activities in Russia
needed to face up to the fact that by 2009 Russia's role in the world had become
dramatically different from the situation in 1994 when the ISTC formally en-

tered onto the world stage. Russia had recovered from the depths of despair—economically, psychologically, and politically. Key Russian officials considered their country among the world's leaders in shaping the security arrangements across the continents. A dangerous weapons brain drain could emerge, but it would not originate in Russia, argued Russian colleagues.

I reflected on the many successful redirection projects supported by the ISTC and on the transparency of Russian institutions where these projects had been carried out. Such transparency was inconceivable at the beginning of the 1990s. I was pleased to have been associated with the ISTC staff, and I reflected on the absence of financial irregularities that we had worked diligently to avoid. I was reluctant to let go of these accomplishments and to abandon this amazing experiment.

At the same time, I could not forget the lingering animosities in Moscow over the political decisions by the Western countries many years earlier to establish a separate science center for the Ukraine and to encourage Georgia to become a member of this center in Kiev, as well as remaining a member of the ISTC. These decisions, made under pressure from the U.S. government, had eventually weakened the ISTC's appeal to the authorities in Moscow. As Russia began to regain its economic viability, these decisions to keep Russia on the sidelines to the extent possible had taken their toll on support for the ISTC.

As noted in chapter 3, I had informally raised two questions in 2001 during discussions with the ISTC Secretariat. How was the center supporting achievement of Russia's national goals? How should the transition to Russian funding of ISTC-type projects be made? In 2009 I reflected on the importance of these two questions.

In short, the international security community did not give sufficient attention to the need for ISTC activities to take into account changing Russian scientific, economic, and political interests until it was too late, and the die for closure had been cast in Moscow. Western and Japanese officials did not seem concerned whether their policies complemented Russian policies. If Western approaches raised friction with Moscow, the Russians would get over their unhappiness, so thought impatient officials from abroad.

As to the need to prepare for a transition in the financial commitments to the ISTC, there was, of course, much discussion over the years when it came to matching financial contributions from the Russian government. However, such a core transition issue required major adjustments of ISTC operations. This step should have been considered in detail from the earliest days of the ISTC.

RESETTING THE U.S.-RUSSIAN RELATIONSHIP

In December 2009 Secretary of State Hillary Clinton finally spoke out about the need to reorient the U.S. relationship with the ISTC: "Progress toward achieving the original objective of the ISTC Agreement has been a resounding success. At the same time, the landscape, internationally and in countries where the center has been active, has undergone profound changes."[15]

But this admonition to pay attention to the changes in Russia and elsewhere was several years too late. By that time, the Russian government had decided on its course of action. Inadequate international attention to changes in Russia was certainly a factor that led to closing of ISTC activities in Russia.

NOTIFICATION OF RUSSIA'S WITHDRAWAL FROM THE ISTC

In August 2010 the Russian Ministry of Foreign Affairs posted on its website a decree signed by President Dmitry Medvedev stating that Russia intended to withdraw from the Provisional Protocol of 1994 and its associated obligations under the ISTC Agreement of 1992. As noted in chapter 1, the protocol had established the ISTC on a temporary basis, pending ratification of the ISTC Agreement by the Duma.[16] The withdrawal was to be effective six months after the Russian government formally notified the other parties to the protocol of its intention.[17]

Of course, withdrawal meant that the ISTC could no longer continue its activities within Russia. The decree was appropriately silent on activities of the center in the other six states that emerged from the former Soviet Union and had joined the center. Future ISTC-sponsored activities in these states would then become a topic of intergovernmental negotiations among these states and the other ISTC parties.

The agreement had been awaiting ratification by the Russian parliament for many years. Even if the legislative branch had taken that step, Russia would have retained the right to withdraw from the agreement with six months' advanced notification to the other signatories of the document. Ratification would have placed a modicum of additional pressure on the Russian authorities, both internationally and internally, to continue the operations of the ISTC in Russia. Withdrawal might have been politically more difficult for President Dmitry Medvedev. But by 2010 President Medvedev and Prime Minister Vladimir Putin were in strong positions within Russia. Most likely they would have imposed their will to withdraw, without encountering political blockage by the Duma or any other Russian entity.

The key leaders of the Medvedev administration never questioned the view of many prominent politicians, nonproliferation experts, and scientific leaders within and outside Russia that the ISTC had been a good idea in the 1990s and that the center had performed well. But they correctly claimed over and over that times had changed. "We need to look to the future and not to the past" was a common refrain. The need for this foreign outpost operating near the heart of the Russian security complex was no longer in Russia's interest, according to some vocal commentators. Also, the Russian leadership had other more important issues to negotiate with the many governments that participated in the ISTC, they added.

As an example of these other mega-issues, the controversy over U.S. intentions to continue to pursue establishment of anti-missile facilities in Europe was in the headlines in Russia at the same time that the Russian government proclaimed the end of the Moscow science center. The revived interest in Washington in anti-missile facilities came forth in the wake of an earlier announcement that the United States would abandon the concept of locating such facilities in Poland and the Czech Republic. Russian officials assumed that the United States had previously changed course in large measure to satisfy Russian concerns. But why the latest reversal? With a focus on such large issues, the Russian authorities were undoubtedly convinced that foreign criticism over their decision to withdraw from the ISTC would soon subside.

To return to the 2006 G8 meeting in Berlin, Russian officials clearly implied there that Russia was reconsidering the need for the center. They underlined that the economic and security situations in their country, which were the original incentives for establishment of the center, had changed significantly.[18] Thus, the signing of the decree four years later by President Medvedev should not have come as a complete surprise to anyone deeply involved in ISTC activities. By that time, the Western governments and Japan had finally realized that they should have paid more attention to views of Russian officials who were, in fact, quite serious about their early warnings of likely withdrawal.

However, the route that the Russian government took in 2010 to inform the thirty-eight other participating states of its pending action—a simple Internet announcement, rather than direct conversations with the key governments that had invested heavily in the ISTC, and certainly with the ISTC executive director—was clearly inappropriate. The diplomatic community in Moscow widely condemned the action as a rude breach of customary diplomatic practice. Some diplomats even contended that Russia's action was inconsistent with its obligations under the Vienna Convention, which provides the framework for diplomatic relations among governments.

Three months earlier, the Russian government had informed many research institutions within Russia that the future of the ISTC was uncertain. The authorities warned about the futility in submitting new proposals to the center. But the Russian authorities did not have the courtesy to inform the center of this action either before or even after it was taken.

Following the Internet posting of the Russian decree concerning withdrawal, the governments of the United States, Japan, Canada, and the European Union, along with the ISTC Secretariat, quickly requested meetings with Russian officials for clarification. Eventually, a few meetings were held. In October 2010 Russian officials had the first technical consultations with the ISTC Secretariat; in June and December 2011 the governing board assessed the implications of the planned withdrawal.

But by then the Russian position was clear and embedded within the bureaucracy. The often-repeated official Russian view was that the need for the ISTC had disappeared. Key officials contended that the threat of uncontrolled proliferation of know-how developed in Russia for weapons of mass destruction had passed; at the same time, Russia was allocating more resources to support its own scientists adequately without the need for external assistance. Many bilateral and multilateral channels were available to pursue scientific efforts of international interest, added Russian spokespeople. Indeed, the government in Moscow had clearly developed an appetite for bilateral arrangements rather than continuing to commit to a long-term multilateral approach through the ISTC when it came to dealing with sensitive technologies.

Warnings of adverse impacts of the withdrawal reverberated throughout Moscow. Articles in leading newspapers, postings on the Internet, and discussions at gatherings of diplomats gave voice to dire predictions of the political and security consequences of withdrawal. Stories of scientists again trolling for support from unsavory sources livened up discussions among officials within and outside Russia.

In 2010 an important Russian nuclear scientist conveyed his views to the Russian government, and indeed to the world, via the Internet: "The decision to withdraw from the ISTC is not good for Russian science, for international scientific cooperation on sensitive technologies, or for grassroots work on nonproliferation. It will lead to renewed isolation of closed cities, while reducing opportunities for cooperation with leading international science centers such as the international nuclear center in Geneva, CERN."[19]

The lack of a Russian champion who was well positioned within the government and who was interested in taking on the responsibility of representing Russia in dealings with the ISTC was undoubtedly a major factor in the decision of the Russian government to withdraw from the center. The Ministry for Atomic Energy (Minatom) was the original champion and had passed the baton to its successor organization, Rosatom. But Rosatom was in large measure evolving into a profit center focused on sales of nuclear reactors abroad and was eager to disentangle from the ISTC. No one wanted to be the *new* godfather of an *old* institution. The excitement of establishing a new entity and shaping it in accordance with personal preferences was not part of the job description.

RUSSIAN VIEWS UNDERLYING THE WITHDRAWAL

Amid nonstop discussions in the hallways of the ISTC headquarters concerning Russia's withdrawal, confusion reigned as to the timing and the approach that the Russian authorities would adopt in phasing out the center's activities in Russia. For many months, the government was not forthcoming in providing ISTC member states and the secretariat with clear indications of how it planned to proceed in developing the details of closing the ISTC headquarters and addressing the fate of ongoing projects. Quickly many staff members of the center began looking for other places of work in Moscow, with the task of preserving the documentation generated by the center over many years only a distant concern that would be left to others.

As soon as President Medvedev's withdrawal decree became public, a cottage industry of ISTC-watchers in Russia, Europe, the United States, and Canada began flooding the Internet and private communication channels with analyses of the reasons behind the Russian decision. Some commentators had been steadily involved in ISTC activities for many years. Others were sporadic participants. Still others had quickly become self-proclaimed experts on brain drain issues and on scientific cooperation in sensitive fields involving important elements of Russia's defense complex.

Each expert had an opinion as to the reasons behind the Russian decision to close the doors, but they always returned to the absence of an ISTC champion within the Russian government. Russian commentators blamed the lack of Western sensitivities as to the rightful place of Russia in a changing global security architecture. At the same time, representatives of a number of countries emphasized that Russia was making a mistake based on (a) Moscow's overly optimistic assessments as to the readiness of Russia to control its dangerous know-how and (b) Moscow's lack of appreciation of the value of international communication channels, built on joint interests of Russian and foreign counterparts, that provided access to international scientific achievements.

A well-informed Russian colleague who was close to the internal deliberations concerning the future of the ISTC provided revealing insights regarding the views of Russian decision makers in May 2010.

> Russia is satisfied with the ISTC and does not have political or other problems with the center. The big problem is the changed environment. When the ISTC was established, there were no competitors. Russian scientists were ready to emigrate with no sources of funds for research. Now Russian scientists have other sources of funds from the Russian government and from bilateral research projects involving not only Western countries but also supported by China, Brazil, India, and other countries.
>
> Transformation of the ISTC requires changing the agreement. The nonproliferation question has been resolved, and there are questions as to why only scientists involved with weapons of mass destruction should benefit from the ISTC. . . . The ISTC's commercialization program has been a complete failure. All intellectual property rights go to Western partners. Thus, partners become international competitors with the Russian institutes. At the same time, foreign companies are more interested in working directly with Russian entities than through the ISTC. . . . No other organization has similar tax and customs privileges, nor do scientific organizations have diplomatic privileges. . . .
>
> There is a need to find a godfather for the ISTC. If an organization does not have an internal champion, it disappears. After Rosatom became a joint stock company, its only interest has been to sell reactors to other countries. The Ministry for Education and Science has its own programs and is a competitor with ISTC. The Academy of Sciences cannot assume control since it is managed by scientists, and it is not a government agency.[20]

A second report concerning a meeting several weeks later between Prime Minister Putin and key government officials again underscored that the lack of a strong advocate for the ISTC within the government was probably the single most important reason that the decision was made to close the ISTC's operations in Russia. According to this report, if any minister had expressed interest in accepting the responsibility for retaining the ISTC, the center would not be shuttering its windows. But the most appropriate official, the minister for education and sciences, was in the midst of a reorganization of his ministry and was not interested in taking on an additional task.[21] An infusion of government funding had increased the ministry's capabilities to support research throughout the country. The ministry probably considered itself as a successful rival of the ISTC, which had lost much of its external financial support. In any event, no one was interested in assuming the headaches of managing the center.

All the while, rumors circulating in Moscow provided a litany of additional reasons why the ISTC could not muster support from an advocate within the Russian government. Explanations included the following:

- After many years of pressure from the United States and other nations for Russia to tighten control over exports of dual-use technologies, the government had implemented effective measures to help ensure that potentially dangerous exports would not fall into the hands of unreliable organizations in other countries. Some ISTC projects, particularly several supported by the European Union, provided access by Western organizations to Russian data that were subject to export control. However, the Western organizations insisted on reserving the right to forward sensitive information to other institutions with unknown histories in distant countries beyond the reach of the ISTC.
- North American, European, and Asian governments treated Russia as just another developing country within the ISTC context, whereas Russia had become a revitalized power on the international scene. Russian officials complained that their country was being considered as an impoverished assistance recipient—together with Belarus, Kazakhstan, Kyrgyzstan, Tajikistan, Georgia, and Armenia—while other countries that were parties to the agreement were treated as donor countries. This lack of respect for Russia's capabilities created a dark shadow over the motivations of the funding parties in helping Russia harness needed technologies.
- The ISTC was established to engage Soviet-trained scientists who had been involved in developing weapons of mass destruction. But after nearly two

decades, most of the scientists who were prepared to give up their defense-
oriented careers, or at least a percentage of their time devoted to such activities, had either converted to civilian endeavors or retired. The pool of
weapons scientists interested in new types of civilian-oriented high-tech
jobs had become quite small.

- Reciprocity was never considered by the Western countries to be an important aspect of projects sited in Russia. Western partners insisted on repeated access to sensitive Russian facilities without offering comparable
access by Russian specialists to facilities in their countries. Some Russian
officials interpreted this imbalance as evidence that espionage was high on
the agenda of many partner organizations.

Russian officials also recognized the steady decline in financial support for
ISTC projects, particularly support from the United States. Indeed, by 2009 the
new U.S. financial contribution for regular ISTC projects (in contrast to partner projects with narrowly defined objectives of interest to a specific external
partner) had dramatically fallen. This was in stark contrast to the twenty to
twenty-five million dollars that the United States pledged annually in the early
years for new research activities in Russia, when competition for internal financial resources in Russia was intense. This funding decline was at least a partial
factor that hastened the Russian government's decision to close the doors. It
also certainly discouraged potential ISTC champions in Russia from taking on
a money-deficient proposition.

UNVEILING THE DETAILS OF THE CLOSURE

Finally, in July 2011 the Russian government informed the ISTC Governing
Board of its plan for withdrawal from the ISTC Agreement and the closure of
the Moscow science center. At long last, the authorities in Moscow were ready
to talk about a timetable and specific issues that needed to be resolved. By
this time, the other parties had already begun to find new uses for most of the
funds that were to have been transferred to the center for support of Russian
scientists, and the center was clearly on the road to shutting down its Russia
operations.

Russian authorities stated that all previously funded projects would be completed. During implementation of active projects, all provisions of the ISTC

Agreement would remain in force. After all projects came to a conclusion, Russia planned to send written notification to the other ISTC parties as to its withdrawal. Six months after such notification (in 2015), the Russian Federation would formally withdraw from the agreement.[22]

The parties agreed that in order to achieve an orderly wind down of the ISTC operations in Russia, they would resolve several critical issues. Of particular interest were (a) arrangements for tax-free transfers to Russian research institutes of equipment and materials that they were using—valued at more than two hundred million dollars—but for which the ISTC still held title, (b) repayment of loans that ISTC extended to the owner of the center's premises, (c) reimbursement of funds that the parties invested in upgrading the ISTC headquarters building, and (d) disposition of the ISTC's archives. At the same time, the governing board noted that in accordance with the ISTC Agreement, during the interim period prior to closing the center, no tariffs, duties, taxes, or other charges related to ISTC activities should be imposed.[23] The governing board asked the Russian government to assist in finding suitable redeployment of the staff members who had accumulated considerable experience in working in an international environment while achieving high levels of project management and financial skills.

The governing board also decided that as soon as projects are completed, ownership of equipment provided through the ISTC should be transferred to the institutes where activities were carried out, provided that the relevant authorities had given assurances that such transfers would not result in any tax liabilities for either the funding parties or the institutions that hosted the projects.[24]

Despite the withdrawal of Russia, the other new independent states that had become members of the center, with the exception of Belarus, agreed that they should continue their activities pursuant to the ISTC Agreement. Their support for continuation of ISTC activities in their countries could not have been stronger. To this end, they decided on a preliminary basis to consider transforming the existing ISTC branch office in Kazakhstan into a new headquarters office for the center at an appropriate time.[25]

The governing board also agreed to continue discussions, with participation by Russia, of possible establishment of a new multilateral framework for scientific and technical cooperation. These conversations were to take place in a variety of venues. They would encompass mechanisms for multilateral cooperative programs in science as well as coordinated nonproliferation efforts.[26]

IMPACTS OF CLOSURE IN RUSSIA

The greatest setback resulting from the closure of the ISTC's operations in Russia will be a partial return to isolation of important institutions throughout the country from the international nonproliferation and scientific communities. The retreat will probably lead to a steady decline of international transparency regarding the programs and intentions of Russian institutions that have both civilian and military dual-use capabilities. Thus, the international trust in and respect for activities carried out in previously closed institutions throughout Russia—trust and respect that the ISTC had nurtured—may quickly erode.

The loss of transparency will be of particular concern in the biological field. The Biological and Toxin Weapons Convention does not have effective compliance mechanisms, and ISTC projects have been important in helping to verify that the country had abandoned important components of its former biological weapons program. Of course, some level of cooperation that touches sensitive biological institutions in Russia and attracts Russian researchers to international meetings will continue. But the ISTC has provided agreed-upon ground rules that facilitate foreign access to facilities, and resident staff members in Moscow have been able to arrange frequent visits to such facilities that both Russian and foreign specialists have welcomed.

Also of special concern is the future orientation of activities in the closed nuclear cities of Russia, where defense and civilian activities take place in close proximity to one another. The ISTC has truly been a pioneer in developing and implementing access procedures that protect the security interests of Russia while providing road maps to genuine cooperation in important areas of nuclear science. The cities have remained off-limits for the general public, but the Russian security services developed procedures for access to conduct ISTC business as necessary in a manner that has been acceptable to all concerned. Perhaps the lab-to-lab program of the U.S. Department of Energy that helped open doors in the closed nuclear cities in 1993, based on reciprocal visits to American nuclear facilities, can be revitalized in a form that is consistent with future U.S. and Russian security procedures.

However, future access to the closed cities, even if there could be an influx of international technology into these isolated municipalities, will not be easy. The Ministry of Finance, while initially agreeing to grant tax-free status for industrial activities in closed cities in the 1990s, had changed its position in 2010. By that time the minister of finance had reportedly learned that each year this tax-free provision had cost the government ten billion dollars in tax exemptions for Russian companies that were registered in the cities. The ministry pointed out that industrial development in the cities was hardly commensurate with this loss of revenue. Thus, tax advantages for focusing science and technology activities in the closed cities, whether financed by domestic or foreign entities or through the ISTC, are no longer a popular topic within important government circles.[27] And without Russian obligations set forth in the ISTC Agreement, pressures for access will decline.

While Russia favors international cooperation in sensitive areas of science, cooperation will be on Russian terms. There will be little room for negotiation. Procedures concerning past cooperative ventures will certainly be modified by the Russian government.

The closure of ISTC activities also signals that the U.S. and other governments will probably encounter increased difficulties carrying out cooperative activities that spill into security-related fields. Ad hoc arrangements will surely be possible from time to time. However, lack of certainty over the long-term continuity of collaboration will likely again become a significant impediment to organizing and effectively carrying out joint efforts.

In short, there is little evidence that the Russian government carefully examined in detail the direct and indirect political as well as financial costs in withdrawing from the ISTC before it announced its decision. The expense of arranging international cooperation will increase for all sides, even though near-term cost-savings from closing the ISTC facility in Russia will presumably be realized. Certainly, Russia will perceive the political benefits of no longer being considered a second-class citizen within the ISTC context. At the same time, however, Russia will lose credibility as a significant international partner in some areas of science and as a reliable partner in countering proliferation. Also, Russia's future statements about technical achievements of its scientists will be clouded with uncertainty in the eyes of scientific peers around the world, who will have increased difficulty in carrying out on the ground verification of Russian assertions.

Undoubtedly, some governments will adopt new approaches to cooperation with Moscow in order to reduce the political and technical losses associated with the closure of the center. They will be concerned that Russia is moving back toward isolation. All the while, other leading countries of the world will be moving toward global integration of scientific capabilities. Without deep involvement in such integration efforts, Russia can expect increased difficulty in keeping up with scientific groups throughout the world.

REACTIONS OF RUSSIA'S RESEARCH AND ACADEMIC LEADERS

In early 2008 Russian staff members of the ISTC, sensing that the Russian government's support for the ISTC was waning, solicited opinions from directors of leading Russian research institutions as to the future of the ISTC. Prominent scientific leaders of key research institutes in a variety of fields sent to the ISTC headquarters more than a dozen ringing endorsements of the importance of the ISTC. Extracts of a few of these comments follow:

> The ISTC is the basis for international scientific, technological, and economic connections and is an important factor in attracting young talent to science.
> —Director, nuclear research institute, Moscow

> The ISTC can assist in guiding leading Russian technologies into the international market through business contacts with foreign scientific and industrial partners.
> —Director, nuclear research center, Leningrad region

> The ISTC has demonstrated to many Russian scientists ways to make contact with foreign scientists that have resulted in joint projects through the ISTC.
> —Director electronics research institute, Fryazino

> With the support of the ISTC, we have been able to maintain our scientific research teams and work in a number of important directions.
> —Director, chemical research institute, Volgograd

> The ISTC has made a large contribution to the reorientation of former defense scientists to the civilian workforce and strengthened contacts among scientists of the entire world.
> —Director, biological research institute, St. Petersburg[28]

A second wave of ISTC program endorsements came from important Russian scientists following the release of President Medvedev's August 2010 decree announcing Russia's withdrawal from the center. The Russian government decided to post several dozen such accolades on the Kremlin's blog. A few examples of these reactions are as follows:

> The ISTC provides the legal, accounting, and management basis for projects, and it provides the business requirements for science.
> —Department chair, Moscow State University

> The ISTC gives Russian scientists the opportunity to work with modern laboratory equipment, to buy reagents and materials not included in regular budgets, to attract young specialists, to receive patents, and to participate in international conferences.
> —Project director for ecological research center, St. Petersburg

> The ISTC enables you to use your ideas at a high methodological level, arrange temporary positions for scientists in foreign laboratories, and broaden international contacts.
> —Medical academician, Primorsky region

> The ISTC provides a national system for submitting and reviewing proposals that balance Russia's interests with interests of financing parties, ensures authoritative international peer review of proposals, recognizes stringent export controls, and fosters anti-corruption practices.
> —Academician, Chelyabinsk region

> It is necessary to preserve the ISTC for development of scientific and business connections in partnership with Western centers and companies.
> —Professor, Murmansk region[29]

Meanwhile, as preparations for signing the decree became known during the summer of 2010, a group of senior scientists who were members of the Presidium of the Russian Academy of Sciences and who had personally participated in successful ISTC projects became concerned over the impending loss of a valuable mechanism for scientific cooperation. However, the leadership of the academy quickly concluded that it was not in a position to serve as the nation's champion for retaining the ISTC. The academy was not a component of the Russian government, and only an arm of the government could orchestrate an effort that involved so many government facilities.

This group of scientists then began lobbying for an enlarged role for the academy's Center for Global Security, which would build on many of the initiatives of the ISTC. Of course, the potential financial commitment of the academy in assuming such an expanded role was of considerable concern. In short order, the advocates within the academy realized that a subordinate unit of the academy would not be up to the task of leading an effort to continue the work of the ISTC. The Center for Global Security would simply not have the necessary clout within government circles nor the management capability to take on such a major task. Scientists working outside the Russian government, even those who have been recipients of prestigious international awards, have seldom been a powerful force in steering the policies of the government when large sums of money are involved.

ALTERNATIVES TO ACHIEVE RELATED GOALS

Following the Russian government's decision to withdraw from the ISTC, the other members of the center considered a number of options to continue selected programs in Russia. However, enthusiasm for continuing to provide multilateral funding to Russian organizations for constraining the leakage of weapons know-how had plummeted. The Russian authorities had declared that they did not need such funding. Therefore, why should international partners use their limited funds for unneeded activities?

But the issue is too important simply to walk away from seventeen years of investments in the ISTC and its many projects. These investments have produced important cadres of Russian scientific advocates for reducing the likelihood of misuse of dual-use technologies. Also, the Russian government contends it is prepared to continue to contribute to achievement of nonproliferation goals and to scientific advances of global interest, presumably drawing on ISTC experience as appropriate.

The most immediate response among the member states of the ISTC when Russian intentions began to emerge was to modify the center's programs to address valid concerns of Russia. *Go global and thereby convince Russia to retract its plans to withdraw from membership in the ISTC* became a popular theme. Already beginning in 2007, the governing board had introduced relevant concepts into its programming. The ISTC Agreement was sufficiently broad to accommodate many program adjustments.

The governments have at times considered modifying the ISTC Agreement. Some representatives have suggested greater recognition of the key role of Russia in addressing global issues. The focus on former weapons scientists could be softened to include more researchers with no past connection to defense activities. The parties could address Russian concerns over foreign domination of intellectual property rights and also acknowledge the importance of reciprocal access to sensitive facilities. But Russia's other objections—tax and custom exemptions and diplomatic status for scientific administrators—were not to be renegotiated, emphasized the international partners. Thus, there was little likelihood of reaching agreement on a new basis for continuing the center's operation in Russia.

A key element in the new thinking about the importance of the center was the recognition accorded the center by the G8 Global Partnership. In each of its annual reports, the partnership emphasized the importance of containing expert knowledge that could be misused to support proliferation activities. On a number of occasions, the partnership explicitly recognized the critical role of the ISTC in worldwide efforts to reduce the likelihood of a misguided brain drain of sensitive expertise.

In May 2011 the Global Partnership again issued a ringing endorsement of the work of the ISTC, as well as the successes of the closely related organization in Kiev, the Science and Technology Center in the Ukraine. The G8 countries committed to completing projects underway in Russia. These projects focused primarily on nuclear and radiological security, biosecurity, and scientist engagement.[30]

However, the parties to the ISTC soon stopped their search for a modified ISTC. For example, the view of a senior National Security Council official in Washington in the fall of 2010 was brief and to the point: "No point in trying to save the ISTC per se. Let's come up with a new name and concept, salvaging what we can from the ISTC."[31]

This statement came at almost the same time that Senator Richard Lugar was praising the center: "ISTC has value beyond removing incentives for a given scientist to proliferate weapons knowledge. The ISTC provides a means through which we can achieve added transparency and greater cooperative engagement on a wide range of weapons of mass destruction issues."[32]

The only realistic approach on the table in the fall of 2011 was continuation through well-established channels of other bilateral and international nonproliferation programs and related scientific exchange programs involving Russian organizations. The ISTC Secretariat had proposed (a) a successor organization focused on cooperation with selected successor states of the former Soviet Union, under a modification of the ISTC charter, or (b) a worldwide scientists' engagement center.[33] But neither proposal attracted significant support.

THE CHANGING RUSSIAN LANDSCAPE

In summary, the decline in Russian support for the ISTC can be attributed largely to the following six factors:

- The view of Russia that the original problem (a potential brain drain involving sensitive information) had been resolved
- Russian confidence that the security infrastructure within Russia had greatly improved, and the need for further international involvement to safeguard dual-use expertise had dramatically declined
- Lack of a Russian organization that was interested in being a champion for the center as Rosatom lost its interest in continuing to be responsible for activities of the center
- Increased opposition within the Russian government to the center's involvement in sensitive security matters
- Decline in international budget support for the center's programs
- Lack of respect for Russia's status as a major player in international security matters

In hindsight, could the ISTC have done a better job in responding to the interests of Russia in a manner that would have significantly increased security and scientific interests of all parties, particularly Russia? Yes. First and foremost, officials of the funding parties could have given higher priority to regular dialogues with key Russian officials on common interests in development and implementation of ISTC programs. The discussions within the governing board during the 1990s and into the early 2000s were quite important and effective. But then as the political and economic situation in Russia changed and the Russian government gave less attention to the center, a revitalization of such discussions through many channels could have been very useful in responding to latent concerns within the Russian government.

Also, attention of the parties and secretariat could have been more effectively focused on a number of operational issues. Greater attention could have been given to the commercialization program of the center in view of Moscow's fixation through the early 2000s in increasing the presence of Russian products on the international market. Also, even as the ISTC budget began to shrink, the center kept expanding the scope of its activities, which was not matched with funding availability, such as the adoption of an overly ambitious sustainability program. It would have been more effective to focus on a few areas of importance and thereby record additional highly visible success stories. But such adjustments were unlikely to have changed the attitude of Russia that the center had come to the end of its useful lifetime in Russia.

Meanwhile, the proliferation threat has become a permanent global landmark. For the foreseeable future, Russia, along with many other countries, will be in the sights of rogue states and terrorist groups searching the planet for advanced weapons technologies. The Russian government must assume full responsibility for resisting the shoppers at its doorsteps. Russian authorities claim that they understand and have accepted this responsibility. But do they recognize the magnitude of the threat and the unique role that the ISTC has played in connecting key security and scientific nodes throughout the entire nation to the mainstream of international nonproliferation efforts?

The ISTC is now an idea whose time has passed in Russia. However, international cooperation involving Russia in security affairs has been and will continue to be in the interest of all countries. The Russian experience has underscored the need to focus not only on past experience of individuals in developing dangerous weapons and weapon components but also on newly acquired capabilities. The threats become more diversified each year. While the Moscow science center may be funding its final projects in Russia that address such threats, the legacy of the center cannot be allowed to vanish from the Russian Federation. This concern is further addressed in chapters 12 and 13.

In conclusion, the program of work for the ISTC during 2012–15 includes the following major challenges:

- Completion of active projects being carried out in Russia: 92 regular projects, 115 partner projects, and 13 communication projects
- Establishment of a new headquarters for the ISTC in another member country of the ISTC, with particular attention to the offer of Kazakhstan to host the center in Almaty
- Dismissal (and to the extent possible job placement) or transfer to the new ISTC headquarters for the 118 remaining members of the secretariat staff

- Transfer (tax free) to Russian research institutions the equipment titles that are currently held by the ISTC
- Retention by a Russian organization of those portions of the ISTC archives that contain information about activities in Russia, taking into account the interest of Rosatom in accepting this responsibility
- Collection of funds owed to the ISTC by the Red Star enterprise, which owns the facility that has housed the ISTC

But as previously underscored, the most important task is to pass on to government institutions and scientific centers throughout Russia and in other countries the lessons learned from the ISTC experiment. They can contribute to evolution of a safer and more prosperous future throughout the world.

The contribution of the ISTC has often been quantified as a one-billion-dollar foreign investment in Russia and an investment of three hundred million dollars in other countries that emerged from the former Soviet Union. These investments have been made by governments and private sector organizations in North America, Europe, and Asia. However, the matching contributions of the institutions and individuals in Russia and other countries that have received financial support have never been quantified. Surely they were much more than the foreign contributions. It is essential that that lessons learned from these investments are reflected in nonproliferation, science, and economic development activities throughout the world.

Signing of the ISTC Agreement, Moscow, 1992.

ISTC Secretariat staff at Moscow headquarters, 2009.

ISTC Scientific Advisory Committee (SAC) at Obninsk Engineering Center, 2007.

Senators Barack Obama and Richard Lugar visit ISTC projects at All-Russia Scientific Research Institute of Phytopathology, Golitsino, 2005.

Project involving gas analyzer based on diode lasers, Institute of General Physics, Moscow, 2008.

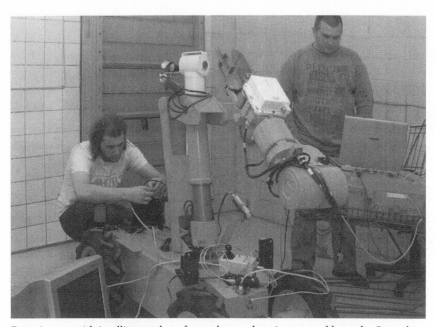

Experiments with intelligent robots for nuclear and environmental hazards, Central Research and Development Institute of Robotics and Technical Cybernetics, Moscow, 2009.

Field investigations to detect and characterize Newcastle Disease and avian influenza viruses, Federal Center of Animal Health, Vladimir, 2009.

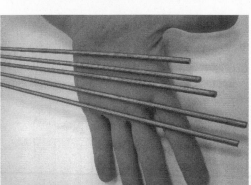

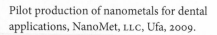

Pilot production of nanometals for dental applications, NanoMet, LLC, Ufa, 2009.

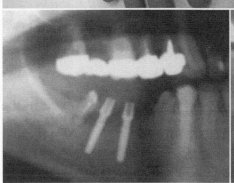

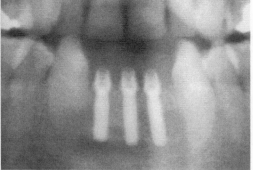

Development of techniques for reducing herbicide impact on crops, All-Russia Research Institute of Biological Plant Protection, Krasnodar, 2008.

Experiments with lightning simulator, All-Russia Research Institute of Experimental Physics, Sarov, 2009.

Developing experimental database for main fuel isotopes, Khoplin Radium Institute, St. Petersburg, 2007.

Investigating nonculturable microorganisms in Siberian Permafrost Soil, Skryabin Institute of Biochemistry and Physiology of Microorganisms, Pushchino, 2006.

Detecting microorganisms in the atmosphere in southwestern Siberia, State Research Center of Virology and Biotechnology, VECTOR, Koltsovo, 2005.

Monitoring atmospheric contamination with novel spectrometers, Kotel'nikov Institute for Radio Engineering and Electronics, Moscow, 2007.

Upgrading of the Large Hadron Collider, CERN, Geneva, Switzerland, 2008.

CHAPTER FIVE

The World Market for High-Tech Expertise

Ivan the Terrible sent 17 young men for study in Europe in order to make Russia rich and strong, but none returned. Peter the Great sent to Europe 50 courtiers, who became admirals and established the Russian Academy of Sciences.

—Russian historian, 1994

The head count of Russian researchers decreased from 878,482 in 1991, to 425,954 in 2000, to 375,804 in 2008. The decrease in technicians was even more dramatic.

—Higher School of Economics, Moscow, 2010

AS THE SOVIET UNION SPLINTERED into fifteen independent nations, "stop the brain drain in Russia" became the mantra of both nonproliferation specialists and promoters of international scientific collaboration in many countries. Indeed, concern over a brain drain in dangerous directions was the primary driver for the establishment of the ISTC. The world's largest scientific community had gone into a cascade of downward organizational and economic spirals, with few hospitable landing sites below.

Applied research institutions suddenly lost most of their financial patrons. They had employed 80 percent of Russia's research and development workforce. At the same time, the institutes that were the focal points for basic research lost more than half of their budgets. According to a UNESCO survey, in 1994 Russian scientists considered that their pay should increase by ten to thirty times to reach international levels.[1] This may have been an exaggeration on the part of the scientists, but nevertheless the general concern was appropriate.

At the same time, the emphasis on commercialization of scientific findings had become a nemesis for scientists, particularly in the basic research institutes.[2] Most scientists were not interested in taking on such a task, nor were they prepared to become responsible for commercialization activities. Given the lack of interest of the scientists in the economic payoff from research, important elements of the cash-strapped population began to consider scientists as losers in a changing world. Political leaders and government officials both increasingly viewed basic research as a method to satisfy individual curiosity at the government's expense.[3]

A number of prominent academicians and educators in the science academies and universities of the former Soviet Union were well known in the West. However, many institutions that were confronted with financial shortfalls were closely tied to the Soviet military complex. Few of their leaders had developed contacts beyond the borders of the former USSR. The ISTC was to help ensure that both known and unknown scientific contributors to the Soviet defense effort who had fallen on hard times could remain busy with civilian tasks in reoriented laboratories, despite the economic chaos, and not be tempted to look for support from rogue countries or international groups with hostile intentions.

COUNTING THE WEAPONS SCIENTISTS

When the ISTC opened its doors, the governments of the United States, the European Community, and Japan significantly underestimated the number of weapons scientists in Russia, and they had only superficial understanding of the economic conditions surrounding these scientists. The Russian government was reluctant to provide help in estimating the size or stability of the manpower pool. The available estimates from open sources in the West indicated that between ten and twenty thousand Russian scientists and engineers had provided the core of the Soviet effort to develop weapons of mass destruction and their delivery systems. And an estimated forty to fifty thousand Russian specialists, including skilled technicians, were engaged in the overall effort.[4] We later learned that these numbers reflected less than 50 percent of the highly skilled workforce linked to weapons of mass destruction in the Russian portion of the USSR. Perhaps a few Western intelligence specialists appreciated the vastness of the military effort, but their insights did not reach those of us who were responsible for managing the startup of the ISTC.

In 1992, at the future headquarters of the ISTC, I set forth my estimate of the number of Russian specialists of concern, which mirrored the erroneous underestimates that others were releasing: "Sixty thousand specialists had many years of direct hands-on experience in the laboratories and on the test ranges where components and materials for thousands of weapons were developed and tested. This manpower pool of potentially dangerous people in Russia includes about 30,000 who learned their trade in the aerospace industry, about 20,000 in the nuclear field, and 10,000 in the biological and chemical sectors."[5]

I was well aware that among the other eight hundred thousand Russian scientists active at the time were many more specialists who had expertise that could contribute to weapons programs. But these skills were not unique. Scientists who possessed them were already spread throughout the world as middle-income countries tried to move toward knowledge-based economies. I questioned whether it was worth the effort to aggressively recruit for participation in ISTC projects underemployed Russian specialists who possessed widespread skills.[6] In retrospect, I was wrong. We should have been more interested in the activities of the larger cadre of savvy scientists, since even modest skills are in short supply in some countries of concern.

A particularly significant miscalculation was the underestimation of the vast array of specialists who had become involved in Soviet activities related to biological weapons, with direct relevance to bioterrorism. That workforce probably exceeded forty thousand scientists, engineers, and technicians—who had dual-use capabilities—rather than the ten thousand I had originally estimated, with the vast majority living in Russia. A few had returned to Russia from other newly independent states after the breakup of the USSR. In numerous instances, their capabilities could be used to protect human health, advance agricultural productivity, or make preparations for destroying lives.

How many scientists with potentially dangerous skills would remain in place? How many would search for more promising sources of funding that might entice them to participate in activities that they knew were inappropriate? Would honorable scientists of the past be forced to become servants of future anarchists who were determined to wreak havoc throughout the world? It now sounds melodramatic. But at the time, the answers were unknown, and we considered the situation quite serious.

DETERIORATION OF THE RUSSIAN SCIENCE INFRASTRUCTURE

In the early 1990s the entire population of Russia was feeling the effects of the sharp decline in gross domestic product (GDP). By 1994 the scientific research allocations of the government, which supported more than 95 percent of activities throughout the country that were classified as research, had fallen far below 1 percent of the dwindling GDP. The international standard was then and remains today between 2 and 3 percent.[7] Many scientists in Europe and the United States, who for years had collaborated with their colleagues employed by Russian academies and universities, were calling for massive international efforts to save Russian science while also addressing the proliferation problem. If weapons scientists were to change their stripes, they needed satisfactory working conditions within a revitalized architecture of the civilian science infrastructure. Thus, the foreign advocates of helping Russian science through a time of crisis persuasively argued that the collapse of Russian science would have a direct impact on security interests of other countries, including the United States.[8] In 1993 a group of American leaders of science summarized the situation:

> The political turmoil and economic tribulations of the past few years pose
> a grave threat to the survival of the best specialists in natural science, social
> science, and engineering in the former Soviet Union. Scientists and engi-
> neers are being forced to leave their professions in order to survive. Old re-
> lationships have been sundered, and new ones are emerging only with great
> difficulty. The physical infrastructure is crumbling or is tragically obsolete.
> The enterprise is in a state of intense crisis.[9]

In short, there were two clear reasons to be concerned about the collapse of the scientific infrastructure of Russia. The most immediate threat to the Western and Japanese governments, as previously noted, was the increasing potential for proliferation of weapons expertise that accompanied such a collapse. A second reason was the impending tragedy of the loss of invaluable contributors to international science. The ISTC was born at precisely the time when an international mechanism was needed to address these concerns. An effective mechanism required that the confrontational legacy of the Cold War give way to the security and scientific imperatives for saving Russian science.

A brief review of the brain drain within Russia and the related atrophy of the overall science and technology infrastructure helps provide a context for judging ISTC impacts. In addition to examining the statistics compiled by international analysts, I have added a few personal observations of developments within Russian institutions. These on-the-ground impressions highlight the spotty conditions in laboratories that existed in Russia in the late 1990s and early 2000s, facilities that are still in a recovery mode in some institutions of the country.

As discussed in other chapters, Russia currently remains behind the major industrial countries in supporting science in a manner that can achieve results to help energize the economy. For decades Russian researchers have been more interested in advancing science than in commercializing their research products. They have considered this entrepreneurial dimension to be the responsibility of others, and they often worry that their involvement in commercial activities detracts from the attention that they can focus on science. "But science for what?" This skepticism of the World Bank in the early 2000s forced a lot of blank looks among Russian investigators. As is discussed in chapter 6, such an attitude became a key factor in Russia's inability to invest successfully in needed products for a free market economy.

DOWNSIZING THE SCIENCE SECTOR

American experts have described the science establishment that the new Russia inherited: "Under the Soviet system, the country's science sector was inflated beyond the economy's capacity to sustain it. Yet the country's leadership expanded the science sector—encouraged by a bureaucracy that rewarded growth for growth's sake. The system did not know or consider the true costs of maintaining its science and engineering institutions and the high prestige that had been attached to science and technology in general."[10]

The Soviet government had begun downsizing the science sector when budgets tumbled in the 1980s and into the 1990s. As the new Russia emerged, layoffs within inflated staffs were required. Involuntary staff reductions affected primarily younger scientists. These reductions were accompanied by (a) emigration, particularly of Jewish scientists who went to Israel and German scientists who went to their German homeland; (b) attrition, as older scientists retired and were not replaced; and (c) an exodus from science of entrepreneurial specialists, who began seeking their fortunes in the commercial sector, where average salaries were two to three times the salaries within the research and development complexes of the country.

This process of streamlining research institutions continued well into the 2000s. For example, from 1989 to 1993 the employment of research and development specialists fell by 40 percent. Within another few years the number of working researchers had declined by another 40 percent. And by 2010 the number of science and technology specialists actively working in the fields for which they were trained was less than 30 percent of the number employed when the Soviet Union collapsed.[11]

In some ways, this painful downsizing of bloated facilities was a healthy trend. However, in many cases those who remained in science were not the most productive or the most talented specialists in their laboratories. Overall, the percentage of innovative and self-starting specialists who remained in the workforce declined substantially. A prestigious advisory committee of the U.S. National Academy of Sciences offered its assessment of developments in Russian science institutions:

> Internal migration to the business sector should be welcomed by institute directors who for various reasons, including responsibility for the social welfare of employees, have not been able to downsize staffs. While continued downsizing is of interest for the Russian science sector, the reductions that have occurred have not necessarily preserved the most competent people. Are the best scientists and engineers leaving? Are the younger scientists and engineers leaving?[12]

All the while, both the Russian government and the scientific institutions undertook a variety of initiatives, often fruitlessly, to develop new income streams while attempting to preserve groups of highly talented but underemployed scientists.

In particular, the government launched large-scale defense conversion programs. They were to provide defense facilities with new sources of income through the production and sale of civilian goods. Suddenly factories that had been manufacturing heavy military equipment were producing bicycles and fishing rods—a development I witnessed at large military enterprises in Perm. The economic successes of these programs were few and far between. Some scientists were ashamed to admit how they were spending their time with such primitive activities that brought few financial returns.

A second stream of activities was the establishment of small private firms that would enable scientists to try to innovate for near-term profit. They were to use their high-tech skills for providing new products, processes, and services for yet-to-be-identified customers. Most scientists were already resorting to some types of moonlighting—from vegetable gardening to taxi driving to providing repair services; and many were interested in using their dormant *technical* skills again, as long as others helped them find markets for their inventions.

As elaborated in chapter 6, hundreds of government research institutes spawned small firms, usually housed in facilities belonging to the institutes. These efforts were sometimes successful in producing consumer items, such as electronic gadgets, and even items of interest to large enterprises, such as automobile parts. But they seldom had significant impact on the unemployment dilemma, nor did they advance the economy in a major way, as imported items continued to flood Russia.

Still, these minimarts provided supplementary employment opportunities for thousands of talented specialists. Also, for-profit enterprises, however small, signaled the beginning of an entrepreneurial culture that had been foreign to most scientists in Russia. At the same time, however, the fledging firms often raised concerns about appropriate use of government facilities where many had laboratories, particularly when private sector activities of the companies were being subsidized for the benefit of a few institute managers who had become owners of the new firms.

MANY DIMENSIONS OF THE BRAIN DRAIN

Analysts have at times divided brain drain into several categories as they continue to wrestle with the definition of the expression. Overlaps between categories are obvious in my framework for considering brain drain issues that I set forth below. Unfortunately, reliable statistics to highlight the significance of the different types of activities are lacking.

1. *Emigration of established Russian scientists for permanent residence abroad.* Such relocation has sometimes involved a continuation of scientific endeavors but at other times has led to departure from scientific careers. In the 1990s an estimated 50 percent of Russian scientists who accepted invitations from foreign institutions remained in their scientific disciplines after they emigrated. For well-qualified scientists who searched for employment after they arrived abroad, analysts have estimated that the placement in jobs that provided opportunities to use well-developed technical skills was on the order of 20 percent.

   These same estimates seemed to persist in the 2000s, although interest in tracking Russian émigrés waned considerably. The number of Russian scientists who emigrated to the West and other foreign destinations in the early 1990s has recently been estimated by the Russian authorities as twenty thousand, although unofficial estimates are much higher. The number of weapons scientists was but a small fraction of this total, but even one or two key Russian scientists could lead an offshore effort to spread sophisticated weapons technologies.

2. *Complete or partial departure from research by established scientists for other professional opportunities within Russia.* The exodus to work in the commercial sector due to salary differentials, with an attendant loss for Russian science, has been a large concern of the government for many years. In the 1990s, for every case of emigration of a Russian scientist, an estimated ten cases of internal migration of scientists took place, usually to the business sector as physicists became bankers, engineers became maintenance specialists, and medical researchers became private doctors. In 2011 the exodus of scientists from their technical careers to other pursuits in Russia remained much larger than the small stream of those who emigrated.

3. *Temporary employment abroad of established Russian scientists.* Often such employment has been arranged through contracts between the scientists and foreign companies. A continuing emphasis has been on foreign recruitment of Russian scientists with computer software skills. At times, temporary employment has led to permanent emigration.

4. *Employment of Russian scientists in Russia by international companies that limit dissemination of scientific findings or methodologies developed by their employees.* Often these Russian scientists have worked in foreign technological enclaves within Russia, dutifully transmitting their proprietary findings to company headquarters in other countries. Thus, their contributions to enrichment of the scope and quality of the Russian scientific infrastructure have been limited.

5. *Departure from scientific careers by highly talented Russian university students* during their periods of advanced study or upon graduation. This switching of professional interests early in careers, often motivated by employment outlooks, has resulted in a significant drop in available midlevel talent.[13]

In the late 1990s a Russian social science researcher described the average emigrant as follows: "A typical science emigrant in 1992–93 was a man 31–45 years of age with the equivalent of a Ph.D. who engaged in theoretical research. In most cases, he had a large number of publications. Physicists and mathematicians accounted for more than 50 percent of the emigrants followed by biologists and chemists. Most were from Moscow, St. Petersburg, and Novosibirsk. The leading recipient countries were, in order, Germany, Israel, and the United States."[14]

This analysis raises questions about the relevance of the early brain drain patterns to the ISTC's proliferation concerns. Still these early emigrants established precedents that were followed by others, with applied as well as theoretical skills. And there was no doubt as to erosion of the scientific infrastructure.

Some motivations driving the ever expanding brain drain were obvious in the early days of economic turmoil and still are of concern. They include the following:

- Low salary levels
- Difficulty in finding housing near research institutions, particularly for young scientists with families
- Obsolete research equipment, inadequate maintenance and supplies, and poor information support
- Decline in prestige associated with being a scientist

An often overlooked dimension of being a satisfied scientist is knowing that others are interested in the results of your work. This aspect of research has been referred to as the "demand" for research results, which is often tied directly to the interests of the organizations that are financing the work. While a financial sponsor of research of course should be interested in the return on investment, often the researcher must stimulate interest in scientific findings beyond the confines of the funding office. Otherwise, the research may have been largely a wasted effort.

Unfortunately, in Russia lack of interest in research results that do not have immediate applications has long been a problem. Too often the government funds research simply because the focus area has become popular internationally rather than because someone is prepared to use the results for further investigations or for commercially oriented activities. Once a project is financed, sponsors frequently move on to the next round of activities, without taking time to track progress in earlier projects. A survey among institutes of the Russian Academy of Sciences reported that during the 1990s the interest of foreign partners in research results (48 percent were highly interested) far exceeded the interest of the Russian government (17 percent) or Russian commercial organizations (10 percent).[15] Unfortunately, a general lack of interest in the results of research financed by the government continues to plague the research system.

Meanwhile, difficulties in obtaining professional positions abroad have been due in large part to limited Western capacity to accept new international researchers, differences in science qualification standards, and shortages of appropriate career paths in foreign countries. While the career fates of emigrants are usually uncertain, it remains clear that the migration of highly trained Russian scientists to the West has been costly for Russia. One estimate in the late 1990s was that the annual economic loss to Russia from brain drain at that time was equivalent to one-third of Russia's foreign debt, or about fifty billion dollars. While the calculations leading to this estimate were not revealed, highly trained Russian specialists have frequently become a valuable commodity in other industrialized countries where they are able to pursue their specialties.[16]

For twenty years, a few Western institutions have been pursuing programs that encourage "brain circulation" as an antidote to brain drain, with Russian scientists repeatedly traveling abroad for short stints and then returning to Russia. Under these programs, Russian scientists spend a few months in Western laboratories and then return to their Russian laboratories—perhaps repeating the experience several years later. French institutions, in particular, have well-developed arrangements for twinning Russian science centers with counterpart French institutions that provide opportunities for such prolonged circulation.

Against this background, effective redirection of Russian weapons scientists to civilian tasks has been a major challenge from the earliest days of the ISTC. Not only do the scientists need appropriate salaries and equipment, but they also must accept personal responsibility for ensuring that their experiments are of interest to other scientists and organizations that are close to the markets for new scientific information and technological approaches. Such an orientation does not come easily to scientists who were accustomed only to look inward and not reach out to the broader community of interested organizations.

ENCOURAGING RUSSIA'S SCIENCE STARS TO REMAIN IN RUSSIA

A dozen or more Western scientific exchange programs have been justified, in part, as preventing brain drain involving weapons scientists, nonweapons scientists, or both. Four programs that I have watched over the years are described here. The impacts—both positive and negative—of these and other exchange programs may take decades to unfold. A few preliminary observations about short-term results follow.

(1) Basic research in biology

One of the most successful international programs for supporting Russian as well as other researchers—in terms of both advancing science and encouraging outstanding scientists to remain in place—was an international program of the Howard Hughes Medical Institute (HHMI) devoted to basic research in the biological sciences. I had a number of opportunities to witness implementation of the program in Russia.

The effort began in the mid-1990s and continued for more than a decade. All the while, HHMI basked in the success of the program. But despite the glowing reports to the institute about the importance of its work, HHMI decided it had made its contribution to supporting science pioneers while combating brain drain from Russia and Eastern Europe. The institute then redirected its resources to support a major expansion of its own activities in the United States.

During my visits to laboratories of several HHMI award recipients in Pushchino, Russia, in the late 1990s, the enthusiasm of the young research teams was infectious. Several scientific leaders had recruited handfuls of very good postdoctoral scholars and graduate students to work on projects financed by HHMI grants. These young teams were carrying the reputations of their entire institutions on their shoulders, as other laboratories at times did not even have the resources to turn on their lights.

The formula for success was (a) HHMI's focus on young investigators willing to take risks in searching for major scientific breakthroughs; (b) long-term grants totaling about a hundred thousand dollars per year for five years, which could be divided to cover several team members; and (c) opportunities for participation in annual scientific conferences in the United States and Europe. Decent pay, participation by rising superstars, and a strict limitation on time spent abroad were good responses to concerns about brain drain—at least for a short period of time. And while the researchers were not former weapons scientists, their chemical and biological skills could certainly have been used to underpin inappropriate efforts to develop weapons.

(2) Biochip development

An ambitious five-year program of cooperation between Russia's Englelhardt Institute of Molecular Biology and Argonne National Laboratory in Illinois began in 1995. The program focused on development of biochips based on three-dimensional microarray technology. The institute had demonstrated that different hydrogels could be used for a variety of applications. A particularly compelling argument for the research was that such biochips could lead to fast and inexpensive biomedical tests for pinpointing the nature of a patient's disease. The information could then be used in determining the best treatment. And when treating multidrug-resistant tuberculosis was announced as a target of the research, interest peaked in Russia and elsewhere.

For a few years the research involved a team of a dozen Russian researchers located at Argonne as well as their Russian colleagues working in the partner institute in Moscow. The team received a variety of grants, and Motorola and Packard Biosciences licensed the results of some of their applied work. However, as other organizations also entered this field of research, the Russian team soon lost its unique international standing; the scientists returned to Moscow to continue their work at their home institute, orienting their research toward the Russian market. There is little question that this cross-ocean teaming strengthened the capability of the institute while providing employment opportunities at a critical time for a number of Russian scientists with broad-ranging skills that they used for peaceful purposes.[17]

(3) Virology and biotechnology

An example of Western efforts to draw on the scientific strengths of former Soviet bioweaponeers was an ambitious international engagement program initiated by the United States with the Center for Virology and Biotechnology Vector in Koltsovo near Novosibirsk. For more than twenty years, Vector had operated as a shadowy component of Russia's biological weapons program. But it was suddenly opening its doors to the outside world, as it too sought ways to obtain new income streams for its poorly paid scientists. Western countries were very interested in learning about its tightly controlled approaches and in taking advantage of its skills in dealing with highly dangerous pathogens.

For more than a decade Vector was one of the largest recipients of ISTC awards. Despite new access to facilities in both countries, Russian officials and the Western partners had lingering suspicions about the motivations for launching joint investigations. "Are the Americans simply spying on our activities?" queried the Russian gatekeepers. "Are the Russians simply after our money so they can continue their biological warfare activities in their undisclosed back rooms?" asked the American visitors.

Russian scientists were frequently caught in the middle of allegations of breaches of security and uncertainties about the duration of international support. Consequently, many of the most talented scientists who had participated in the program gradually left Vector for other destinations in Russia and occasionally for positions abroad. Then in the 2000s, as Russia's secret biological legacy continued to unfold, a new management team at Vector—the former symbol of research on deadly biological pathogens—felt more comfortable receding from public scrutiny; thereafter international contracts rapidly dwindled in size and frequency. By 2011, however, the international outreach of Vector seemed to be slowly returning.

(4) Applied science

Another program was not nearly as successful. In the late 1990s the U.S. Agency for International Development (USAID) was interested in quickly bringing dozens of Russian applied researchers to the United States for one-year stints in U.S. laboratories. I objected to this approach as a certain formula for brain drain, suggesting as an alternative the strengthening of research centers in Russia.

But my arguments fell on deaf ears. We reluctantly acquiesced to the insistence of USAID officials, who controlled the funds, that training in the United States was an urgent priority. We brought 150 Russian nonweapons and former weapons researchers to laboratories throughout the United States. Initially, I thought the USAID officials had been correct in moving forward with the program. The participants were well qualified, about one-half were rising stars under the age of forty, and the visits helped U.S. host institutions to leverage other funds for expanding, or at least continuing, the cooperation that had been initiated.

Over the longer term, however, reports increased concerning the limited opportunities for the Russian participants to use newly acquired skills when they returned to Russia and subsequent plans of many to emigrate. The conditions in Russia simply were not up to the standards that the participants had encountered in the United States. USAID thereupon shifted its funding priorities to other endeavors, with the hope that at least a few of the Russian scientists in the program would return and become important pillars of a revived research base in their home country.

RESTLESSNESS IN THE MISSILE TOWNS

While most of the ISTC's early attention was directed to the underemployment of scientists in Russia's nuclear centers, the economic crises of the 1990s also had a dramatic effect in the towns where the primary employers were enterprises that designed and manufactured components of missiles and rockets. Opportunities for working abroad became a lively topic among thousands of skilled specialists who were in jeopardy of soon becoming unemployed. There was general sympathy among the workers when their colleagues announced plans to seek employment elsewhere, including in foreign countries. They wished their colleagues well as they lamented their own inability to move to other locations.

A team of Moscow social scientists conducted an important survey of attitudes in three missile-related centers at the end of the 1990s and published their report in 2001.[18] They carried out the survey in the following three towns:

- Korolev, a suburb of Moscow, where the Korolev Rocket and Space Corporation designed outer-space systems and orbiting stations, employing about ten thousand specialists
- Miass, in the southern Urals, where the Makeev Design Bureau participated in the development of submarine-launched missiles, employing about five hundred specialists
- Votkinsk, in the western sector of the central Urals, where Topol ballistic missiles were produced, with a specialized workforce that included about seventeen hundred scientists and engineers

In 1999 the average monthly wages for technical personnel were as follows: Korolev, $115; Miass, $50; and Votkinsk, $40. Both Miass and Votkinsk suffered from lengthy delays in distribution of paychecks. In general, the employees considered that they were receiving about 25 percent of the wages that they deserved. After a few years of deprivation, many were angry, and a growing number of highly qualified young specialists had left for other towns and cities.

As to trends during the 1990s, over one half of the survey respondents believed there had been a dramatic economic decline, even from the near-poverty levels in 1992. The residents of Korolev, paid more than twice what those in Miass and Votkinsk received and with easy access to Moscow, considered their situations less desperate than residents of the other two towns. This was partially explained by an urban environment's greater opportunities for moonlighting as well as the wage differentials.[19]

The survey revealed considerable interest in working abroad: in Korolev, 28 percent of the scientists and engineers were interested; in Votkinsk, 12 percent; and in Miass, 32 percent. Of these specialists, more than 85 percent were prepared to work in the United States or Europe. Few offered a definitive "no" as to whether they would work for foreign defense industries. More than half would not rule out any country as a potential place of employment. China and Pakistan had the highest rejection rates. Others said they would not go to Iran, Iraq, India, North Korea, or Libya.[20]

ROGUE SCIENTISTS WAITING IN RUSSIA?

The U.S. government commissioned a survey carried out in late 2002 and early 2003, which produced an important report that was aptly titled "Will Russian Scientists Go Rogue?" The survey targeted 602 Russian physicists, biologists, and chemists at twenty institutes. All had been involved in ISTC projects. Thus, they were presumed to have expertise of relevance to development of weapons of mass destruction. At the same time, the survey was not fully representative of attitudes throughout the former Soviet weapons complex, particularly since (a) institutes of Minatom were not allowed to participate, and (b) views of scientists at only twenty institutes were but a small sampling of the differing opinions throughout the entire research complex of the country.[21]

Nevertheless, the results provided valuable insights into the core issue that was the primary focus of attention of the ISTC since its establishment—the attitudes of former weapons scientists.

The survey was a timely supplement to the largely anecdotal evidence concerning the likelihood of leakage of important technological information. While many Russian scientists were reporting considerable satisfaction with new opportunities to sell their civilian research results to Western countries, others continued to complain that as in the past their newly designed products simply decorated the shelves of their institutes. At the same time, some Russian skeptics doubted the value of Western nonproliferation programs, which they considered to be fronts for espionage activities and for plots to steal Russia's intellectual property.

The survey asked whether each scientist would consider taking a job in any of eight foreign countries, if the job required him or her to move there for at least one year. Interest in taking jobs in Germany was overwhelmingly positive, along with substantial interest in moving to Israel or India. The interest in going to a rogue country (i.e., Iran, Iraq, Syria, North Korea) was much lower, ranging from 6 percent who expressed interest in Iraq to 14 percent in North Korea. By combining responses for all four rogue countries, the results indicated that about 21 percent of the respondents would consider moving to at least one of these four countries.[22]

While this result was disturbing, the survey also indicated that participation in foreign grant programs reduced the propensity of Russian scientists to consider living in a rogue country. For those scientists who had never applied for foreign grants, about 26 percent said that they would go. For those who had applied but were unsuccessful, the number of interested scientists increased to 28 percent. For those who received grants as participating scientists, the number fell to 15 percent. For those who became principal investigators on foreign grants, the number declined to 12 percent.

Based on statistical analysis of the data, the bottom line was as follows: 25 percent of the respondents indicated that they would consider going to rogue countries if they did not receive foreign grants, whereas only 11 percent would consider such an option if they received foreign grants.[23]

Another important conclusion from the data concerned the age of the scientists. Younger scientists were more inclined to go rogue. They did not feel as strong a sense of responsibility to their profession or their country as their more senior counterparts. They were more willing to simply cast aside their roots and seek their fortunes abroad, including working in a rogue nation.[24]

The report's authors concluded that the data provided solid empirical evidence that international programs reduced the likelihood of a brain drain of expertise concerning weapons of mass destruction. At the same time, their queries indicated that access to *Russian* grants had little effect on attitudes. Therefore, in the view of the authors, foreign nonproliferation grant programs should be maintained and even enhanced.[25]

Regretfully, such surveys have been rare. However, anecdotal evidence confirming the nonproliferation importance of ISTC programs continued to accumulate until the decision to close the ISTC headquarters in Moscow became a reality. By then the concern was less centered on scientists moving abroad for a period of at least one year, but rather on their participation in a variety of ways at home or abroad in the spread of highly dangerous dual-use technologies throughout the world.

But by 2002 the threat of a weapons brain drain had begun to slowly fade from the center of attention of many key officials in the West. The ISTC still considered the brain drain a significant security concern. The center increasingly focused on scientific benefits of its programs while continuing to engage former weapons scientists.

Perhaps this decline in interest in a possible weapons brain drain was warranted, due to effective administration of the programs of the ISTC and other nonproliferation organizations, which reduced the likelihood of leakage of weapons knowledge. Fortunately, some leaders of the center realized that they were not fully in touch with on-the-ground developments, particularly the employment outlook of former weapons scientists and others in Russia after 9/11. They welcomed fresh insights regarding the possibilities for collaboration between terrorist groups and disgruntled scientists. Thus, the ISTC embraced the results of the survey concerning interest in working in rogue countries, realizing that scientists were still facing economic hardships and bleak outlooks for nondefense employment.

WHITHER THE BRAIN DRAIN

The ISTC arrived on the scene at a critical time. It has repeatedly demonstrated how scientifically challenging and carefully designed programs can play a central role in tempering both emigration of accomplished researchers and internal migration of talented young scientists and engineers to professional pursuits that are distant from science. Due in part to the efforts of the ISTC, the ominous warnings of the early 1990s, as illustrated in the following excerpt from an article in the *New York Times*, disappeared long ago.

> The disintegration of the infrastructure within the closed nuclear cities is now seen as threatening to send scientists and materials flying into foreign hands in a new kind of international peril. Foment is real as Russian nuclear experts have received job offers from Iraq and Libya. Bomb makers in the secret cities are striving to invent new ways of making money at home. Some of the initiatives would hinder atomic leakage. Others encourage it.

But lifting secrecy, they now want to go commercial. They are ready to embark on joint projects with the west and do nearly anything in their power to survive and avoid falling apart.[26]

But many of the scientific cadres with dual-use skills in Russia and other countries of the world are larger than ever before. They continue to grow. A summary of the trends in the brain drain across Russia underscores several important points.

In the early years of the new Russia, the overstaffing of institutions was steadily reduced; but complete rationalization of the nation's science system would take time since in the Soviet era, one-fourth of the world's scientists honed their skills in the USSR, which had rigid structures. New systems of financing science have gradually evolved to complement the growth of long-standing approaches of science support from the ministries: first from foreign sources, then from new competitive grant systems of the Russian government, and finally from both Russian foundations and the Russian private sector. Meanwhile, Russian specialists are increasingly addressing problems related to the geography of Russia and to other unique features of the country that raise international interest in Russian science. The entire country, including the defense sector, has become more open, thereby attracting additional funding from abroad, including funding through the ISTC.[27]

Finally, a well-considered assessment of the brain drain dilemma taken from a survey of hard-core weapons scientists ends with the following suggested approach: "The number of residents of closed cities to leave Russia has not been large. But now there is only one obvious way out—to draw on the experience of the United States which has classified research institutions and enterprises but no closed cities."[28] The notion that an entire reorientation of the current Russian approach to classified research is needed deserves attention, even fifteen years later.

In 1992 former secretary of state James Baker made the following comment to the press while visiting the closed nuclear city of Snezhinsk: "Rather than thinking of efforts by some countries to obtain Russian secrets as a brain drain problem, we should think of it as an opportunity for brain gain, in which the international community works with Russia and other independent states to help you turn your talents to interesting and useful civilian projects."[29]

Nearly two decades later, Russia is still trying to recover scientifically. Building alliances with Western partners and reducing the size of its research workforce have been steps in the right direction. However, the record for scientific publications is disappointing, as Russian output continues to slip. Russian scientists produced only 2.6 percent of the world's total scientific publications from 2004 to 2008, a dramatic drop from times past.[30]

On the positive side, the methods for financing research in Russia are slowly becoming more flexible. The government recognizes the gaps between research and innovation and is trying to encourage researchers to address these gaps. Most important, the entire system is becoming more open. But Russia has not yet turned the corner toward a science infrastructure that will spur and sustain economic growth. Real signs of improvement of the science infrastructure will become clear when the young scientists stop looking for a better life outside the science sector and outside the country and are able to make a comfortable and satisfying living within scientific laboratories.

CHAPTER SIX

The Long Road to a Silicon Valley in Russia

Rather than the science and technology sector pulling up the rest of the Russian economy, the rest of the economy pulls down the science and technology sector.
—Organization for Economic Cooperation and Development, Paris, 2000

Research transforms money into knowledge, while innovation should transform knowledge into money.
—Russian technology transfer specialist, 2011

THOMAS EDISON OFTEN SAID, "If I can't sell it, I don't want to invent it."[1] Both aging Russian researchers and the new generation of scientists now realize that a successful transition to a market economy requires more attention to Edison's practical philosophy. For the time being, with very few exceptions, Russian researchers should keep in the distant background their dreams of emulating the theoretical findings of Albert Einstein.

As noted in previous chapters, the Soviet system frequently separated the organizational responsibilities for technological invention from responsibilities for converting new technologies into practical applications. Government authorities determined the technological approaches that were to be developed, often by industrial branch design institutes and occasionally by universities or academy institutes; and they also decided which enterprises were to use the results in their production activities. Costs were important, but frequently costs were not the decisive factor in applying the outcomes of the research process to production of better products and improved manufacturing processes.

This Soviet legacy of disconnected steps in the innovation process, glued together by the government, has complicated efforts of the new Russia to penetrate advanced technology markets at home and abroad with the inventions of talented Russian researchers. These researchers traditionally had been comfortable working in their laboratories, knowing that the state would help induce manufacturing enterprises to use their discoveries. Now the scientists have no choice but to take the initiative in looking for economic and technically oriented allies who will help guide and finance the transfer of their novel ideas into viable products. These products must meet the marketplace's cost, quality, and functionality requirements; and such requirements should be taken into account during the earliest stage of the research process.

Aware of stagnation of an evolving innovation system that has often resisted rather than supported the efforts of the new breed of young entrepreneurs of the country, President Dmitry Medvedev announced in 2006 his intention to improve the international competitiveness of Russian technologies, a theme that Russian leaders had trumpeted many times previously. At the top of his list of projects was establishment of a new mega-incubator at Skolkovo for nurturing promising technologies of interest to Russia's restless cadre of young entrepreneurs.

In 2010 a close aide of the president, supported by the leadership of the country, compared the initiative to the development of Silicon Valley. He described the initiative as follows: "Our flagship project is the creation of the new innovation center in Skolkovo, near Moscow. Our goal is not just to build good facilities and spend taxpayer money on the development of this piece of land. The purpose is to create a window and a vehicle for driving innovations across Russia. This is a window for those people who are afraid to go to other regions in the Russian Federation, who are afraid of Russian bureaucracy and corruption—a window for people who did not believe it was possible to start doing real research and doing real innovation in Russia."[2]

This chapter considers the context for the development of the new mega-incubator. Can the Skolkovo initiative transform into market reality some of the seeds of innovation fertilized by the ISTC? Or will the effort be dominated by Russia's entrenched financial magnates who focus on discoveries of their own constituents that may be distant from the ISTC's pioneering efforts? Fortunately, many scientists who are eager to become involved in activities of potential interest to both themselves and the oligarchs who surround the Skolkovo project are alumni of ISTC projects. With their perseverance, perhaps there will be success stories with roots in the Moscow science center.

REALITIES OF INNOVATING FOR PROFIT

When the ISTC opened its doors in 1994, managers of many scientific research institutes throughout Russia believed that a new mechanism was in place to help transform their inventions into commercial products and manufacturing technologies, which in turn would support rapid rehabilitation of the nation's aging industrial base. They had long lived with the government-orchestrated Soviet approach that gave short shrift to costs and, at times, even quality. But now cost and quality are critical determinants of user interest in nearly every product.

During the preparatory phase for establishing the ISTC, I visited several dozen research centers, beginning in Moscow and its environs. I then extended my explorations to St. Petersburg, the Urals, Siberia, the Volga region, and southern areas of the country. In the institutes and related facilities, I saw displays of electronic and mechanical components for industrial machinery; new materials based on graphite, titanium, and silicon; biological and chemical compounds that could provide the basis for new drugs; and other technological achievements. Almost all of the novel items were labeled by their inventors as innovation successes of the future.

These displays, I was told, featured "user-ready" technologies. According to the directors of the research centers, the scientists had successfully completed the innovation process except for one critical step—finding a company that would produce and sell the inventions to waiting customers, while rewarding the centers with substantial payments. Could the ISTC offer help or advice?

Unfortunately, in almost every case the scientists had been spending too much time innovating for display purposes rather than for eventual profit. The likelihood of transforming their well-honed products into commercial successes seemed remote. They had little evidence of market demand for the products at home or abroad, particularly in the aftermath of the collapse of the Soviet Union.

Foreign businessmen already had seen most of the scientists' exhibits and had congratulated the inventors on their achievements. While these international visitors were indeed impressed by the scientists' ingenuity, they had numerous questions about the marketability of the research results. Questioning the sales potential of unwanted items that were on display, they quickly decided to look elsewhere for technological winners.

What the scientists failed to realize is that product innovation is not simply invention. It includes adoption by customers of inventions, ideas, and research results. Innovating for profit—not simply to demonstrate how advanced technologies can be developed—should be the mantra in the approach.[3]

The ISTC Governing Board and Secretariat have repeatedly underscored the importance of implanting the results of their sponsored research into better products, processes, or services that then effectively enter the marketplace. Of course, this is easier said than done. As noted in earlier chapters, the ISTC has consistently been the target of criticism for not having major successes in this regard.

Unfortunately, the ISTC, mirroring the outlook of many other foreign organizations interested in revitalizing Russia's scientific infrastructure, has often been overly optimistic in predicting that its modest research projects would become significant contributors to Russia's economic advancement. In many cases, projects have made small contributions, and this book highlights a number of these contributions. But the center still awaits the news of a blockbuster invention that has been adopted, grabbing the headlines away from discovery of yet another oil or gas field.

On a larger scale during the 1990s, Moscow's leading politicians repeatedly voiced their frustrations with the failure of Russia's technology-oriented companies to compete successfully with foreign firms. These international manufacturers were sending all types of products into Russia and had little interest in encouraging domestic competition. At the same time, economic advisers from abroad were recommending against the adoption by Russian companies of import-substitution strategies when selecting the products that they would upgrade and manufacture, even though some Russian firms had adopted this tactic on a limited scale.

Too often, high-priced Western consultants, along with Russian managers of scientific programs, had convinced Russian politicians and economic czars that Russian ingenuity is unmatched. Therefore, the country should not revert to simply duplicating imports. They argued that in the long run, Russia would fall further behind by imitating the achievements of others. Forget about reverse engineering and target the international marketplace for your completely new products, urged the voices from abroad.

However, during the early 2000s some local politicians began to advocate that Russian firms should first of all take over the domestic market, which was being dominated by imported goods. Then they could begin to spread their technological wherewithal throughout the world. Many Russian companies agreed. But they pleaded with the government to provide them—and their Western consultants—enough money to prime the pumps for both tasks.

At the same time, the Russian political leadership had serious reservations about increasing subsidies for research activities of public sector research institutes that had yet to demonstrate their abilities to achieve near-term economic impact. Consequently, the budgets for these institutes did not increase significantly even as the economy began to expand and the international markets were attracting considerable attention. Successful business practices had to be compatible with Russian realities and not Western models, explained the politicians.

Then, in 2002, President Vladimir Putin complained—not about money to support new discoveries but about the lack of good projects that responded to Russian needs—as follows: "The rich science and technology potential that Russia possesses is not being used. There are very few worthwhile and long-term projects in our economy meeting this potential. We need to create conditions for healthy commercialization of applied science."[4]

Clearly, for many years neither the ISTC nor the Russian government had given sufficient attention to bridging the divide between research and its applications. Perhaps more aggressive efforts by the center to promote this mutual interest in successful shepherding of technical innovations to market might have carried some weight during internal Russian discussions of the lack of economic relevance of the center. The center was widely viewed as interested only in immediate redirection of weapons scientists.

At the same time, Russia was engaging Western technology firms on its own terms through other mechanisms. Requirements were dictated by individual ministries and not embedded in formal intergovernmental agreements. Unfortunately, such interactions too often gave priority to the personal profit motives and not to Russia's broader interests.

ROLE OF SMALL HIGH-TECH FIRMS

In 1998, at the height of yet another financial crisis that engulfed Russia along with many other countries, I met with a colleague who owned a small science-oriented firm that had received a jump-start three years earlier from ISTC support. Sadly, one of his remarks accurately described the situation that prevailed throughout Russia at the time: "More than 90 percent of Russian scientists simply wait for someone to give them money. They are not interested in search-ing for research contracts or grants. They believe that the government owes them the financial support needed to conduct research. They assume that in-troducing research results into practice is someone else's responsibility. I had difficulty changing my attitude. I hope that other scientists will also change their outlook."[5]

Meanwhile, two developments with both positive and negative impacts were unfolding in Russia. First, the international financial crisis in the late 1990s, which initially was considered to be a disaster for Russia, was becoming a benefit for Russian industry and for the economy in general. In fact, it was the onset of an industrial opportunity that had been ignited by the devalua-tion of the ruble, the associated decline in competition from foreign imports, and the expansion of domestic markets. While the quality of Russian prod-ucts of many types was inferior to that of imported goods, prices had fallen to less than one half of Western prices, and quality considerations faded into the background.

Second, a number of small firms established by scientists seeking new in-come streams were just beginning to break even and at times flourish, benefit-ing at least the science entrepreneurs who owned the firms. A number of the owners and their employees had left their research institutes during the early 1990s, setting up small-scale operations either within premises provided by the institutes or in technoparks or incubators organized by local governments, universities, and research institutes. Availability of security-protected facili-ties was usually critical to their success. Injections of grant funding, sometimes from Russian government entities and sometimes from abroad, were frequently needed during their earliest days. In time, more consistent funding—in the form of grants, loans, or equity investments—came from financing institutions established by the government. Some firms succeeded in obtaining outsourcing contracts from large Russian enterprises, such as automobile enterprises seek-ing electrical components, mechanical devices, or other appendages to cars and trucks. In time, small firms began producing dental equipment, prefabricated laboratories, housing construction materials, medical diagnostic kits, motion-detector burglar alarms, advanced coatings for eyeglasses, language translation software, new forms of animal feed, and other items.[6] Still, viewed from a broad perspective, these activities had limited economic impact.

An important aspect for entrepreneurial success was assurance of political and economic stability. New entrepreneurs were usually less concerned about administrative harassment and tax collectors, which were often cited in the press as major barriers toward success. Of course, they considered inspections excessive, sometimes describing inspectors as "flies going in all directions."

In general, new high-tech firms were usually reluctant to engage in blatantly corrupt business practices, although the limits of acceptable practices were poorly defined. The payment of fees (or bribes) to accelerate licensing procedures was a particularly murky area. And it was common to have two sets of books—one for the business and one for the auditors. Meanwhile, expansion of activities was nearly always a problem due to the lack of finances for covering the initial costs to build facilities and purchase new supplies and equipment.

But frugal approaches of new entrepreneurs sometimes paid off. For example, a few physicists developing computer software programs banded together in a secluded tower of Moscow State University and quickly learned how to become accountants and handle their own books. They had no need for patent lawyers, since they decided that they would not become involved in developing ideas that might be claimed by others as intellectual property. They worked for deferred income. Sometimes barter replaced cash transactions, thus reducing the need for security guards. They did not charge overhead until they became established businessmen. In short, they were content simply to make a living and not try to participate in a technology revolution.[7] The ISTC and other funders welcomed the example of such cost-cutting efforts.

During the 2000s the Foundation for Assistance to Small Innovative Enterprises, which the Russian government established in 1994, reached impressive heights as a source of financial support for new entrepreneurs. By the early 2000s its annual budget exceeded seventy-five million dollars, with hundreds of small firms becoming beneficiaries. It developed a good record of helping small businesses both survive and thrive. At times, the foundation has partnered with the ISTC in supporting innovative proposals.

But managers have had problems in scaling up firms that received small grants. This difficulty has resulted from both their inexperience and from uncertain conditions within the private sector. Some scientists recklessly chased after available investment funds, whatever the source, so that they could have a major presence in the emerging market economy, at least for a few months.

Among the programs that the foundation has supported over many years are the following:

- Start-up program for new firms that called for three phases: development, testing, and patenting of a product prototype; registration of firms and elaboration of two-year business plans; and implementation of plans
- Young scientist competitions: research projects carried out by students and scientists between the ages of eighteen and twenty-eight
- Partnerships of companies and universities: innovation projects carried out by small firms using technical talent of universities
- Small-firm acquisitions from universities of industrial engineering solutions: research carried out under licensing arrangements with universities
- Development activities of enterprises: partial funding by the foundation of enterprise research projects
- Reimbursement of interest on loans: small enterprises simultaneously carrying out loan-supported production and interest-supported related research[8]

Related to the foundation's activities, the government has long supported incubators, technoparks, and innovation technology centers with overlapping types of activities. These innovation-oriented institutions number in the many hundreds and are distributed throughout the country. An example of a successful technopark is Akadem-Park in Novosibirsk. By 2009 it had attracted more than sixty companies engaged in microelectronics, communication and computer technologies, biotechnologies, and nanotechnologies. Sales exceeded twenty-five million dollars per year. It has been billed as a prototype for Skolkovo, even though it is very small-scale in comparison.[9]

RUSSIA CONTINUES TO LAG BEHIND

Despite these modest successes during the 1990s and continuing into the 2000s, many experienced business leaders in the United States and Europe have hesitated to consider economic investments in Russia. Why should they waste time with problems in Russia where the likelihood of indigenous technology benefiting the United States or contributing to economic development in the near term has been low? They point out that globalization of modern technology is taking place in Europe and Asia, and that is where they should concentrate attention. Even other transition countries, such as Poland and Hungary, offer more promise than Russia as technology partners for the United States, they argue.

At the same time, Western economic experts have emphasized that investments by both Russian and foreign companies are essential if a stable industrial base is to emerge. Such a base would help guarantee permanent employment for recipients of ISTC funds for their projects, they sometimes add.

There have been notable exceptions to the general pessimism over successful business ventures in Russia. Boeing, United Technologies, Alcoa, and Chevron, for example, have shown that carefully designed partnerships can be profitable for the participants on both sides of the ocean, while enhancing the high-tech labor pool in Russia. And other firms from Europe and Asia have found niches in Russia. Nevertheless, many Western government officials have been skeptical about the economic value to industrialized countries of science and technology engagement with Russia. They have considered the successes to date to have been small in number and limited in overall impact.

Turning to basic science, the Russian government has claimed at least some of the credit for the achievements of two Russian-born and Russian-educated physicists who shared the Nobel Prize in physics in 2010. However, when asked about their Russian heritage, the new laureates promptly responded that had they not moved to the West at early stages in their research careers, they would not have had opportunities to carry out their pathfinding research.[10] Their experience suggests that the areas for cross-ocean cooperation that are of interest to potential Western partners working on the leading edges of modern technologies are limited in number. Russia has simply been falling farther behind the other industrialized countries for two to three decades. Even in physics, which for many years had been the pride of the USSR, the decline in Russian achievements is increasingly noticeable.

The role that advanced technologies play worldwide in economic development has been rapidly expanding—often to the detriment of a lagging Russia, which has many secluded industrial complexes isolated from the networks of other nations. As globalization spreads, the pace of technological change is increasing, and product life-cycles are shortening. The international search for talent is growing, and the competition for leading-edge skills is intensifying. Can Russia ever catch up?

While the Russian government is determined to penetrate the international marketplace, particularly in a few priority areas, the road ahead is long and elusive. At times, there will be no available on-ramps to roads that lead to technology success. Recognizing this reality, the Russian government has repeatedly pledged substantial increases in its support of science and engineering as it tries to build new points of entry. Also, it has promised new financial incentives and streamlined procedures for international access to the latent expertise of Russian specialists in many fields, in an effort to encourage foreign organizations to increase their investments in Russia.

Unfortunately for the scientists, the government's actions have not backed up pronouncements about the importance of innovation. In 2010 Russian financial support for research and development activities was only 1 percent of gross domestic product (GDP), while the norm for industrialized countries is 2 to 3 percent. The government was contributing more than two-thirds of this investment, with the Russian private sector providing only a portion of the remainder.[11] Such private sector investment in research is well below expected levels in the United States, Europe, and industrialized countries of Asia, and private sector commitments are essential for building an internationally competitive advanced-technology economy.

While money is important, it is only one aspect of establishing an innovation culture that underpins the success of developed countries—a culture of attitudes, goals, and practices. The requisite environment includes strong leadership and entrepreneurship at many levels. It reflects a commitment to delivering improved processes and products at competitive prices. And it is based on an ability to move quickly and to adapt readily to a changing world, while adopting a willingness to accept failures. Russia is lagging in all these areas.

What then supports the case for a robust level of continued engagement by the United States and other industrialized countries with Russia in science and technology? International concern over proliferation of weapons technology that has roots in Russia is no longer on a rapid rise. And as noted earlier, the economic payoff from technological cooperation with Russia is highly uncertain.

That said, Russia retains potent defense capabilities, including a broad range of dual-use technologies that may encompass commercial nuggets, which have not yet emerged. Its vast geographic expanse is unrivaled. And its tradition of somehow mounting megaprojects, which achieve seemingly impossible goals, should not be dismissed simply because Russia currently is a lagging partner. These reasons for a robust program of bilateral and multilateral engagement may not persuade many skeptics, but the arguments cannot be cast aside lightly.

In addition, Russia is eager to engage in the technological arena with other advanced countries, and particularly the United States. In 2008 it announced a political commitment to spend billions of dollars for narrowing the ever-widening technological gap between Russia and the United States, Europe, and Japan by working in a variety of fields with these countries. As is frequently the case, by the end of 2010 the lack of follow-through in Moscow became obvious as the government announced that it was scaling back its financial commitments to science and technology in view of a depressed economy. But the political commitment still remains, and a gradual upsurge in financial resources provided by the government is noticeable.

RUSSIAN ASPIRATIONS AND ISTC EXPERIENCES

By 2005 the Russian political leadership had tired of the unsuccessful searches for international interest in products based on Russian technologies. At home, locally bred products reached the commercial market only when better products could not be imported. The Russian government gradually accepted the suggestions of foreign mentors who had slowly adjusted their earlier advice, now urging concentration of technology efforts on Russia's true market potential, while continuing to search internationally for yet-to-be-convinced customers.

Meanwhile, the international technology gurus repeatedly recited the key ingredients of the information technology (IT) revolution in the West and in Asia as the passport to high-tech commercial success. They underscored that innovative activities, venture capital, and entrepreneurship must be brought together within a framework of small- and medium-sized companies with special privileges received from the government. Western specialists contended that in some countries that used this approach, 10 percent of GDP could be traced to the impetus of new technologies.[12]

But the details embodied in this concept are critically important and have posed several stumbling blocks. For example, innovation is defined by many Russian practitioners simply as "technological" innovation, whereas "organizational" innovation and "marketing" innovation may be equally important. Second, there are different sources for venture capital, each with requirements for rewarding the financiers. The government may provide the funding in its quest for a thriving and competitive economy, while private financial institutions seek to invest funds in products and services that show promise in generating healthy returns. Another approach is for large manufacturing companies to accumulate their own venture capital funds, which are then dedicated to products of direct interest to the companies.[13]

Recognizing the challenges holding back Russian product development, the ISTC had taken on the task of more aggressively moving the technological achievements of the center's grantees into the marketplace during the late 1990s. First, the center recognized that its partner program, discussed in chapter 3, was becoming a successful effort. From the outset, an international partner that wanted either to use or market the results of the particular research was financially embedded in each project—a market-pull approach that shaped the character of research to meet the carefully articulated customer needs.

But the majority of ISTC projects have been technology-push projects. The grantees develop technologies that correspond with their personal interests and skills. Too often the interests of potential users are not taken into account until the very end of the research process, when the users are to miraculously appear on the scene with cash in hand to market the "user-ready" results. This approach has had few immediate rewards.

Now, as the Moscow science center winds down, it is attempting to focus attention on commercialization of some of the most promising technology-push projects supported in recent years, such as energy efficiency projects that are consistent with current government priorities. With rare exception, it is simply too late to market technologies developed many years ago that did not adequately take into account market demand.

Still, the number of commercial follow-on endeavors in the wake of regular projects that survived after ISTC funding ended has been surprisingly high. The newly minted entrepreneurs managing commercially oriented projects were not wide-eyed visionaries trying to penetrate global markets with unwanted products. Most had been considering rather modest—but realistic and practical—goals of limited improvements and cost reductions of existing products or processes that could be made and sold in Russia.

But neither the ISTC nor its critics have been satisfied with such limited achievements, even if they sustained some energetic scientists for a few years. Small pathfinding achievements were important and may have been more than could have been reasonably expected from the relatively small investments made by the center.[14] In short, the commercialization program of the ISTC simply did not provide the needed results to persuade skeptics of the soundness of the efforts.

THE INGREDIENTS FOR INNOVATION SUCCESS

Neglect of the marketing dimension of innovation is at the top of the list of missing elements in the development of an overarching culture of innovation in Russia. As mentioned, hundreds of small product successes can be seen in many cities of Russia. These achievements have on some occasions been supported by the ISTC and other international programs. Usually, however, Russian organizations with little experience in a free market have been on their own in finding markets for their unique products. At the same time, small successes need to be scaled up to have a discernible impact on the economy, in addition to increasing paychecks for previously subsidized pioneers now suddenly working in a free market economy.

By 2002 the World Bank recognized Russia's struggles in establishing an economy based on manufacturing and internal distribution of Russian products. The bank's Russian experts began to develop an action plan to promote innovation on a broad basis. The plan was based on the following framework:

- Transform the wealth generated from extraction of natural resources into investments that will foster the emergence of a knowledge-based economy. But who will transfer these surpluses from one sector to another, and is it simply a question of redistributing financial flows? Or will transfer require fundamental changes in the system of commercializing research and development and in improving the capacity of Russian enterprises to absorb and use technologies?
- Commercialize the country's research capability and harness Russia's science and technology assets for the job of creating a knowledge-intensive domestic economy. Two parallel systems have been developing: (a) an enterprise sector that occasionally finds financial resources to purchase modern equipment abroad and (b) a science and technology sector that occasionally manages to sell knowledge and equipment abroad. Shouldn't these systems be more integrated to serve the Russian market?
- Develop linkages between science-intensive small and medium enterprises and large national and international firms that can help local firms develop a high value-added niche in the global value chain. Linkages between the small and medium enterprises and the remainder of the Russian industrial community are only slowly developing, thereby depriving the large firms of access to some of the most creative institutions in the country.

- Change the business climate. Improving the investment environment is a prerequisite. It includes easing the entry of new firms into the approved community of businesses and establishing better intra-industry linkages.
- Invest in education. While the interest of the youth in enrolling in the elite Russian universities is very high, much of the motivation is tied to a belief that such education eases the acquisition of visas for emigration to other countries. Until there are greater opportunities to use high-tech skills in Russia, the brain drain will continue to be a problem in moving toward a knowledge-based economy.[15]

In large measure, the fundamental problem in improving prospects for meaningful innovation has been the lack of synchronization among the efforts of the science and technology sector, the education sector, and the commercial sector. The World Bank has repeatedly underscored that the objective should be not only to ensure that the restructuring of the enterprise sector proceeds but that such efforts also drive the restructuring of the science and technology sector.[16]

In 2010 a UNESCO report on the Russian science infrastructure picked up both similar and additional themes in chronicling the country's weaknesses, as follows:

- Excessive dependence on exports of raw materials
- Structural imbalances in the economy and a technology gap with leading industrial nations
- Monopolization of local markets, which suppresses incentives to improve productivity
- Barriers to entrepreneurship, and inadequate protection of ownership rights
- Lack of incentives to foster a coalition among business, the government, and the public
- Low level of confidence in state authorities
- Glaring economic differences among regions
- Inequality in income distribution and in development of the social infrastructure[17]

Reflecting on previous national reports devoted to upgrading the science and technology infrastructure, the UNESCO report set forth four general policy objectives:

- Promoting industrial demand for new technology and innovation
- Increasing the quality and scale of national research and development output
- Developing human capital capable of meeting requirements of an innovation economy
- Establishing an effective system for adjusting research and development objectives and for setting long-term priorities[18]

The UNESCO report concluded with the following warning: "Russia has no choice but to improve substantially the efficiency of its national science and technology sector and innovation policies. All necessary transformation processes have undoubtedly been set in motion. They call for a stronger focus on the part of all stakeholders; direct and indirect systemic support from the government; forward-looking innovation-based company strategies; and monitoring of both the steps taken and the impacts."[19]

A CONTEMPORARY FRAMEWORK FOR SCIENCE AND TECHNOLOGY IN RUSSIA

Throughout its lifetime, the ISTC gave only limited attention to the strengths and weaknesses of the overall Russian infrastructure for supporting science and technology activities.[20] While most ISTC-funded projects have been housed in important government research institutions within this infrastructure, analyses of the overall direction of science and technology policy and implementation have been conspicuously absent from the center's portfolio. Such overarching concerns were left to the various ministries and agencies within the Russian government.

Greater attention by the ISTC as to the impacts of ongoing projects and proposed projects in strengthening the infrastructure would have been useful. It could have helped in targeting resources, in sustaining activities, and in developing larger cadres within the Russian government and the scientific community of important supporters for the center.

By 2010 several trends in financing Russian research and development were clear. Overall, funding levels had more than doubled (in purchasing power parity) since 2000 but still hovered at only about 1 percent of GDP. The businesses had reduced their financing of research and development to about 28 percent of the national total, which remained very low by Western standards but was higher than in earlier years. Foreign financing of Russia's research activities had fallen from 17 percent in 1999 to less than 6 percent in 2010. And the much-heralded *new* government approach of competitive funding of research remained low, at about 25 percent of all research.

Turning to the technical workforce, the outflow of researchers from science continued during the 2000s, with many aging researchers but a decreasing number of middle-aged researchers remaining in place. Few researchers trained in Russia but working abroad returned to Russia.

As to publications, Russian authors continued to slip further behind colleagues in other countries in almost all fields. For example, between 1999 and 2008 the percentage of the total world output of publications that could be claimed by Russia had fallen to 7.0 percent in physics, 2.3 percent in engineering, and 0.6 percent in clinical medicine.

One of the most significant changes in recent years was the designation of a number of Russian universities as research universities, with the number growing to twenty-nine by 2011. The ISTC has supported activities at many of these universities, strengthening capabilities at some institutions that may have helped them win the intense nationwide competitions for obtaining the new status. Significant additional funding from the Ministry of Education and Science has begun flowing to the newly named universities. The initial allocations of supplemental funding have focused on developing innovation infrastructures, establishing world-class laboratories, and carrying out large projects aimed at eventually creating a high-tech industrial base.

Of course, with the distribution of additional funds, a number of questions arose. What should be the character of new laboratories? How can the universities expand collaboration with industry? Can large projects be carried out at universities that have limited technical bases for research? Are the intellectual property regulations, which give the universities control over inventions, acceptable to industry? Since the ISTC worked with institutions of all types, it repeatedly became involved in addressing such questions.

Public attitudes toward science are often an interesting, although somewhat less than reliable, barometer of the success of the government's efforts to move the country forward toward a knowledge-based economy. In particular, in 2009 scientists and engineers ranked far down on the list of well-regarded professions, giving way to lawyers, politicians, businessmen, and doctors, all of whom commanded much greater respect. As to introduction of technologies into daily life, Russia was considered by its population as far weaker than other advanced countries. And more than one half of the population considered that it would take Russia ten years or longer to reach the technological levels of other advanced countries, with the key factors being better discipline in the laboratories, enforcement of the law, and maintenance of social order. Assistance from the West was not considered important by most respondents to polling efforts. Overall, this was not a good report card.[21]

Turning to innovation indicators, the statisticians finally focused on sales of innovative products—not levels of government funding—as the key indicator, with surveys showing that only 5 percent of total sales were linked to new innovations. At the same time, expenditures on nontechnical innovative activities—defined to include marketing and managerial innovations—were recorded as about 1 percent of sales, which is quite low by Western standards.

According to one Russian analyst, the foregoing trends and supporting documentation suggest the following:

- Decisions are often based on political rather than economic criteria.
- There is inadequate understanding of foreign experience that should be incorporated in the approach to the Skolkovo project.
- Retrospective analyses are needed to understand why previously created infrastructures did not bring expected results.
- Since the demand for innovation is weak and not properly encouraged, business enterprises are not very engaged in the national innovation system.[22]

SKOLKOVO: THE INNOVATION CITY

In 2010 a leading advocate for spreading Russian technologies throughout the world proclaimed, "Skolkovo is a step to stop the brain drain from our country. It will give confidence to all scholars and researchers that the results of their labor are in demand in Russia and are protected according to international standards of intellectual property protection."[23]

Heeding such optimistic words, many Russian politicians rallied behind President Dmitry Medvedev's drive to establish the new innovation city located on three hundred hectares of land thirty miles to the west of Moscow. Breakthrough technologies are to receive priority for government funding. The research priorities run in parallel with the nationwide focus pronounced by the government: energy efficiency and energy conservation, nuclear technology, space systems including navigation and telecommunication networks, strategic computer technologies and software, and biomedical devices and pharmaceuticals.

From the beginning, Skolkovo advocates insisted on new premises. They were simply not interested in locating the new research and education center in tax-free zones where high-tech companies were already congregating and where collaborations among companies and universities were developing. For example, the new technology center in Novosibirsk discussed earlier had received more than $113 million of federal funds for infrastructure investments.

The president apparently was firm when he criticized Russian innovation centers in Novosibirsk, Dubna, Zelenograd, Tomsk, St. Petersburg, and elsewhere as not sufficiently successful to support the Skolkovo effort. He argued that it was easier to start from scratch than to rehabilitate weak attempts to advance an innovation agenda for the country. In time, however, he retreated and acknowledged that activities could be carried out in regional centers under the Skolkovo banner. Of course, he wanted personal nationwide identification with this mega-initiative, raising the issue as to the viability of the center after he steps down as president of the country. Thus, the headquarters of Skolkovo was established thirty miles from Moscow with satellite centers to be organized in a number of other locations throughout the country.

What success can President Medvedev thus far claim in developing the Russian version of Silicon Valley? His principal metric seems to be the number and stature of the international corporations that are prepared to invest significant resources in the new facility. As of 2011 more than a dozen large technology-oriented Western firms committed on paper to establishing facilities at Skolkovo, while a few leading Russian industrial enterprises also committed to establishing innovation centers for nanotechnology, railway car improvement, and development of better construction materials and designs, for example.

The strong Russian political commitment to the new city is impressive; it has been fully embraced by Kremlin leaders. However, extending anticipated benefits not only to Skolkovo but throughout the country will require the Russian government to create a more attractive nationwide investment climate by reducing corruption, decreasing the likelihood of corporate raiding of top talent, and improving the functioning of the domestic financial sector, beginning with the banking systems.

Was the selection of Silicon Valley as the model a wise decision? It has certainly captured the imagination of Russians as well as other populations. But would it not have been better to select as the model the high-technology approaches in Taiwan, Korea, or India? They may be less well known to the public, but they have successful track records and in some ways seem more relevant to Russian realities of beginning slowly and building momentum.

In addition to its grassroots free-market history, Silicon Valley contrasts dramatically with Russia's top-down approach to strengthening the country's science infrastructure. It remains to be seen whether the Russian government will allow market forces to determine the activities at Skolkovo. The private investors will certainly play an important role in determining the success of Skolkovo. The international firms have been slowly lining up, but reserving their positions on the size of their investments.

Many are surely interested in the future markets in Russia as well as access to high-tech Russian talent. But are they truly optimistic that Skolkovo will be a successful endeavor? And is the following formula, which helps explain the successes in Silicon Valley, relevant to Skolkovo?

- *Give a lot of money to brilliant people*—and stay out of their way. Entrepreneurs who became rich in one wave in Silicon Valley turned around and invested in the next wave.
- *Find yourself a top-notch university*, preferably one with room to spare. Stanford University has graduated more chief executive officers of high-tech companies than any other single institution in the world. Google and Yahoo, for example, started when their founders were still graduate students at Stanford University.
- *Don't forget that location matters*, and people vote with their feet. Today's high-tech workers choose to move around the globe in search of the right job in the right place. The cities that can't provide competitive amenities will lose out. But at present, Skolkovo is largely a barren landscape.[24]

The leaders of Skolkovo point out that since the center will have satellite activities throughout the country, the foregoing criteria are not relevant. But there will be a concentration of offices and the hub of the support network for Skolkovo at the Moscow location.

In 2011 the Skolkovo leadership enlisted the Massachusetts Institute of Technology (MIT) to help fill the current educational void. MIT is to serve as the designer of a new graduate school—the Skolkovo Institute of Science and Technology (SkTech). SkTech will be equipped with its own laboratories and will also be linked to fifteen collaborating research centers in various regions of Russia. Each center in turn will be networked with a university beyond the borders of Russia. In short, SkTech will orchestrate a number of networks, with its new laboratories benefiting from expertise available in Russia and throughout the world. While this novel approach has raised considerable interest in science circles, the complications of putting the networks in place are formidable.[25]

An interesting novelty is the heavy emphasis on young entrepreneurs. At a Kremlin meeting in 2009 to stir enthusiasm for the venture, attendance was limited to five hundred Russian specialists. All were younger than thirty. But one Kremlin meeting, while highly visible, does not guarantee that the older generation will take back seats in the new enterprise.

Many unanswered questions remain. They relate to the availability of qualified workers wherever the activities take place—in Skolkovo proper or in remote locations. Will capital be readily available for projects? Will government policies be supportive and not disruptive? And will the government be prepared to risk venture capital and other funds on projects that may fail to penetrate international markets, the likely fate of many projects?

In short, Skolkovo focuses attention on important aspects of the innovation process. On the optimist side, the business community will have a chance to press for reforms of financing mechanisms. The engineers will be able to demonstrate their ability to handle cutting-edge technologies. And the business community will show whether it is ready to play a role in globalization using its own resources, as well as those of the government.

In June 2011 the *Moscow Times* made the following observation: "President Medvedev hopes that Skolkovo will be the Noah's Ark for Russia's oil-flooded economy. Companies that have joined the project have remained optimistic while others have preferred to observe from afar, content with their Russian business and contributions to the economy."[26]

As of December 2011 the following steps had been taken to expedite development of Skolkovo and to initiate research activities within the framework of the project, recognizing that research would be conducted off-site until the center becomes an operational facility:

- The Russian government had allocated $2.8 billion to develop Skolkovo.
- Venture fund commitments had reached $266 million.
- The government-financed Skolkovo Foundation had awarded $163 million to the first wave of applicants for research projects.

- The Russian government had granted exemptions from income tax and property tax, while value-added-tax will be required only on imported items.
- The Russian government had granted exemptions from payments by employers to the Social Insurance Fund and Health Insurance Fund.
- The Customs Service had established expedited procedures for customs clearance.
- The Russian government had issued regulations eliminating the need for government permission to hire foreign nationals, while assistance will be offered for obtaining work permits. The government agreed to eliminate quotas for foreign workers and not place restrictions on salaries for highly qualified Russian specialists.[27]

ASPIRATIONS FOR A KNOWLEDGE-BASED ECONOMY

Russia has many of the assets that can provide building blocks for a knowledge-based economy—the type of economy that Skolkovo is meant to epitomize. They include the following assets:

- Large and well-defined reserves of raw materials that can provide the financial basis for boosting industrial development and for ensuring energy security
- Extensive facilities for processing raw materials that can be expanded to facilitate innovations that improve efficiency
- Advanced technologies in the defense-related industries, including leading-edge achievements that are relevant to further development of the nuclear, space, aviation, shipbuilding, biological, and chemical sectors
- High educational level of the population
- Availability of qualified research personnel and world-acknowledged scientific schools in fundamental science

The leadership of the country recognizes that Russia is maintaining resource dependence that reduces incentives for modernization of many industries. And it is slowly realizing that more resources are needed to transform research products into new income streams. Nevertheless, optimistic predictions of the future of nanotechnology, biotechnology, cyber technology, and energy technology developed in Russia in cooperation with other countries are the order of the day. According to the minister of education and science, the state's policy provides new conditions for commercialization of science-intensive technologies, development of high-tech branches of industry, growth of the quality of human resources, and trade in advanced technologies and high-technology goods. It will be interesting to witness whether these new conditions will be significant in stimulating international cooperation in many of the areas that have been of priority importance to the ISTC.[28]

At the same time, experienced Western investors bring much reality to the forefront. For example, a long-time industrial representative of a major American manufacturing company who has been based in Moscow observed in 2009: "Russia will have to make fairly dramatic changes (the sooner the better) in the business-law regime to encourage research and development in what will hopefully be a vibrant private sector—which in turn will be able to flourish in a stable, transparent, and legally based economic system."[29]

In its quest for an innovation economy, Russia has many important assets. But it is lagging in the most important asset of all—an innovation culture. Such a culture emphasizes innovating for profit in an internationally responsible manner that will benefit the Russian population on a broad scale while rewarding those who take financial risks and are successful. Whether or not the culture will shift from adherence to bureaucratic commands to working with the international community in searching for new innovation opportunities remains to be seen.

The immediate challenge for Russia is to effectively (a) increase the low economic and social payoffs from government investments in science while increasing the investments of the private sector in research and development, (b) strengthen the weak links between government-supported science and the interests of the business community, (c) improve the technological links among economic sectors, (d) reverse the waste of material and energy consumption, and (e) reduce dramatically the high level of corruption that corrodes the entire economic base.[30] The ISTC has interesting experiences in some of these key areas that should not be simply lost chapters in manuscripts that will continue to undergird Russia's progress toward a knowledge-based economy.

CHAPTER SEVEN

U.S.-Russia Bilateral Engagement Programs

The lab-to-lab program in Russia will jump-start the ISTC.
—Director, Los Alamos National Laboratory, June 1994

Our Biological Engagement Program endeavors to transfer sustainable programs to host governments and establish a culture of responsibility among dual-use scientists, while also securing high-risk pathogens.
—U.S. Department of State, January 2011

AS THE ISTC WAS BEING ESTABLISHED in the early 1990s, a number of U.S. government departments and agencies were rapidly increasing their expenditures for technology-related contracts with Russian organizations. These expenditures soon climbed into the tens of millions of dollars each year. Within a few years, annual U.S. government spending levels had reached hundreds of millions of dollars for bilateral projects involving Russian facilities that had previously depended for survival on the country's defense budget, which was rapidly shrinking.

A large portion of this spending from abroad was to help ensure that dangerous Russian materials would not surreptitiously become available to unreliable governments or to rogue groups. However, some Russian officials were convinced that U.S. programs, characterized as safeguarding Russian assets, were designed simply to gain access to technological know-how. In their view, prevention of proliferation of weapons technologies was only a secondary consideration.

Whatever the U.S. motivations, the overlaps of large bilateral efforts with many projects being considered for financing by the ISTC have been obvious throughout the lifetime of the center. Initially, Washington did not give coordination between programs high priority, as the center raced to begin operations. However, once the ISTC had earned a seat at the table of important nonproliferation organizations by demonstrating effective programs, the center became a key player in promoting coordination.

THE SCOPE OF BILATERAL PROGRAMS

The bilateral nonproliferation programs of the United States carried out in Russia have been large in comparison with the relatively modest U.S. investments in the regular projects and support activities of the ISTC targeted on Russia. The Department of Defense (DOD), the Department of State (DOS), and the Department of Energy (DOE) have supported the largest bilateral programs. At times, the departments have implemented these programs through the ISTC as a series of partner projects. Then consistency among related programs has usually been assured. At other times, the departments have carried out programs without adequate consultation with the center, occasionally funding Russian scientists to conduct work that overlapped with tasks being addressed by the same scientific teams that were supported through the ISTC.

Of course, the United States was not alone in initiating bilateral programs that had similar objectives to the multilateral approaches carried out through the ISTC. Several countries of the European Union (EU) and Japan, in particular, have carried out a variety of programs to redirect weapons expertise to civilian endeavors. They have addressed many of the same coordination issues that confronted the United States. For example, Russian institutions have (a) participated in the European Commission's long-standing Framework Program that helps build science capacity in Russia as well as expanding the international outreach of member states of the EU, (b) become deeply embedded in the nuclear programs of CERN in Geneva and in related activities of several European countries, and (c) developed strong direct interactions with Japanese scientists who share interests in advanced nuclear reactor technologies. In these and many other international endeavors, the issue of coordination of all efforts became, and should remain, an important issue—both to avoid unnecessary duplicative expenditures of funds and to capitalize on synergistic effects of related programs.

This chapter focuses on bilateral activities financed primarily by the U.S. government. The emphasis is on both (a) scientist redirection programs and (b) other programs designed to help reduce the vulnerabilities of Russia's weapons arsenals and weapons-related technologies developed in Russia. The latter category of activities has inevitably involved Russian scientists with expert knowledge, including scientists who would have otherwise been underemployed.

The bilateral nonproliferation activities financed by the United States have been the most far-reaching programs targeted on Russia of any country and have exceeded even the combined efforts of all members of the EU. The U.S. activities probably provide examples of almost every type of success and every problem encountered in Russia by foreign governments that have carried out cooperative programs related directly or indirectly to security concerns. Analysts residing in Europe, Asia, and Canada have better access to information concerning bilateral programs of their governments and have closer contacts with their local practitioners than do I. Therefore, I leave to them the task of documenting ISTC's overlapping interests with programs sponsored by organizations based in their regions.

In general, the objectives of most externally financed nonproliferation efforts in Russia seem to have been consistent. Of course, many countries have shared common interests in coordination. However, the political and technical realities in engaging Russian institutions have varied widely, according to the objectives and technological capabilities of the participating organizations.

This chapter briefly mentions cooperative U.S. programs that have been technology-oriented but have not focused on traditional nonproliferation approaches. For example, the external brain drain from Russia, including expertise relevant to weapons systems, depends to some degree on whether there are attractive professional opportunities at home for technical specialists who are on the fence as to whether to remain in Russia. Cooperative activities involving U.S. government organizations have often created such professional opportunities through programs that have not been labeled as nonproliferation programs. Also, a number of programs have drawn on talent that resides in Russia in exploring new research methodologies that are relevant to the discussion of brain drain. At times the U.S. agencies have provided modern equipment and laboratory supplies to bolster Russian efforts that have been of interest to former weapons scientists seeking new career paths.

Now, as the ISTC begins to fade from the scene in Russia, an important issue is whether the other programs involving advanced technologies and financed in large measure by the United States and the European countries will continue to operate in Russia. To what extent will they be cut back in response to changing interests of the Russian government? Many relevant programs have already reoriented their financial sails and have reduced their presence in Russia in response to the worldwide spread of interest in applying dual-use technologies to spur economic development. In short, a steady diversion of international funding for nonproliferation efforts away from Russia is well underway.

Meanwhile, authorities in Moscow repeatedly announce that Russia is no longer interested in foreign assistance. But will funding by Russia for strengthening its technological base for development and production activities in the country increase significantly as support from abroad declines? There are certainly indications of increases by the Ministry of Education and Science in support of research. However, the talk in Moscow of dramatic increases for science related to nanotechnology, biomedical issues, and energy efficiency, for example, is far ahead of the commitment of funds to follow through on official pronouncements.

RELEVANT INTERESTS OF MANY U.S. ORGANIZATIONS

Among the U.S. agencies that have been involved in scientific and technological developments in Russia, but are not deeply concerned with nonproliferation, are the National Aeronautics and Space Administration (NASA), National Institutes of Health, U.S. Agency for International Development, National Science Foundation, and Department of Education. Their activities have occasionally been loosely coupled with ISTC programs. For example, NASA has invested heavily in cooperation with Russian counterparts in the following areas, which have also been areas of interest to the center:

- Lunar exploration: Russian neutron detectors have been built for NASA missions.
- Earth sciences: Joint projects using space-based sensors have investigated forest, land surface, and coastal changes.
- Space sciences: Cooperation has included exploration of Mars and cosmic gamma ray bursts.
- Life sciences: Biomedical challenges have included research on single-celled organisms and analog studies of behavioral health and performance experiments.[1]

In addition, several U.S. nongovernmental organizations have goals in Russia that are relevant to interests of the ISTC. They include, for example, the

Civilian Research and Development Foundation (e.g., strengthening Russian research universities), the Nuclear Threat Initiative (e.g., supporting projects to reduce nuclear weapons stockpiles); and the Rostropovich Foundation (e.g., protecting children from common diseases). In addition, several grant-giving Western foundations have occasionally supported cooperative projects involving think tanks in both countries, particularly projects that address policy issues of widespread concern, ranging from biosecurity to limitations on tactical nuclear weapons.

The political and economic leaderships of Russia have long espoused the importance of U.S. private-sector investments in Russia. However, the business environment in Russia has many shortcomings. Consequently the level of foreign company investments has not been high in comparison with investments in a number of middle-income countries.

Now, senior Russian officials are intensely interested in the experience gained through international cooperation that will help them better understand the details of successful U.S. approaches in spurring advanced technology investments in Silicon Valley, as discussed in chapter 6. A few modest joint ventures and other technology-sharing arrangements have benefited all parties in the past. Russia seems determined to replicate such successes, while avoiding demands by potential partners for special status concerning ownership of intellectual property rights that would deprive Russian scientists of claims to their own achievements.

Russia's concerns over new business opportunities and protection of intellectual property intersect with the long-standing interests of the U.S. Department of Commerce, Overseas Private Investment Corporation, and Export-Import Bank. For many years, these organizations have promoted U.S. investments in Russia—including support of feasibility studies, often costing hundreds of thousands of dollars each. In some cases the studies should have been of considerable interest to the ISTC but were little known to the center, which in its early days stayed generally aloof from potential trade arrangements. For example, during the early 1990s the center was largely unaware of U.S. government support of information-gathering activities of American pharmaceutical firms interested in capitalizing on the research capabilities of secluded Russian institutions. However, in recent years the center has sponsored many events explicitly designed to stimulate international trade.

While the search for business opportunities in Russia by international companies will continue, the ground rules for operating in Russia may change. Russia is increasingly focused on opportunities for its own industries, and this orientation should be taken into account by foreign investors. As discussed in earlier chapters, commercialization of Russian technologies has been on the screen of the ISTC for many years. Let us hope that nonproprietary information about commercial opportunities in Russia accumulated by the center will continue to be available for helping both Russian and Western companies find interested partners.

OVERLOADING MANAGERS OF INTERNATIONAL PROGRAMS

As funding by many countries for cooperation involving Russia increased, interested U.S. government agencies should have been more attuned to the possibility of overloading senior Russian scientists with new international management and coordination responsibilities. Over the years, experienced and effective Russian managers/coordinators of sensitive programs have been in short supply. The turnover has been frequent, often leading to inexperienced managers/coordinators on the Russian side for international programs.

For many years, ISTC specialists with relevant experience have helped fill coordination voids. They have usually been available to assist when asked. They have provided advice to Western governments, both on substantive aspects of projects and on logistics. They have organized meetings in Russia—often free of charge—on opportunities for working with Russian institutions without inadvertently stumbling over ongoing activities. Unfortunately, government agencies of the United States and other countries have not adequately used this reservoir of expertise when seeking new paths into Russia's science and technology infrastructure. Even brief telephone calls to the ISTC Secretariat can at times save newcomers to the Russian scene considerable effort in finding promising pathways for exploring their interests.

In the 1990s the sudden U.S. interest in capitalizing on technology bargains in Russia, and particularly on the low wages that could be paid to Russian scientists for high-quality work, triggered warning buttons of some American skeptics, who questioned the value of Russian technology. They doubted that Russian achievements would be of much use to the United States. They argued that U.S. funds flowing to Moscow could assist the weakened Russian military complex in again aiming its weaponry toward the countries of NATO. And such skepticism remains.

Still, more than thirty-five organizations of the Department of Defense

(DOD), for example, have at times been given authorization to search for technologies in Russia. And search they did—for high-strength materials, for night vision devices, and for cold weather lubricants—with mixed results. The explorations that evolved into useful collaborations almost always depended, in the first instance, on the interest and capability of a Russian leader of the proposed activity. Too often, the American side thought that they could manage the collaboration on their own with only token involvement of Russian managers/coordinators, an attitude that usually led down dead-end streets, but an attitude that still persists among bargain hunters.[2]

In summary, many thousands of Americans living in Russia or regularly visiting the country have been engaged in a wide variety of intergovernmental, commercial, and academic activities that have drawn on the advanced technology skills of Russia's workforce. Some efforts have complemented ISTC projects. Others have ignored the center's activities even though they have depended on the same pools of Russian specialists that had been energized by the center for carrying out tasks of international interest.

The center has done a good job in organizing many international conferences, workshops, and consultations to bring together specialists with common interests being supported by many different organizations. Now, as the center fades from the scene, the U.S. and other governments should be vitally concerned as to how they will help prevent costly missteps by organizations interested in interacting with Russia's high-tech workforce. Without the assistance of the ISTC, many will be disappointed.

LAB-TO-LAB PATHFINDERS

That said, the initiatives of a number of U.S. scientific organizations have been of special significance in promoting nonproliferation objectives.

As an important early example, in June 1993 I made my first visit to Arzamas-16, the long-standing code name for the city of Sarov. A half-century earlier it had become the cradle for incubation of Soviet nuclear weaponry. The purpose of my visit was to explain to the nuclear scientists of this closed community the anticipated ISTC requirements for obtaining financial support, which could encourage the redirection of research activities of weapons scientists to civilian-oriented endeavors. The economic situation in Russia was at a low ebb; and the interest of previously prosperous scientists in Sarov in new income streams was high.

During a short airplane flight from a military airport on the eastern edge of Moscow to Sarov, I unexpectedly encountered the director of the Los Alamos National Laboratory (LANL), who was making one of his many trips to the secluded city. Rumors had been circulating within the ISTC planning group in Moscow that LANL claimed exclusive U.S. rights to engage the scientists of Sarov in civilian-oriented tasks and wanted the ISTC to concentrate its efforts elsewhere. At the same time, it seemed clear to our staff that the Los Alamos scientists would like to receive funding from ISTC, as long as they had free rein on the use of the funds and would not be required to compete with others for undertaking international projects centered in Sarov.

I was pleased to learn during the flight that such a self-centered view to limit contacts with Sarov-based scientists was not shared by the leadership of LANL. The director explained that his visit to Sarov was an early step in establishing a lab-to-lab program sponsored by the DOE. Under this program, Russian nuclear scientists who were interested in applying their skills to civilian challenges would host American counterparts and then would make reciprocal visits to U.S. weapons laboratories. Reciprocity for peace was the concept. Still, when he noted that the areas of interest for cooperative ventures that could emerge from the lab-to-lab contacts were environmental protection, nuclear reactor safety, and medical applications of isotopes, I wondered why we were both focusing on the same topics for projects involving the same Russian scientists.

He shared my concern that the number of Russian scientists capable of leading international projects was limited and that we should not be competing for their time. He viewed the lab-to-lab program as providing a jump start for the more bureaucratically encumbered ISTC. He persuasively argued that the U.S. weapons laboratories would quickly modify the independent approach of their lab-to-lab program as soon as the center became fully operational. Then DOE would bring the laboratory interactions under the umbrella of the ISTC, at least for coordination purposes, to prevent duplication and to encourage complimentary approaches.

However, the U.S. Congress, encouraged by the staffs of LANL and other DOE laboratories that had little appetite for sharing ownership of programs that they developed, had different ideas. In 1996 DOE allocated millions of dollars provided by the Congress to promote direct cooperation of the national laboratories with Russian counterpart institutions. Soon this lab-to-lab linkage, which was a formidable success in introducing specialists from the two countries to each other, expanded to a program for upgrading the control of nuclear materials at Russian facilities. It soon encompassed even more ambitious interactions through large-scale projects developed by DOE. The bilateral programs of DOE and several other U.S. departments were destined to play important roles in redirecting Russian specialists from weapons-related research to cooperative activities, thereby facilitating achievement of goals that were very similar to those of the center, with a decided DOE preference not to become entangled with the ISTC.

In short, I have always given high marks to the LANL director for being an invaluable pioneer in blazing new trails for cooperation that in time benefited the ISTC greatly, whatever the lack of clarity in the bureaucratic arrangements. He had considerable credibility with his Russian colleagues in Sarov. His steadfast support of the center for many years helped convince the most conservative Russian scientific leaders that the ISTC had important objectives that would benefit both countries.

NUNN-LUGAR PROGRAM

The Nunn-Lugar Program (formally named the Cooperative Threat Reduction, or CTR, Program) has been a signature cooperative activity of the United States for two decades in dismantling weapons infrastructures and in promoting nonproliferation throughout the territory of the former Soviet Union. The program provided the initial U.S. funding for the ISTC, and the many visits of the two senators to Russian facilities actively involved in security projects contributed to the high visibility in Russia of the center. The cumulative funding from 1991 to 2011 for Nunn-Lugar projects involving Russia was more than six billion dollars.

The initial legislatively mandated objectives of the program were the following: (a) help former Soviet states destroy nuclear, chemical, and other weapons including transporting, storing, disabling, and safeguarding weapons in connection with their destruction; and (b) establish verifiable safeguards against the proliferation of such weapons. These two objectives were subsequently amended to include dismantling missiles and missile launchers; destroying provocative conventional weapons; preventing diversion of weapons-related scientific expertise; establishing science and technology centers (e.g., ISTC); facilitating conversion of defense industries; and expanding military-to-military contacts.[3]

Much of the U.S. funding has provided support for thousands of Russian specialists who possessed extensive experience in designing and handling various types of weapons systems but who were engaged in civilian projects beyond the extent of ISTC projects. While their dismantlement of weapons systems was very important, the relationship of such activity to the mission of the center in supporting redirection of scientists was never fully recognized. Destroying rather than building weapons systems has important psychological implications for the careers of the dismantlers. Hopefully, such implications bode well for future activities of this cohort of specialists, who can become strong advocates of responsible science.

The specific components of the Nunn-Lugar program have varied in character and size over the years. In recent times the budget for activities in Russia has declined as new activities were launched in other states. During 2011 the following activities were being carried out in Russia at funding levels in the tens of millions of dollars for each activity:

- Elimination of solid propellant missile systems
- Elimination of liquid propellant missile systems
- Dismantlement of submarine-based missile systems
- Support for destruction of chemical weapon stockpiles
- Improvement of security and safety at nuclear weapons storage sites
- Enhancement of safety and security of nuclear warheads being transported to storage and dismantlement facilities
- Certification of nuclear weapon rail transport cars
- Disposition of spent naval nuclear fuel and missile material
- Enhancement of security at nuclear storage sites[4]

The long-term efforts of the CTR program to strengthen biosecurity in the former Soviet Union were a particularly significant activity. The ISTC provided an important mechanism for facilitation of the program. DOD even assigned specialists to the ISTC Secretariat to assist in implementation.

For fifteen years the CTR program supported a broad range of dismantlement, research, and surveillance activities in Russia. But by 2011 the program had almost shut down in Russia. Important Russian officials were concerned over DOD intrusions into activities under the purview of the civilian-oriented health authorities.

Despite the enthusiastic support of many Russian scientists for continuation of the biosecurity program, it simply was not possible to continue along the lines that had long been in place. At the same time, leading Russian institutions urged DOD to find new ways to continue cooperation.

As the program began to shrink in 2007, a prominent Russian biological scientist commented: "The Department of Defense invested tens of millions of dollars in restoring to international levels the capabilities of a dozen key Russian biological research institutions. Now the U.S. program should take advantage of this investment and support joint activities of the scientists at these laboratories with their American colleagues."[5]

The loss of official Russian interest in the program was undoubtedly rooted in mistrust among important Russian officials of DOD's motivations. In particular, the linkage of Russia's civilian health issues with DOD biomedical activities was not palatable to some Russian organizations, even though it made sense to address threats from both naturally occurring and deliberately triggered outbreaks of dangerous diseases within a comprehensive program. Also, Russian leaders did not share DOD's concerns over the scale of the threat of bioterrorism efforts that could be attributed to Russian weapons capabilities.

Nevertheless, the results of the activities of the biosecurity program were impressive. They were reflected in enhanced security and modernization of research centers as well as production facilities. Perhaps most important, personal interactions among scientists from the two countries developed to the point that some would probably continue indefinitely. Indeed, a few leading Russian scientists and American counterparts who had been financed initially through the CTR program found other channels for joint efforts.

NUCLEAR NONPROLIFERATION ACTIVITIES

As would be expected, DOE has been the leading U.S. organization for bilateral cooperation with Russia in nuclear nonproliferation throughout the lifetime of the ISTC. During the early 1990s, DOE had a strong interest and a financial investment in the activities of the center, since nuclear nonproliferation was at the top of ISTC's agenda. However, in 1996 DOS assumed primary responsibility within the U.S. government for funding ISTC activities and took a stronger role in managing the affairs of the center.

In time, DOE's interest in ISTC activities declined as it developed its own large nonproliferation programs, particularly in the nuclear field. However, DOS continued to rely on specialists from the national laboratories, such as LANL, to assess Russian proposals for ISTC support, with particular attention to (a) significance of the commitment of important weapons scientists to work on civilian tasks and (b) potential contributions of proposed projects to the advancement of international science. But the policy aspects of supporting the ISTC were clearly in the hands of DOS.

Since the early 1990s DOE has spent billions of dollars on nuclear nonproliferation programs focused on Russia, which have been carried out in parallel with the smaller programs of the ISTC. These DOE programs have involved thousands of Russian specialists. Many undoubtedly abandoned their weapons-oriented careers to participate in the DOE-supported activities. On a few occasions, DOE has relied on the ISTC to facilitate implementation. In 2010 DOE issued the following important summary of achievements:

> We have installed security upgrades at 93 percent of Russia's nuclear material and warhead sites. We have verifiably down-blended over 375 metric tons of former Soviet weapons-origin highly enriched uranium (HEU), enough for 15,000 nuclear weapons. Together, the United States and Russia have minimized the use of HEU in civilian applications worldwide. Since 2002, the United States and Russia have returned 910 kilograms of Russian-origin HEU fuel from third countries to Russia, and more than 1,215 kilograms of U.S.-origin HEU have been returned to the United States. Together this is enough HEU for more than 85 nuclear weapons.[6]

The annual funding level for DOE's Russia-oriented activities in 2010–11 exceeded four hundred million dollars. The major programs were as follows (listed in descending order beginning with the most highly funded activity):

- Material Protection Control and Accounting: enhances security of nuclear weapons and weapon-usable material and consolidates material
- Global Threat Reduction Initiative: converts research reactors from use of HEU to LEU (low enriched uranium) fuel, disposes excess nuclear and radiological materials, and protects nuclear and radiological materials from theft and sabotage
- Second line of defense: strengthens Russia's capability to deter, detect, and interdict illicit trafficking in nuclear and other radioactive material across its international borders
- Elimination of Weapons Grade Plutonium Production: oversees shutdowns of three Russian weapons-grade plutonium production reactors
- HEU Transparency Program: monitors down-blending of HEU into LEU

- Global Initiative for Proliferation Prevention: helps prevent migration or recruitment of Russia's technical experts that could lead to exploitation of weapons expertise by rogue states or groups
- Health Studies: assesses health effects suffered by populations living near or working at Russia's nuclear weapons production facilities
- Warhead and Fissile Material Transparency Program: promotes development of technical measures, negotiates agreements, and monitors transparency obligations[7]

Smaller programs rounded out a broad array of activities that covered many aspects of the handling of nuclear weapons and fissile material. They included technical research collaboration involving institutes of the Russian Academy of Sciences, exchange visitors in the fields of high energy physics and nuclear physics, and cooperation in development of fusion-based energy sources. Also, the Initiative for Proliferation Prevention (IPP) program, discussed below, was active. Thus, collaboration through ISTC was but one venue, and generally a secondary venue, for scientific interactions.

Problems with access to sensitive Russian facilities have often inhibited implementation of intrusive bilateral activities. Sometimes, ISTC projects have been the most successful in providing important insights as to otherwise unknown Russian nuclear activities. Capitalizing on this capability, DOE has at times carried out bilateral programs through the ISTC, including (a) research related to materials protection, control, and accounting, and (b) implementation of some components of the IPP program, with redirection of expertise a primary objective.[8]

While the security-related returns for investments in Russia by DOE have been impressive, some programs had shortcomings. For example, from the outset of DOE's involvement in Russia, repeated complaints from American and Russian experts have underscored that too large a portion of DOE's nonproliferation funding has been used to pay the salaries of an excessive number of specialists from the DOE laboratories, who at times become addicted to travel to remote destinations in Russia. These critics have even contended that some American specialists have been more interested in nuclear tourism than in serious technical work.

As early as 2001 several highly respected specialists from DOE laboratories commented to me that the reports of scientific tourism were accurate, but that DOE had made a concerted effort to limit the number of visitors to Russian sites.

They refreshingly asserted that this limitation was a very positive development. They cited an example of a DOE denial of a request from Sandia National Laboratory to send fifteen specialists on a two-week mission to witness safeguarding of fissile material at a single Russian laboratory. They added that DOE then insisted on a modified request to send only seven specialists. The personal opinion of my colleagues was that four specialists were enough; but in order for several DOE laboratories to participate in the visit, it was necessary to send seven. Despite the problem with excessive travel, the overall program proceeded with only limited difficulty.

At about the same time, a senior official of Rosatom commented to me that while DOE had supported more than five hundred joint research projects involving Russian institutions, the contract terms were unfairly slanted to benefit DOE (i.e., DOE retained exclusive intellectual property rights for any patentable discoveries) with little payoff for the Russian institutions. As a result, the Russian participants had no incentive to pursue innovative approaches. Thus, not a single patent application had been prepared by the Russian participants since they knew that they would not be beneficiaries of successful commercialization activities.

ENGAGING SMALL U.S. COMPANIES

DOE created the IPP program in 1994. The objective was to engage former Soviet weapons scientists in nonmilitary work in the short term and create private-sector jobs for these scientists in the long term. These objectives are quite compatible with ISTC objectives.

Under this program, DOE's national laboratories have spent many years searching for promising technologies in Russia, and their scientists have long believed that some technologies would be of interest to small U.S. companies. When there appeared to be good matches of interests of Russian developers of technologies and American companies, the DOE laboratories have helped make necessary commercial arrangements and then encourage steps to bring the technologies to market. The concept has been quite simple, but commercializing even the most promising technologies has not been an easy task, as evidenced by ISTC experience.

The IPP program has led to a number of small successes in marketing Russian-developed products. These successes have been important in developing science entrepreneurs in Russia while earning profit for the associated

American companies. Perhaps in time the sales levels for some products will reach the tens of millions of dollars that were originally anticipated.[9]

However, in 2007 the U.S. government's General Accountability Office (GAO) prepared a critical report of the program, including the following commentary:

> DOE has overstated accomplishments for the two critical measures it uses to assess the IPP program's progress and performance—the number of scientists receiving DOE support and the number of long-term, private sector jobs created. First, although DOE claims to have engaged over 16,770 scientists in Russia and other countries, this total includes both scientists with and without weapons-related experience. GAO's analysis of 97 IPP projects involving about 6,450 scientists showed that more than half did not claim to possess any weapons-related experience. . . . Second, although DOE asserts that the IPP program helped create 2,790 long-term private sector jobs for former weapon scientists, the credibility of this number is uncertain because DOE relies on "good-faith" reporting from U.S. industry partners and foreign institutes on the number of jobs created. DOE has not developed criteria to determine when scientists, institutes, or countries should graduate from the program. In contrast, DOS, which supports a similar program to assist Soviet-era weapon scientists through the ISTC, has assessed participating institutes and developed a strategy to graduate certain institutes from its program. DOE should seek cost-sharing for all IPP projects. The absence of a joint plan between IPP and ISTC's Commercialization Support Program raises questions about the lack of coordination.[10]

The GAO report raised important issues concerning measurement of the impacts of nonproliferation efforts, whether supported by DOE, ISTC, or others. This issue is addressed in chapter 11, which is devoted to metrics. In short, the report is somewhat naive as it greatly simplifies the feasibility of implementation of programs in Russia involving sensitive facilities and sensitive technologies. Also, it fails to recognize the importance of establishing a robust technology base in Russia, even along a drawn-out timeline, as an essential component of sustainable nonproliferation initiatives.

The IPP program has certainly opened many closed doors in Russia at a time when small U.S. firms could not have penetrated on their own the security rings surrounding many research centers. While contacts in basic science have been generally easy to establish, moving into the applied commercial areas, which are the realm of this program, has been difficult. Nevertheless, a number of

American firms, which would not otherwise have found technologies of interest, have succeeded in capitalizing on Russian technical skills. While the profits have been modest and the number of Russian weapons scientists who have been permanently redirected has been relatively small, the program has nevertheless focused considerable attention on the cupboards filled with technology that exist in Russia and the practical aspects of bringing such technologies to the marketplace.[11]

OTHER INTERFACES WITH ISTC OBJECTIVES

After the collapse of the Soviet Union, the DOS began a long-term expansion of its nonproliferation and related efforts directed to the states of the former Soviet Union. Unlike the newness of the ISTC approach that focused primarily on the behavior of individuals with expert knowledge of military-relevant technologies, many DOS activities were continuations and expansions of longstanding policy and program efforts to control the spread of military technologies through transfers of materials and equipment. As DOS increased project funding for many aspects of nonproliferation efforts, the interfaces between bilateral and multilateral activities, including ISTC activities, expanded rapidly. The importance of coordination increased accordingly.

Projects financed by DOS soon covered many aspects of nuclear, chemical, and biological weapons proliferation and control of missile technologies. DOS repeatedly underscored Russia's responsibility to develop and enforce at the national and local levels stronger controls over its military-related assets. These assets have been scattered throughout Russia's huge geographical expanse.

Highlighted here are three DOS programs that have been closely linked with ISTC activities in Russia. DOS was the responsible department within the U.S. government for providing support for the center. Therefore, DOS was in a good position to ensure that its activities were consistent with approaches advocated through the ISTC.

(1) Export control

Control of access to sensitive materials, equipment, and technical information was extraordinarily tight in the Soviet Union. Extreme measures were often applied to protect items that in the West would not have been considered sensitive, such as civilian transportation equipment. Physical security at the institute and enterprise levels was rigorous, and the isolation of military-related research and production activities, both from each other and from civilian activities, was a common practice. The scientists and engineers working in sensitive areas were well aware of the harsh consequences of violating security procedures, and personal compliance with required practices was a way of life.[12]

At the national level, Soviet decisions concerning trade and other international technology transfer arrangements were highly centralized. The likelihood was small that low-level officials or even ministers might individually make decisions to send sensitive technologies abroad. In short, the Soviet government had little interest in modifying its procedures to comply with Western export-control requirements, which were designed in the first instance to deny Moscow Western technologies. At the same time, the Western countries were not interested in providing the USSR a seat during their deliberations as to how to hold the USSR at bay. In short, international export-control limitations were developed with little Soviet involvement.

Then as Russia unlocked many of its doors and directors of enterprises and institutes focused on potential monetary returns for their dual-use technologies, the iron-clad procedures of Moscow for containing technologies gave way to free-form entrepreneurship. Money trumped protection of sensitive technology time and again. The Western governments, while eager to share in the access to Soviet-era technologies, also became concerned that these same technologies were falling into the hands of their future adversaries.

Under the leadership of DOS, the United States initiated in the early 1990s an aggressive program of training, persuasion, and financial coercion—facilitated with international travel and prestige-related benefits for Russian participants in the program—to bring Russian export procedures into line with Western approaches. While about five hundred Russian enterprises were to remain under the direct control of the state, more than fifteen hundred major technology-oriented enterprises were being privatized in a manner that raised concerns in the West that criminal elements would gain footholds in at least some of the firms. In the view of many Western experts, attraction of paying customers with questionable motivations was outweighing interests of Russian entrepreneurs in complying with Western-style export controls.

At the same time, a few Russian officials became increasingly concerned that Russia needed to polish its international reputation as a responsible trading partner in order to attract foreign investment, and Moscow slowly responded to repeated U.S. overtures for joint efforts in upgrading export controls within

Russia. DOS, in cooperation with the Department of Commerce, DOE, and DOD, expanded efforts to encourage modernization of Russia's approach to export control. Russia became a willing and, in time, an active participant in international training efforts and in discussions at international forums, as it took steps to bring its programs into line with Western concepts. As a participant in several international arrangements for enhancing export controls—the Nuclear Suppliers Group, the Australia Group, the Missile Technology Control Regime, and the Wassenaar Arrangement—Russia increased its efforts to limit diffusion of military-sensitive items through upgrading its own regulatory and enforcement structures.

Of particular importance, American specialists introduced Russian colleagues to the well-developed concept of internal company programs for compliance with national export controls. These programs were particularly significant as newly privatized companies emerged from the economic chaos. This approach emphasized clear designation of responsibilities within a company for (a) ensuring compliance with regulations, (b) keeping accurate records for exports, (c) training of key company personnel, (d) carrying out internal audits, (e) notifying authorities of questionable transactions under consideration, and (f) establishing comprehensive approaches to determining and fulfilling licensing requirements. In short, the active involvement of U.S. specialists stimulated and accelerated the establishment of effective controls in Russia years earlier than would have otherwise been the case.

The linkages between the export control program led by DOS and related ISTC activities were several-fold. First, a central concern of ISTC was to help prevent dangerous legal and illegal exports of sensitive technologies encompassed in hardware and in the knowledge of weapons scientists. The ISTC relied heavily on Russian judgments whether specific projects involving Russian institutions were consistent with Russian export control laws, which in turn were influenced by Russia's acceptance of international standards of decision making and enforcement.

Second, international partners in the center's projects frequently obtained access to Russian technologies that were on watch lists of international export-control organizations. In these instances, the partners had a responsibility to limit dissemination of technology to third-party countries. At times, the Russian government contended that the partners (alleged to be primarily from Europe) were not taking this responsibility seriously enough.

Finally, in the mid-2000s, several Russian officials who had been important participants in the development of Russia's export control regulations became involved in the discussions leading up to the government's decision to withdraw from the ISTC. They argued that export controls had been successfully implanted in Moscow. This step significantly reduced the need for the ISTC, they contended.

(2) Biological engagement

For several decades DOS has been concerned with the inadequacy of international arrangements for verifying compliance with the Biological and Toxin Weapons Convention. Establishment of an effective inspection/verification system has simply eluded diplomatic efforts and continues to be a seemingly unattainable goal. This deficiency in the international regime for controlling dangerous biological pathogens became particularly acute as the vast extent of the Soviet biological weapons (BW) program was revealed, following the collapse of the USSR. During the early 1990s evidence continued to mount that Russia was pursuing prohibited activities to further develop its BW capabilities, despite its commitments to discontinue such activities.

While the ISTC initially planned to focus its major efforts on reducing the threat of nuclear proliferation, by 1994 the U.S. government had decided to expand the portfolio of ISTC projects into the biological field. I first visited one of the Soviet Union's leading BW research institutes in the fall of 1994—the Center of Virology and Biotechnology Vector—as it celebrated the twentieth anniversary of its establishment. It was emphasizing its new role as an important component of the civilian biological research network of Russia. Reflecting Vector's history as a pioneer in developing military-relevant programs, a large number of Russian military representatives at the jubilee underscored Vector's historic ties with the defense establishment. My visit helped signal the readiness of the ISTC to begin support of redirection efforts at Russian biological facilities that had disbanded military activities, with the hope that eventually bygones would become bygones.

At about the same time, DOS led the U.S. policy effort to expand bilateral nonproliferation programs to encompass biological activities. By the end of the 1990s DOD, working through the ISTC, was putting in place a robust disease-oriented research and surveillance program as a component of the CTR program that involved redirection of former Soviet weapons scientists. It attracted participants from a number of important Russian biological research institutions (as discussed in chapter 9). In parallel, DOS decided to focus smaller efforts on activities that linked research to manufacturing in accordance with international standards, focusing on drugs, vaccines, and medical devices. It provided support for infrastructure improvement within selected Russian institutions that would enhance the interest of foreign customers in drawing on the extensive research facilities, which had originally been built to support the BW effort. The goal was to help ensure that redirection efforts at selected institutions rapidly became sustainable, without the need for financial assistance from Western governments for the indefinite future.

A particularly significant DOS program was the BioIndustry Initiative (BII) carried out during the early 2000s. Through aggressive outreach within Russia backed by a readiness to promptly fund applied research and related projects, DOS soon became a major player to turn a number of networks of financially struggling biological research institutions into networks of institutions focusing on civilian aspects of biological research, while being well on their way to sustainability. Testimonials from Russian scientific leaders about the contributions of BII in enabling institutions to find niche markets became commonplace.

As DOS took center stage in enhancing capabilities of Russian institutions to offer products and services, it also introduced throughout the U.S. government an awareness of the importance of a comprehensive approach in reducing risks of bioterrorism. Addressing potential vulnerabilities throughout the research, development, and manufacturing cycle was important. But not to be neglected was the need to detect and control disease outbreaks whether or not they were triggered by man-induced causes. This systems approach to disease prevention, detection, containment, and treatment had already been adopted by the ISTC and was the standard for biological nonproliferation programs—as well as public health programs more generally—throughout the Western countries.

(3) Engagement of other U.S. agencies in nonproliferation activities

Related to the interest of DOS in expanding its biology-related activities in Russia was recognition by the department of the special skills of other U.S. government agencies in addressing nonproliferation issues, and particularly the capabilities of the Departments of Health and Human Services (HHS) and

Agriculture (USDA). Both of these departments have extensive international networks of collaborators for addressing civilian-related international problems. They long ago recognized that their efforts to control naturally occurring human and animal diseases were relevant to concerns over bioterrorism, on the territory of the former Soviet Union and more broadly throughout the world. Also, for many years they have been concerned over what seemed to be excessive reliance by DOD's CTR program on private contractor organizations that provided advice on diseases for which the governmental departments had unique experiences and international contacts.

DOS thereupon led the effort to convince the U.S. Congress to include in the foreign affairs appropriations legislation a special provision for funding nonproliferation activities by the two departments and also engage the Environmental Protection Agency in the effort. Since this legislation was administered by DOS, Congress was confident that the nontraditional approaches of other governmental organizations would be closely coupled to the government's broad nonproliferation efforts. Congress was correct in its assessment.

Thus, for a number of years HHS received a charter and funding to support U.S. nonproliferation efforts through establishment of joint projects with a range of research institutions in Russia and other newly independent states. The presence of HHS in these efforts was particularly important in Moscow, where Russian health authorities had become wary of having DOD as a partner. HHS had the needed credibility in the eyes of Russian skeptics as to the U.S. government's objectives, and the U.S. government as a whole benefited from the department's participation in the program.

Similarly, a number of Russian agricultural centers welcomed nonproliferation programs administered by USDA at the request of DOS. The USDA approach was frequently hailed in Washington as a model to be emulated. An essential requirement of each project was that a USDA scientist must be sufficiently interested in the topic under consideration to take responsibility for the U.S. side of the collaboration, without receiving additional personal compensation. Second, there was a "get-acquainted" phase of two or three weeks of working together to develop each project before serious collaboration began. On occasion, projects were not implemented because the meshing of interests during this preliminary stage was not sufficiently strong. Finally, from the outset of each project, consideration was given as to how the activities stimulated by the project could be sustained over the long term. But the record in this regard was mixed.

JOINT COMMISSIONS

In 1993 the U.S. and Russian governments established a Joint Commission on Economic and Technological Cooperation, with Vice President Al Gore and Prime Minister Victor Chernomyrdin serving as cochairs. The commission continued its work until 2001 when President Bush, with the acquiescence of the Russian government, decided that such a commission had outlived its use-fulness. Critics blamed many of the shortcomings in U.S.-Russian relations during the later years of the Clinton administration on the lack of effectiveness of the commission, even though this consultation mechanism had little respon-sibility for the vexing problems that were cited (e.g., Russia's nuclear dealings with Iran, Russia's position on the war in the former Yugoslavia).[13] The record shows that the commission was more effective than had been anticipated and had won support among even the skeptical career government officials, at least in Washington, who at times ironically were drowning in paperwork required by the commission.[14]

In its role for promoting cooperative activities among technical specialists, the commission quickly became a real boon for science and technology proj-ects, which dominated many bilateral discussions. Originally the commission's goal was to "enhance cooperation in space, energy, and high technology activi-ties." But the scope of its activities quickly expanded to eight subcommittees: space, business development, energy, defense conversion, science and tech-nology, environment, health, and agribusiness. Dozens of agreements and proj-ects were brought under the umbrella of the commission. As new intergovern-mental projects developed, some were included in the commission's portfolio while many other new projects, particularly those supported by DOD, were car-ried out without the commission's involvement.[15]

Russian officials welcomed the concept of considering at the highest levels of government the project proposals being promoted by the agencies of the two governments. Centralized orchestration of important activities had long been a familiar style in Moscow. Russian advocates of cooperation thought that the prime minister, using the commission as leverage, could apply pressure on the Ministry of Finance to provide needed funding to carry out their favorite projects.[16]

Most senior American officials also were enthusiastic about the commis-sion, despite the added burden of taking projects through yet another bureau-cratic level of review. In their view, the commission facilitated and fertilized business-like bilateral interactions. They considered the political stakes to be high enough so that agreements reached through the commission would be followed up with actions that could signal progress in strengthening bilateral relations.[17]

After some initial hesitancy over yet another coordinating mechanism, most of the lower-level officials in both governments became strong supporters of the commission. The organization's activism in clearing obstacles to cooperation was impressive and added impetus to budget requests in both capitals. The ringing endorsements of long-time veterans in the trenches of science and technology cooperation policy indicated that this organizational innovation worked. Outside skeptics sometimes called the commission "political symbolism," but these critics may have been unaware of the benefits to the working-level participants in both countries.[18]

What was the impact of the commission on ISTC activities? The center facilitated a number of U.S. government partner projects in the late 1990s, but it seems likely that these projects would have moved forward with or without the commission. However, the commission stirred considerable interest in Washington in encouraging financial support for science cooperation with Russia; and this interest was reflected in significant growth in budgets, including the nonproliferation budget of DOS, which also funded the ISTC. This high-level attention to the commission's work in many areas of interest for the center was probably a contributory factor in the decisions within the U.S. government to fund the center at a significant level during the late 1990s, even though there were no apparent ISTC program approaches that were direct outcomes of commission deliberations.

In July 2009 Presidents Obama and Medvedev created a new commission, which appeared to many observers to be a revival of the Gore-Chernomyrdin approach. This new Bilateral Presidential Commission was to be an important mechanism for helping to reset the U.S.-Russia relationship, which in the eyes of the two leaders had gone downhill. Similar to the approach of the earlier commission, the new structure called for working groups, with many of the twenty groups having responsibilities related to science and technology that overlap with the interests of the ISTC. The working groups included the following:

- Nuclear Energy and Nuclear Security
- Arms Control and International Security

- Counterterrorism
- Business Development and Economic Relations
- Energy
- Environment
- Agriculture
- Science and Technology
- Space Cooperation
- Health
- Emergency Situations
- Education, Culture, Sports, and Media[19]

Is the new commission simply a rerun of the Gore-Chernomyrdin effort with new players and broad updated agendas? To some degree, yes. But this similarity does not negate the importance of high-level dialogues on a continuing basis. The working groups can focus attention on the continuation of long-standing common interests in many problems confronting the countries and the broader global community, and they can also identify new problems that deserve increased attention. Gaining positive political attention is the first step toward successful implementation.

I participated in activities of three of the working groups, namely (a) Science and Technology, (b) Education, Culture, Sports, and Media, and (c) Health. From the U.S. vantage point, all three working groups faced an omnipresent problem. There was no new money to initiate additional activities or even to continue some well-established collaborations. That meant that much of the U.S. effort would be devoted to repackaging existing and planned programs so that they would at least appear to be newly energized starts, even though they would have been carried out without a new commission.

On the other hand, the Russian government announced the availability of new funding streams for international scientific cooperation and an interest in discussing how this increased funding could be brought under the umbrella of the commission. Over the years the U.S. government had become accustomed to paying more than its fair share of the costs of cooperative activities. So the changed Russian position set a good tone for implementation of planned activities. The hope on the U.S. side was that the Russian position could help uncover hidden U.S. funds for promoting new projects of mutual interest.

As to areas of interest, the working group on Education, Culture, Sports, and Media devoted considerable effort to responding to the Russian interest in linking the country's newly designated national research universities with U.S. counterparts. The U.S. response pivoted around two programs. First, the long-standing Fulbright program has a number of segments that can readily accommodate higher percentages of participants from the natural sciences. Second, the Department of Education quickly announced its intention to expand funding for university-to-university collaboration, a program that had begun in 2007. Unfortunately, this program gave excessive attention to curriculum development and did not adequately recognize the importance of strong research capabilities as an essential component of modern research universities. The Russian Ministry of Education and Science, which was undergoing a major restructuring of its administrative responsibilities, assured the science advocates within the working group that the ministry would work with the Department of Education in the future to overcome this shortcoming.

The working group on Science and Technology initially embraced ongoing activities pursuant to the long-standing bilateral U.S.-Russian agreement on science and technology, which had been renewed for ten years in 2008. About a dozen U.S. departments and agencies have been supporting with Russian counterparts bilateral activities that could be readily embedded in the new working group portfolios. A particularly important task of the working group was to continue efforts to overcome barriers to scientific cooperation, including visa difficulties, tax and customs issues, and ownership of proprietary results of joint efforts.

The working group on Health focused on several areas of long-term interest to the U.S. government. For example, a healthy lifestyle was a concept that eluded significant portions of the populations of both countries, and the working group did a good job in defining many of the problems. A second theme of interest was comparison of food-related regulatory requirements in the two countries. Unfortunately, the working group has had little interest in directly related achievements of the ISTC over many years.

SIGNIFICANT CONCLUSIONS FROM PAST COOPERATIVE EFFORTS

U.S.-Russia commissions, GAO, and nongovernmental organizations—as well as the U.S. and Russian departments and agencies themselves—have frequently reviewed U.S.-Russia cooperative programs. Many conclusions of these reviews have resonated favorably within the halls of the ISTC. An interesting review carried out during the late 1990s reached the following conclusions, which were particularly relevant to ISTC approaches:

- "Assistance" is a donor-recipient concept that is not an appropriate basis for programs with Russia, particularly in science and technology. Rather, programs should be based on mutual scientific interests and genuine cooperation.
- Placing Russia in the same category as other states of the former Soviet Union leads to distortions in science and technology program approaches that may not be appreciated in Moscow.
- Selection of targets of opportunity for cooperative efforts often diverts attention from more meaningful, although more difficult, cooperation opportunities.
- Even for activities funded primarily by the United States, project details should be worked out in Russia, as well as in Washington, to ensure buy-in on both sides.
- Serious questions remain as to whether generous international grants to scientists in weak Russian institutions will result in high-quality work. Scientists reviewing proposals for financial support should carefully consider the quality of the supporting infrastructures as well as the capability of the individual scientists.[20]

Commercial joint ventures remain a priority in Moscow as the Russian government pursues Skolkovo and other projects in a number of regions. A related assessment included the following observations:

- There have been successful joint efforts in manufacturing, but successes in research or software development are easier to achieve.
- Market-driven projects are usually more successful than technology-driven projects.
- Component projects or projects that provide equipment for further use appear to be more successful than end-product projects.
- Russian enterprises that are willing to decentralize, delegate, and spin off units are better at attracting and working with U.S. partners than less flexible companies. The level of privatization of the Russian entities is less important than these factors.[21]

Still, U.S. companies have held a variety of views on seeking help from the U.S. government for establishing joint efforts in Russia. Many companies will keep considerable distance from government programs. Others find government support necessary for investing company resources. Still others are engaged in joint projects, primarily because of the availability of U.S. government funding to cover some of their expenses.

An interesting commentary on Russia's failure to become an important high-tech global player and on the Russian approach to collaboration came from the U.S. Embassy in Moscow in 2010:

> A number of Russian experts on science policy believe that Russia wasted two decades by neglecting science and education. Many talented people have left Russia and will not return. Many Russian scientists and engineers ruthlessly criticize the trend for initiating grandiose innovation projects, which are perceived as a colossal waste of sparse resources. Most administrators, managers, and scientists agree that what is desperately needed for improvement of Russia's research competitiveness on a global scale is expertise in science management. Hence they place much of their hope on the U.S. experience. U.S.-Russia cooperation is now viewed in a meaningfully new context. Both U.S. and Russian scientists and administrators should seek equal authority with their counterparts in all U.S.-Russia collaborative projects to ensure actual partnership rather than a no longer valid tradition of charity.[22]

During recent years, the ISTC has worked diligently to address these issues. Russian specialists have recognized the weaknesses of the separation of science, education, and production activities—a separation that they had inherited from the USSR as discussed in chapter 6. They also recognize the importance of reaching out to other advanced countries that have left Russia far behind. The ISTC has made a number of contributions in these precise areas in galvanizing the scientific community to help rehabilitate an obsolete system.

CHAPTER EIGHT

The Nuclear File

U.S. pays millions to Russian scientists not to sell A-secrets.
—*Washington Post*, 1994

For now, sound economic arguments for opening the closed nuclear cities
in the Urals are trumped by national security concerns and by nostalgia for
the past.
—U.S. Consulate General, Yekaterinburg, 2010

WHEN DIPLOMATS FIRST RAISED the concept in 1991 of an international
center to support redirection of Russian weapons scientists' expertise to civilian tasks, the threat of primitive nuclear bombs constructed by disenfranchised
rogue groups was in the forefront of the discussions. The possibility of a nuclear
catastrophe dominated ISTC deliberations for many years. Even when other
types of proliferation threats moved onto center stage, the nuclear issue was repeatedly cited as a principal rationale in Washington, Brussels, and Tokyo for
continuation of ISTC programs.

Beginning in 1992, Russian nuclear authorities in the Ministry of Atomic
Energy (Minatom) had the host-country responsibility for supporting the ISTC.
For ten years, they provided bureaucratic muscle for promoting the general
perception within the Russian and other interested governments that financial
support for redirection of nuclear scientists was the center's most urgent task.
And the ISTC parties generally shared this view.

A decade later in the early 2000s, however, international financial commitments to the ISTC began to decline as concerns over proliferation of weapons of
mass destruction spread in many directions around the world. Also, American
and European scientists encouraged Russian biologists to compete more aggressively for available ISTC funds, and a smaller share of the already reduced funding went to the nuclear establishment in Russia. The advocates within Minatom

and its successor organization, Rosatom, then began to change their stripes. They gradually became somewhat skeptical about the need for the high-visibility role of an ISTC that was now losing some of its financial clout. They led the steady erosion of political support within the Russian government for the center.

As discussed in chapter 4, the reasons for the decline in interest in the ISTC among Russian officials extended beyond reductions in the center's financial base, although the shrinking budget repeatedly disappointed key nuclear scientists in Russia and abroad. In contrast, the Russian treasury was providing the institutions of Minatom and then Rosatom with increased financial resources. And by that time, the security systems at nuclear facilities had been substantially tightened. The Russian government had developed alternative international mechanisms for addressing nuclear issues, particularly through bilateral programs with the United States, Japan, and the European Union. Thus, the Russian government, and particularly Rosatom, gave less and less weight to the importance of the ISTC as a source of external financing or as a mechanism for coordination of activities of interested states. Indeed, within a few years, whenever an outsider asked a knowledgeable Russian scientist about the identity of the officials who argued against maintaining the center's programs in Russia, the finger of the insider inevitably pointed to staff members of Rosatom.

ASSESSING THE EXTENT OF THE NUCLEAR THREAT

Observing developments in North Korea, Iran, Syria, Pakistan, and elsewhere, officials in Washington, Brussels, and Tokyo have consistently emphasized that the advancing scientific capabilities of rogue countries with nuclear ambitions are a grave danger for the world. The policies and programs of these four rogue states dominated early discussions of the need for the ISTC. While the countries were following different paths to master the art of bomb building, each could benefit from the experience and know-how of renegade Russian scientists, argued the center's advocates.

The nuclear issue continues to be the focus of the spotlight that shines on potential disasters looming over the horizon. To many, the possibility of a nuclear calamity increases anxieties far more than other worldwide threats of the modern era. Frequently, the international community has singled out for special attention a dozen countries that could soon have the capability to assemble nuclear weapons in a short period. At other times, the list has been expanded to include as many as two dozen countries with worrisome levels of nuclear capabilities and uncertain ambitions.

The specter of a devastating nuclear event is a powerful motivator of international action. Suspicion of a nuclear threat propelled the U.S.-led invasion of Iraq. Then it provided a persuasive argument for maintaining NATO troops in Afghanistan, next door to the Pakistan nuclear tinder box. Even Myanmar (formerly Burma) is on some ever-growing suspect lists of potential hideaways for dangerous nuclear activities. In each case, access to fissionable material and know-how has been the central concern; and Russia has long had all of the know-how and technological devices that are needed to support almost every nuclear scenario.

Clearly the nuclear potentials of North Korea and Iran are now at the forefront of international concern. Russian support years ago of the nuclear aspirations of these countries has been a front-burner item in some Western and Asian capitals for more than two decades. The U.S. and other like-minded governments have scrutinized the dual-use capabilities of Russian scientists and engineers and their students from abroad many times in recent years. The spillover of technical expertise from supporting nuclear power to supporting nuclear weapons remains a controversial issue.

Are international concerns that at times extend to nuclear weapons hidden in deep jungle enclaves within the poorest countries a stretch of the imagination? Are extreme scenarios simply intended to scare policy officials who then become more amenable to providing funding to alarmists for new defensive measures? Or, by minimizing the threat do we miss a chance to thwart emerging threats before it is too late? The Western founders of the ISTC thought that any Russian involvement in nuclear transactions with countries on the U.S. threat lists and those of its allies certainly needed prompt attention and that the center's interactions with the Russian nuclear community would help clarify concerns.

In short, all serious analysts conclude that the nuclear threat is a high-priority issue. The danger is both near term and long term. Many voices have long urged governments from around the world to step up efforts to obstruct various proliferation pathways. In recent years the ISTC has occupied an important position in such debates.[1]

Efforts to counter this threat have many dimensions. For example, all countries that possess nuclear weapons should reduce their inventories as rapidly as possible. Production of fissionable material should be tightly controlled.

Stockpiles of dangerous material should be locked down. The Additional Protocol for the Nuclear Nonproliferation Treaty that provides for intrusive policing of the behavior of countries should be universally adopted. Interdiction of nuclear smugglers deserves high priority. Thus, pressures in all direction are needed to limit the number of hostile countries or renegade groups that are in positions to misuse nuclear know-how.

The lists of needed steps to block proliferation continue to grow. But at times, the advocates of greater attention to nuclear dangers can go too far in their calls for action by asserting the presence of mythical hidden activities in some countries. Their cause may be undercut when such exaggerations are unveiled.[2]

In recent years the leadership of the United Nations has joined the chorus in the daily warnings of impending nuclear dangers, as exemplified by former U.N. secretary general Kofi Annan, who proclaimed the following in 2005: "We live in a world of excess hazardous materials and abundant technological know-how, in which some terrorists clearly state their intention to inflict catastrophic casualties. Were a nuclear attack to occur, it would not only cause widespread death and destruction, but would stagger the world economy."[3]

At the same time, many experts have continued to decry the hesitancy of governments to take more active roles in collaring highly enriched uranium. But are the terrorists who now threaten to attack the world up to the task? Perhaps such malevolent behavior is out of the question today, but tomorrow may be another story. Experts cite the following impediments to a global lockdown of nuclear materials, technologies, and expertise—a lockdown that could change the ending of the story in a positive direction:

- Complacency: Many officials in Russia and elsewhere consider that it would be absolutely impossible for inexperienced terrorists to make a nuclear bomb, even if they obtained the needed material.
- Political disputes: Some countries that should be cooperating to develop a global culture of nuclear security have political disagreements with the United States and other concerned countries, and these disagreements inhibit progress.
- Secrecy: Most countries consider some specific aspects of their nuclear activities as closely guarded secrets.
- Sovereignty: Many states want to make their own nuclear security decisions, without other countries or international agencies intervening.

- Cost: Every dollar spent on nuclear security is a dollar not spent on activities that will bring in revenue.
- Commercial interests: Steps to prevent proliferation inevitably raise costs of nuclear activities designed to make civilian products available for the international and domestic markets.
- Bureaucracy: Disputes over which national agency has authority, disputes between countries over taxes and liability associated with collaboration, and sluggish processes for approving international agreements and even visa applications delay cooperation.[4]

At the same time, however, terrorists must overcome many obstacles in launching a nuclear attack. One scenario in carrying out an attack could pose the following challenges for the perpetrators:

- The terrorists engage dissidents who locate an inadequately secured source of highly enriched uranium. These hired perpetrators corrupt several insiders who then lead an undetected entry involving outsiders into the storage area.
- The insiders, who are loyal to the mission and avoid leaks, successfully seize the material and transfer the loot to an untested team with transportation capability, which takes it across unfamiliar terrain.
- The terrorists hire smugglers who then move the contraband across international borders, while avoiding other smugglers using the same routes and while remaining loyal in resisting massive bribes or reward money en route.
- The plotters arrange for technically trained collaborators to establish a machine shop with sophisticated equipment.
- A team of high-tech trained scientists and technicians who swear loyalty to the mission and who have no interpersonal or financial conflicts, secretly assemble the device at the machine shop, with the bomb fabrication processes taking many months or years.
- The terrorists arrange for the theft of precise blueprints on how to design a device that are followed without opportunities to test results of the efforts at critical stages.
- Nothing significant goes wrong, and no leaks occur.
- The conspirators avoid local and international police, perhaps on high alert, who do not detect the activity with traditional and probably sophisticated detection equipment.

- A nuclear device weighing a ton or more is finally assembled and smuggled out of the machine shop to another international border and transported to the target country as either conventional or clandestine cargo without raising suspicions.
- Technically accomplished coconspirators prepare the device for detonation.
- A detonation team is assembled and transports the device to the target area where the team secretly sets the device off. The much-traveled device proves not to be a dud.[5]

Over the years the ISTC has considered this scenario and other approaches to clandestine detonation of nuclear devices. What are the technical choke points that inhibit the unfolding of disaster? Can the center help ensure that technologies for overcoming such barriers are kept away from malevolent forces?

In sum, the acquisition of nuclear devices by additional countries in the years ahead is of serious concern. But in the immediate future, it will be difficult for a government that wants to become a newcomer on the nuclear weapons platform to carry out all elements of a weapons program clandestinely. And for terrorists operating without access to government facilities, the task will be very difficult.

While a low-probability event, the detonation of a clandestinely acquired or assembled nuclear device would cause incalculable damage. The number of human deaths could be very large, economic losses devastating, and psychological trauma of indefinite duration. Thus, all responsible governments must join forces to prevent such a development. Contributing to such an international effort has been an important goal of the ISTC throughout its lifetime.

ISTC'S RESPONSE TO RUSSIA'S NUCLEAR SCIENTISTS

When the United States, the European Community, and Japan were working with the Russian Ministry of Foreign Affairs and other Russian ministries to establish the ISTC in the early 1990s, the Russian nuclear complex was in a state of turmoil. It was suffering cut after cut of its budgetary allocations. Minatom was looking far and wide for new income streams during the economic decline.

For the first time, the privileged nuclear workforce had fallen on difficult financial times. The pantries of the special supply shops that serviced the nuclear facilities were suddenly barren. Paychecks were delayed for many months. At some facilities nonessential work had slowed to a crawl. The nuclear centers were among the most powerful institutions in the country, and the loud protests of their scientists over the decline in their professional challenges and in their remuneration needed to sustain their families resonated throughout Moscow.

Initially, suspicions about Western motivations in setting up the ISTC were widespread, both in Moscow and in remote nuclear research centers. But these apprehensions quickly gave way to the prospects of new international supply lines that would allow the scientists to return to meaningful work. Foraging for food, which had become the order of the day for many scientists, was simply degrading and unacceptable.

Many groups of nuclear weaponeers seized upon the much heralded ISTC as "their" program, which would revitalize their professional lives while restoring respect for Russian science. But they would be alert and would quickly ascertain how serious an enterprise the center would be. They would be the first to know if the center was a supportive and energetic organization or simply a new stop for foreign diplomats who would repeat well-worn calls for financial belt tightening and patience while awaiting the arrival of a market economy and increased paychecks.

Fortunately, the underemployed nuclear scientists were not disappointed, as a high level of excitement and optimism permeated ISTC headquarters in Moscow. Without support of nuclear elites of Russia, who continued to have significant clout with government officials throughout the financial crises of the 1990s and beyond, the ISTC would not have been successfully launched or sustained. Nor would it have been able to exceed expectations as an effective international organization in harnessing Russian weapons expertise in many beneficial ways for Russia and for other countries with civilian nuclear infrastructures in various stages of development. Throughout the history of the center, the level of support from the Russian nuclear complex was an important indicator of the likely fortunes of the institution in the years ahead.

RUSSIA'S CLOSED NUCLEAR CITIES

Returning to 1992, several Russian colleagues working with me at the Preparatory Committee for the ISTC (Prep Com) were taken aback by the downward spiral of economic conditions in the ten closed nuclear cities of Russia, where there were more than seven hundred thousand inhabitants. They strongly urged that we press for a special program to help sustain a minimum level of economic support for the scientists in these isolated enclaves, who had been accustomed to receiving special shipments of low-cost household items and food products. They needed reliable supplies, and they wanted a fast track for obtaining ISTC support rather than looking to inappropriate suppliers, argued their colleagues in Moscow. After all, their economic plight was the primary reason that the center was established, accurately claimed their friends within the Prep Com, who began to develop a special program for the closed nuclear cities. The plan of these supporters was to present a well-developed program to the parties to the ISTC Agreement as soon as possible.

The arguments seemed persuasive. We decided to test the idea within the Russian nuclear community and with representatives of the member governments who were developing their own approaches for supporting ISTC projects. In principle, we could take steps to ensure that once the center was in business, a special set of projects for the closed cities would be on the top of the pile of proposed projects awaiting approval.

But I was soon surprised by the resistance to the concept. The idea of a special program for the closed cities resonated well with me and with my colleagues who had lived and worked in the closed cities. But the suggestion went nowhere when it was raised with Russian officials. Indeed, scientific leaders in several of the ten closed cities were not enthusiastic about the concept.

Singling out ten cities as special cases in need of resuscitation did not make political sense to them. While in desperate economic straits, the nuclear scientists in the cities were no worse off than their colleagues in the open nuclear cities. Why should they receive preferential treatment? Was it just because under the Soviet system they received favored treatment? If so, wasn't it time for a change?

As would be expected, the concept did not appeal to the financiers. After all, there were forty-five closed cities with defense orientations, including those in the nuclear complex. (The cities were called ZATOS, the Russian acronym for "closed areas." The Ministry of Defense controls most of them.) What would be done in parallel to help residents of the other thirty-five cities behind high fences?

A decisive factor in abandoning the concept of special treatment was the confidence exuded by the scientists in the closed nuclear cities that they could effectively compete with colleagues in other cities for the new financial resources that would be available through the ISTC or other mechanisms. They proved to be correct. Their success record was impressive.

Five years later, despite the experience of the ISTC, the U.S. Department of Energy (DOE) decided that it would launch a special program for several of the closed nuclear cities. After lengthy discussions with skeptical Minatom officials, DOE succeeded in initiating a number of small projects in several of the cities, with the department paying the bill. DOE attempted to interest international companies in locating facilities in the cities. They were to be the flagship efforts of the program. But access problems on the tightly guarded property of the cities were very serious.

It soon became clear that the program was going to be plagued with administrative difficulties and that the small projects would not make much of a difference—either scientifically or economically. The cities were not ready to take the necessary steps to enable private investments within the cities on a significant scale, particularly investments from abroad. DOE nevertheless continued its efforts to interest foreign enterprises in investing in the closed cities—although it was far from clear that investments would be possible.

Finally, the program was closed when the five-year agreement for the program came to an end. Tax and liability issues were the stated reasons for termination. However, Russian concerns over the intentions of DOE, perhaps linked with intelligence gathering, were strong and probably were among the drivers of Russia's reluctance to continue.

In any event, the new jobs that were to be created were difficult to identify. Most of the U.S. funding had been turned over to DOE laboratories and contractors that enlisted American specialists of many types, and they increased the time they spent in three of the cities selected as sites for pilot projects. Even the American nongovernmental organization (NGO) advocates, who received funding from both the U.S. government and private foundations to support the effort, soon gave up promoting the program.[6] But the ISTC did not give up on its efforts to include the institutes in the cities high on the lists of recipients of research awards.

In competition with grant-seeking activities of institutions throughout Russia, the institutes and enterprises in the closed cities soon became hosts for many ISTC projects. But this was not because there were special financial earmarks for the cities. Rather, it was because the scientists had been core members of the Russian military effort, had strong dual-use skills, and presented good ideas for redirecting their skills to promoting civilian applications of nuclear science and technology—a mix that attracted high marks from the funding parties. The Institute for Experimental Physics in Sarov, for example, soon became the recipient of more ISTC project awards than any other institution, eventually receiving more than seventy-three million dollars of financing from the ISTC. The Institute for Technical Physics in Snezhinsk captured second place with project awards totaling more than thirty million dollars. Scientists in other closed cities also received financial support, although on a much smaller scale.

In the late 1990s several Russian colleagues and I carried out a comparative study of conditions in several nuclear cities—closed, semiclosed, and open. One of our interesting conclusions concerning the closed city of Snezhinsk was as follows:

> The residents of Snezhinsk will band together to withstand economic pressure. While a few will reach out in their commercial endeavors, most will remain a tightly knit community. They like the personal safety in the city in contrast to the crime elsewhere, and they are accustomed to the strict security governing nuclear secrets. On the practical side, they recognize the importance of retaining rights to apartments both for themselves and for their relatives. Some of the wealthiest residents nearing retirement age may follow their children to Moscow and other cities, while outsiders from Moscow and from abroad will be a growing presence on the streets and in the laboratories. But, for at least the next decade, Snezhinsk will remain largely aloof from the mainstream of Russian life.[7]

In 2010 the Russian government was once again considering long-standing proposals to open some or all of the closed nuclear cities. A Rosatom spokesman announced the following: "Restructuring of the nuclear sector is going on, and specialists are being released, in need of further employment. Closed cities must be granted an opportunity to develop private enterprise and an innovative sector. Such conditions under which our parents agreed to live there are not suitable for our children, and changes are necessary."[8]

However, it seemed unlikely that such a drastic change would occur in the near future. Nevertheless, international projects had begun in a number of the cities. For example, in 2010 the Russian Press Service announced, "Zelenogorsk, a remote Siberian center of nuclear technology, is a closed city with big ambitions. A French multinational has arrived with new technology and an eye toward renewable energy."[9]

ISTC PROJECT FUNDING

Almost 30 percent of ISTC funding for research projects has been awarded to institutes of Minatom/Rosatom. The total value of these awards has exceeded $240 million. Many, but far from all, awards have been directed to projects for advancing nuclear science and technology. Some have addressed alternative energy sources, energy efficiency and conservation, environmental monitoring and cleanup, and climate change, for example. Such projects focus on developments well beyond the boundaries of nuclear topics, while building on the technical flexibility of the nuclear workforce.

At the same time, organizations other than those under the purview of Minatom/Rosatom have also been actively engaged in nuclear projects. These organizations have included Russian universities, institutes of the Russian Academy of Sciences, and institutions of a variety of Russian ministries and agencies. The dividing line between projects that are classified by the ISTC as nuclear and those that are considered nonnuclear projects is somewhat blurred. A reasonable estimate of the funding that has been devoted to nuclear science and technology projects is about $150 million. This support has been distributed through three hundred projects. Most of these funds have been provided by the parties to the ISTC Agreement through contributions to the regular core program. In addition, within the overall number of projects, some have been funded by partners such as CERN.

An important survey of ISTC projects in 2010 categorized ongoing activity in nuclear science and technology into the following topical areas:

- Responsible science: Improvement of understanding by the nuclear workforce of the scientific and technical aspects of safeguards, export control, and dual-use technology monitoring. University courses on nonproliferation principles, ethics, and international approaches. Analyses and activism of think tanks involved in raising public awareness of nonproliferation and related issues. (Also discussed in chapter 4.)
- Severe accident management: Interactions of corium systems with different components of reactor and concrete shafts. Experimental modeling of destructive processes within nuclear reactors, fuel rods, and structural materials. Analyses of materials for safe reactor barriers. Mathematical modeling of reactor-core molten materials.
- Power-plant life management: Development of models concerning

deformation properties of steel. Investigations of embrittlement phenomena. Assessments of relevant international experience.

- Medical physics: Diagnostics for and treatment of cancer, including neutron-capture therapy, gamma irradiation, and electron beam irradiation. Production of medical radioisotopes and modification of research reactors. Computer codes for optimization of doses and beam parameters for individual patients.

- Heavy metal technology: Hydrodynamics and heat transfer in liquid metals. Corrosion resistance of steel to liquid lead and lead-bismuth alloys. Laser separation of lead isotopes. Control of oxygen content in lead coolants

- Gas-cooled fast breeder reactor: Basic reactor design requirements taking into account thermal efficiency, prevention of radiation consequences of severe accidents, and reactivity effects.

- High-temperature gas-cooled reactor: Validation of safety and inherent self-protection of reactors using uranium fuel. Development of technology for helium systems.

- Molten salt technologies. Measurement of principal parameters. Studies of curium in molten chlorides. Handling of radioactive waste, including production of solid molten-like matrices.[10]

Over the years the ISTC has provided an important international platform for promoting cooperation between Russian and international partners in these and other areas. The ISTC has established international contact groups that have held consultations around the world. While the center's financial resources have been useful in promoting civilian-oriented research in Russia, its international outreach of the ISTC has been no less important in helping to ensure Russian awareness of approaches and interests of potential partners. Whether the topic be nuclear safety, decommissioning of nuclear plants, plutonium disposition, novel reactors and technologies, or partitioning and transmutation, the ISTC has become an important component of the international networks of nuclear scientific institutions.

Other areas of ISTC activity during its lifetime are also worth mentioning. They address many issues of worldwide interest—both scientifically and politically. They include the following:[11]

1. *Nuclear power in space*: The ISTC has sponsored a number of projects devoted to preparations for manned flight to far space (Mission to Mars).

Among the topics of interest are life-support systems, flight architecture, robotics, radiation, and meteorite and other safety issues. On-board energy supply options have included solar and nuclear technologies. The nuclear systems show some advantages. The ISTC was represented at a number of seminars in the early 2000s in France, the United States, and the Netherlands; and the ISTC organized a capstone conference in Moscow in 2003. The topic of nuclear power in space will remain on the international agenda for decades into the future, and the early efforts of the ISTC should help shape future debates.

2. *Fusion*: From its earliest days, the ISTC has supported a variety of fusion projects at Russian institutions, which have been international leaders in the field. Among the topics have been plasma physics, transport of thermonuclear neutrons, handling of tritium, and the role of small machines such as Globus. Most recently the center has supported projects of interest to the newly established International Thermonuclear Experimental Reactor (ITER) project.

3. *Y2K program*: During 1999–2000, the center purchased novel computers and software for nine Russian nuclear power plants in anticipation of possible technical problems during the end-of-the-century electronic time transition. Fortunately, the transition was largely uneventful.

4. *Radiation legacy*: During the early years the ISTC devoted considerable attention to nuclear legacies of the former Soviet Union. Of particular concern were the environmental effects associated with widespread contamination of both marine and land areas. The center supported a broad range of projects devoted to different aspects of this legacy. They included inadequately controlled disposal of nuclear wastes; contamination of coastal areas of the Arctic region; water contamination from underground nuclear testing for peaceful purposes such as identification of gas storage sites; and contamination associated with nuclear accidents, particularly in the Urals.

Of considerable importance has been the unknown fate of tens of thousands of radiation sources that were abandoned by organizations that encountered difficult financial situations during the early 1990s. Some sources were sold as components of metal scrap that was being recovered. But even now, other orphan sources could threaten their unsuspecting custodians of metals and components of equipment that are radioactive. Also, there have been a number of incidents wherein such sources were used for criminal purposes, both in Russia and across Russian borders.

5. CERN: This Geneva-based complex has been the ISTC partner that has supported the largest number of projects jointly with the center—as of 2010, a total of forty-five projects cofunded by the two organizations, plus multiple project extensions. CERN contributed nineteen million dollars and the ISTC twelve million dollars to these projects. Taking the Atlas Detector as an example of the joint efforts, the center's contribution was focused on the bus bars, muon wheel support, Ti rods for Toreoid magnets, feet and rails, spines and moulds for the inner detector, tiles, w-rods, and the absorber. A similar number of contributions characterized the center's involvement with the Alice Detector. The center was particularly pleased that one ISTC-funded project generated commercial contracts between CERN and Russian institutions valued at thirty-six million dollars.

6. *Chernobyl.* Russian scientists have been deeply involved in the aftermath of the Chernobyl accident for twenty-five years. The ISTC has supported a variety of projects concerning the causes and consequences of the accident that have been of broad interest throughout the global nuclear reactor community. The Science and Technology Center in the Ukraine has collaborated on several projects. Recent efforts of the ISTC include (a) compilation of more than seven thousand measurements by Russian and other scientists during twenty years of analyzing the reactor failure and monitoring the spread of nuclear contamination; (b) creation of specialized data bases, particularly those related to the state of corium, including concentrations of uranium and zirconium in metal corium; and (c) validation of updated models for corium formation following the accident and into the future. This program should be of considerable importance as a new steel arch is constructed and put into place over the failed reactor to reduce the continued radiological contamination in the surrounding area, and indeed deep into nearby areas of Ukraine.[12]

An example of the seriousness of some of the radiation legacy issues comes from the following report from a radiation inspector in the Urals in 2003: "Each spring we must collect radiation sources that have been tossed into the snow by irresponsible citizens who have discovered them in abandoned buildings, which they have taken over during the changes in the economic structure of our region."[13]

On the other hand, an enthusiastic report from the director general of CERN in 2010 stated the following: "We express our appreciation for the 15 years of fruitful collaboration with Russian institutes made possible thanks to ISTC programs. The center has helped carry out a number of common projects during this period. CERN has profited from the expertise in Russian institutes and from their high-tech equipment and unique technological developments, mainly for the Large Hadron collider project."[14]

ALLIANCE WITH THE INTERNATIONAL ATOMIC ENERGY AGENCY

After years of informal consultations, joint workshops, and other collaborative efforts, the International Atomic Energy Agency (IAEA) and the ISTC entered into a Memorandum of Understanding in June 2009. They agreed to enhance cooperation in support of nonproliferation, nuclear security, nuclear safety, and nuclear energy technologies, as well as in nuclear science applications. Among the new activities to be carried out are training and capacity building, including development of joint educational programs; deployment of nuclear instrumentation and technology for national safeguards and security and international verification; and assistance in deployment of nuclear energy technologies, including reactor, fuel cycle, and radioactive waste technologies.[15]

Following the signing of the Memorandum of Understanding, the two organizations identified the following priority areas for cooperation:

- Research and development of advanced safeguards and verification techniques. This priority includes advanced safeguards approaches; unattended and remote monitoring systems; information-driven safeguards; and proliferation risk assessments, including proliferation network analysis.
- Training and capacity building, including the development of joint educational and training courses. The ISTC is to assist the IAEA in training, capacity building, and education activities. These areas of interest are compatible with the center's programs on responsible science and outreach.
- Development and deployment of nuclear instrumentation and technology for national control and accounting systems, nuclear security, and international verification activities. Implementation of additional safeguards and relevant technologies is an integral part of this initiative.

The program, with an estimated cost to the ISTC of three million dollars over three years, is intended to benefit international efforts for an improved and a more efficient nuclear nonproliferation regime. Also, through ISTC's international management capability, the program should contribute to trust and confidence building among the major parties in nuclear nonproliferation activities.[16]

However, with the announcement of Russia's withdrawal from the ISTC, considerable uncertainty has arisen as to the extent to which the laudable goals of the collaboration will be achieved. Russia has a long history of working closely with the IAEA. Its specialists have a great deal to offer to the international community, as exemplified by this initiative. The Russian government is having some difficulty explaining why it does not believe that a successor organization to the ISTC is needed—precisely for the types of activities set forth here.

IMPORTANCE OF A NUCLEAR SECURITY CULTURE

When considering extreme measures to stop the proliferation of nuclear weapons capabilities, Mohamed El Baradei, the former director general of the IAEA and recipient of the Nobel Peace Prize, has frequently commented, "You can't bomb knowledge." Nevertheless, some governments have been determined to attack or intimidate nuclear scientists who are involved in weapons programs. Motorcycle bombs, kidnappings, bans on international travel, and freezing of personal bank accounts are apparently being used to persuade Iranian scientists, for example, to abandon their research efforts that do not comply with international norms.

A. Q. Kahn, the Pakistani metallurgist who created an elaborate international network for illicit trade in nuclear materials and equipment, focused considerable attention on the need to control highly skilled specialists. Some have been interested not only in assisting their own countries develop nuclear weapons capabilities but also in profiting personally from illicit trade in dangerous nuclear commodities. While Khan's activities apparently did not involve misuse of Russian technology, this type of activity has long been of concern to the ISTC.

Of special relevance to the ISTC experience in focusing on the human dimension of proliferation is the following passage in the communiqué of the Washington Nuclear Security Summit in April 2010: "We acknowledge the need for capacity building for nuclear security and cooperation at bilateral, regional, and multilateral levels for the promotion of a nuclear security culture through technology development, human resource development, education, and training; and we stress the importance of optimizing internal cooperation and coordination of assistance."

Projects of the ISTC have enabled thousands of scientists to become involved in advancing civilian science. While financial incentives are usually decisive in encouraging scientists to participate in specific projects, ensuring sustainability of the scientists' interests in such activities depends on other factors as well, including peer recognition, access to leading-edge research carried out around the globe, opportunities to participate in important meetings and conferences, and satisfaction from witnessing the use of research results for promoting social and economic advancement.

Most important, ISTC projects have focused on technical challenges that are near the top of the research agendas of many countries. Very few, if any, of the projects can be characterized as busy work. Publishers and conference organizers around the world are often eager to learn about the results of the investigations.

In an innovative approach to development of a nuclear security culture, the ISTC program on Responsible Science recognizes that sustainable nonproliferation efforts depend heavily on the attitudes and commitments of individual scientists that are nurtured during early stages of their careers. This program offers considerable promise as an important component of the broad portfolio of nonproliferation activities, even if it is only short-lived in Russia under the ISTC umbrella. Hopefully, its impact will be quickly apparent, and other funding sources will sustain the program indefinitely.

By any measure, the nuclear file of the ISTC deserves high accolades. Relatively small investments have leveraged large in-kind and matching investments from other organizations. The Russian scientific community has become a significant component of many of the most important international nuclear efforts. The ISTC has played a limited, but nevertheless critical, role in the process.

In summary, the skills and experience that the Russian specialists have brought to the table are undeniable. The results of their cooperative activities are impressive. The likelihood that they will strongly support nonproliferation efforts of the Russian government for the indefinite future is very promising.

CHAPTER NINE

The Biosecurity File

We don't know more about the biological weapons threat than we did five years ago, and five years from now we will know even less.
—U.S. Intelligence Community, 2005

The United States should be less concerned that terrorists will become biologists and far more concerned that biologists will become terrorists.
—U.S. Commission on Prevention of Proliferation and Terrorism, 2008

Rapid advances in the biological sciences and biotechnology hold the promise of dramatically improving human health, the food supply, environmental conditions, and other aspects of life. Most biological advances and innovations have originated in the industrialized countries. Now, broad diffusion of biological knowledge and biotechnology capabilities is under way. This trend provides new opportunities for less advanced countries to use achievements of others.

The spread of advanced biotechnology techniques, however, is accompanied by potential risks. Skills that contribute to advances in medicine, agriculture, and environmental preservation overlap with know-how that could be used for adapting dangerous biological pathogens for nefarious purposes. In addition, different types of equipment and facilities are versatile. Some vaccine facilities, for example, could be converted to produce biological agents for terrorists. According to the U.S. Army Chemical School: "Infectious organisms can be modified to bring about diseases in different ways. There is enormous potential—based on advances in modern molecular biology, fermentation, and drug delivery technology—for making sophisticated weapons. The biological weapon agents may emerge in two likely categories: man-made manipulations of classic weapon agents, and pathogens associated with newly discovered or emerging infectious diseases."[1]

Russia, with one-eighth of the world's land mass and a rich heritage of achievements in the biological sciences, has long had unique experiences in controlling the spread of diseases in different ecological and human environments. For many years, the ISTC has provided a mechanism for encouraging the redirection of Russia's biological expertise, which supported in large measure the development of weapons programs to civilian-oriented efforts. Former Soviet weapons scientists are now playing a central role in upgrading Russia's civilian capabilities for coping with endemic and emerging diseases, while at the same time enhancing the nation's capabilities to limit opportunities for terrorists to misuse biological agents that could wreak harm in Russia or elsewhere.

Some of the most important accomplishments of the ISTC have resulted from reorientation of biological skills that were honed in weapons programs. Now they are being directed to frontline applications in the prevention of the spread of debilitating diseases and the treatment of other maladies, whatever the source of the pathogens that are causing the suffering. While the number of professionally active former biological weapons scientists has been decreasing each year in Russia, the following warning in 2008 by a leader of the Russian biological research community is of considerable importance:

> Scientists with many years of experience working with the most dangerous pathogens could certainly create problems if they were to decide, or were forced, to use these skills elsewhere, say in countries governed by regimes with questionable track records. Their colleagues, who have worked at "open" institutes, usually have only general knowledge of group A pathogens. Weapons scientists possess specific skills sets, and they may have access to dangerous strains of microorganisms. Both cadres of specialists could of course become potential threats; but in the case of weapon scientists, the threat would be significantly higher to the point of becoming realistic.[2]

EARLY ISTC INTEREST IN REDIRECTION OF BIOWEAPON SCIENTISTS

During the initial planning stages for the ISTC in 1992 and 1993, the Western parties and Japan directed their attention primarily to engaging Russian nuclear scientists in the development of civilian-oriented projects that could be funded when the center became operational. We had few contacts with the Russian biological science and biotechnology communities. Neither Russian nor international specialists initially assigned to the planning group for the center had strong capabilities or interests in developing programs in the biological field.

At the same time, officials in Russia, the United States, and England were engaged in bitter political standoffs as they attempted to demonstrate for the global community that their countries were not involved in research, development, or production activities that would violate the Biological and Toxin Weapons Convention. Western officials accused the Russian government of hiding some research and production facilities from the eyes of inspection teams that had arrived from the West. Russian officials accused the Americans of concealing activities of private pharmaceutical companies, which were producing medical products—allegedly for peaceful uses—under contracts with the U.S. government. The Russian officials did not accept the U.S. position in prohibiting visits to company facilities. U.S. officials contended that the companies could lose control of their intellectual property through intrusive international inspections.

Meanwhile, at least two defectors from the Russian biological weapons program had made their way to the West. Embracement of these turncoats in London and Washington had raised considerable anger in Moscow and in other Russian cities where the individuals had previously been involved in the Soviet weapons program. Given this development and the continued secrecy cloaking weapons-related activities in the United States as well as in Russia, the atmosphere for discussions among Russian and Western officials about the possibility of joint research efforts financed through the ISTC did not seem conducive for moving forward.

Nevertheless, in 1993 the Preparatory Committee for the ISTC (Prep Com) reached out to the leaders of the Russian program—for example, the director and deputy director of Biopreparat. The Soviet Union had established this research and production conglomerate many years earlier to assume responsibility for investigating and producing important contagious materials in support of the biological weapons program. But the complex of enterprises and institutes was falling on economic hard times, along with the rest of the country. And it was soon clear that Biopreparat was eager to accept financial support from its former archenemies.

As a result of this outreach by the Prep Com, Biopreparat's research institute directors began to visit the temporary headquarters of the future ISTC. The directors entered into serious discussions with Western specialists assigned to the

Prep Com. In time, Biopreparat, along with other biology-oriented organizations in Russia, proposed many ideas for redirecting their scientists to civilian-oriented jobs.

By the time the ISTC formally opened its doors, a number of proposals for putting redirected bioscientists to work were ready for immediate attention. Thus, during the first few meetings of the ISTC Governing Board, the parties approved the funding of several large biological research projects. The institutes and the secretariat soon signed project agreements.

Two strands of ISTC's biosecurity history are important in understanding the center's strategy to modify and modernize Russia's research, development, and manufacturing infrastructure.

First, biology-oriented regular projects, financed primarily by the U.S. government, quickly increased in number. These activities started the process of serious international engagement in biosecurity while calling on Russian scientists to take the initiative in coming forward with topics of priority interest. In time, all parties wanted to have some role in the biological arena.

Second, partner projects financed by U.S. government departments dominated the ISTC's biosecurity portfolio in the late 1990s. These projects were instrumental in pioneering new cooperative approaches through novel research projects developed by Russian specialists. Also, they provided new opportunities to bring together scientists from a large number of organizations in Russia and abroad with overlapping research agendas.

The emerging U.S. leadership in the field of biosecurity was due in significant measure to increasing confidence in Washington that the ISTC was becoming a reliable and convenient mechanism for facilitating joint efforts with sensitive Russian institutions in a field shrouded in political drama.

For example, were Iranian agents really making arrangements for Russian biologists to work in Tehran? Was the Russian government allowing its retired generals with specialized knowledge to publish research papers on sensitive biosecurity topics? Had shadowy Russian businessmen used deadly pathogens to contaminate agricultural products at a popular Moscow outdoor market in an attempt to close the market that competed with a nearby mafia-controlled market? As bioengagement gained traction and introduced transparency, such fears subsided.

When Canada became a party to the ISTC Agreement, Ottawa quickly joined Washington in focusing on biosecurity projects. Canada directed much of its attention to improving the biosecurity infrastructures of several Central Asian countries, which had joined the center, rather than searching for niches in the crowded Russian scene. Thus, the United States remained the principal supporter of upgrades of facilities and related research in Russia.

Given the foregoing interests, U.S.-financed activities dominate this chapter. The levels of U.S. expenditures in Russia through 2010 on regular projects that were classified by the ISTC as biology-redirection projects included the following:

- Environment-oriented projects: $45.4 million
- Industry-oriented projects: $19.9 million
- Health-oriented projects: $17.9 million
- Agriculture-oriented projects: $3.1 million[3]

As to U.S.-funded partner projects implemented in Russia, they too were justified as contributing to nonproliferation and counterterrorism objectives through strengthening Russia's biology infrastructure. The partners and funding levels through 2010 were as follows:

- Department of Defense: $36.5 million
- Department of Health and Human Services: $30.7 million
- Agriculture Research Service: $23.2 million
- Department of State: $12.5 million
- Department of Energy: $8.8 million
- Environmental Protection Agency: $6.8 million
- Defense Advanced Research Program Agency: $3.8 million[4]

All governments have rejected the concept of establishing independent surveillance and research systems for coping with bioterrorism that are separate from the public health and agricultural systems of a country. Thus, Russia and others have been working to upgrade their established public health and agricultural systems on a broad basis. The objective is to have these systems become sufficiently robust to deal with all threats, whether they be naturally occurring disease outbreaks or outbreaks triggered by misguided individuals or organizations. Of course, when an incident is identified as a terrorist attack, the security services quickly assume a lead role in responding to the event.

In promoting sustainable redirection of expertise in biosecurity, the ISTC Secretariat took into account the potential impacts of both partner and regular projects. At times the participating Russian institutions and even the individual investigators received support through both types of projects. In many cases, the Russian government also provided special funds for the participating institutions, a practice that has been enthusiastically welcomed, although it complicates the determination of just how important the ISTC contributions have been.

SETTING THE STAGE FOR PARTNER PROJECTS

Returning to 1997, the U.S. National Academy of Sciences, in cooperation with Biopreparat, initiated through the ISTC eight pilot projects. The objective was to demonstrate how U.S. and Russian specialists could work together in investigating the properties of some of the deadliest pathogens that had been considered as bioterrorism agents as well as causing harm in their natural state. The Department of Defense provided financial support. The total commitment of the department for these start-up efforts was about five hundred thousand dollars.

1. Five projects were sited at the Center for Virology and Biotechnology Vector in Koltsovo:
   - Prevalence, genotype distribution, and molecular variability of isolates of hepatitis C virus in the Asian part of Russia
   - Monkeypox virus genome
   - Genetic and serologic diversity of hantavirus in the Asian part of Russia
   - Advanced diagnostic kit for opisthorchiasis in human patients
   - Antiviral activities of glycyrrhyzic acid derivatives against Marburg, Ebola, and human immunodeficiency viruses
2. The other three projects were carried out at the Center for Applied Microbiology in Obolensk:
   - Microbiological and immunochemical analysis of clinical strains of tuberculosis and mycobacteriosis
   - Immunological effectiveness of delivery in vivo of the Brucella main outer membrane protein by anthrax toxic components
   - Monitoring of anthrax[5]

At the time, the ISTC already had several large biosecurity research projects in place, including, for example, investigations on new immune assays. However, the new pilot project initiative involving two institutions, which were close to the Soviet bioweapons program for many years, was of considerable importance and attracted a great deal of attention within Russia, as well as within the

United States and Europe. The initiative was intended to demonstrate whether it was possible to penetrate the walls of secrecy that had surrounded the most sensitive biological research facilities in Russia with projects that in principle should be of considerable interest to both Russian and Western scientists. At the same time, it was to demonstrate the feasibility of close monitoring by the ISTC staff of projects that would be carried out behind high fences, which surrounded the participating Russian research facilities.

The projects were successful in both regards, as well as in generating scientific results of international interest. Impressive Russian and American scientists, who had years of experience in working with dangerous pathogens, carried out the projects. The Russian institutions were surprisingly receptive to hosting American collaborators on a regular basis. The scientific findings resulting from the projects provided a good basis for continuing the collaborations.

Also the joint activities clarified the limits of such efforts when it came to the inevitable constraints on full partnerships intent on probing dark secrets of the past. For example, the Russian government took the position that export controls put in place in response to pressure from the U.S. government several years earlier prevented the shipment of anthrax strains from Russia to the United States for scientific investigations. U.S. regulations prohibited the sending of many types of strains to Russia.

The Russian and U.S. governments and participants considered seven of the eight demonstration projects successful in demonstrating that research in very sensitive areas carried out in former biological warfare research centers can be of mutual interest and benefit to both countries. The seven successes were followed by more ambitious efforts at these two sites and at other locations. The eighth project devoted to opisthorchiasis was discontinued.

The demonstration projects helped set the stage for an eventual investment by the United States and other ISTC parties and partners of more than two hundred million dollars in biosecurity projects carried out in Russia over a decade beginning in 1998. Larger efforts extended the U.S. reach from the original projects at two institutes to laboratories in ten institutes. Several of these laboratories also had been key research facilities in the center of the Soviet biological weapons program.

The successful demonstration projects highlighted some of the criteria that were used in judging the priority of projects proposed for funding through the ISTC—whatever the field of interest. They include the following:

- Scientific importance of topic
- Quality of the research approach
- Capacity of the research team
- Provision for strong international collaboration
- Engagement of former Soviet weapons expertise
- Promotion of transparency
- Likely sustainability of successful research[6]

The ISTC staff did an excellent job in facilitating the implementation of the demonstration projects. The time from submission to the ISTC of a project proposal until the signing of a project agreement averaged three months. Unfortunately, subsequent to these project proposals passing through the center's system, the average time for processing proposal submissions that led to project agreements was usually much longer. Four to six months was considered extraordinarily fast, with one year eventually becoming the norm. This delay in launching projects soon became a constant irritant for the Russian and international scientists who were awaiting decisions on their proposals, not only in the field of biosecurity but in all fields of interest to the ISTC.

What factors explain the administrative efficiency reflected in the abbreviated timeline for beginning work on the pilot projects? First and foremost, former ISTC staff members had assumed responsibility for shepherding the pilot project proposals through the center, and they understood the internal workings of the secretariat. They were able to cajole ISTC colleagues into moving the proposals quickly from their in-boxes to their out-boxes. However, as the secretariat's workload increased and new staff arrivals had to learn how the project approval system functioned, repeating this success was not possible.

The interest of DOD rapidly expanded from supporting (a) research to improve approaches for identification, characterization, prophylaxis, and therapy of diseases to also include (b) activities that would have a more immediate impact on biosecurity. Laboratory safety and security quickly became focal points for cooperative projects.

Examples of activities of special interest both to the laboratories and to potential financial sponsors included (a) upgrades of physical security systems including new sensors, fences, and locks; (b) installation of pathogen tracking systems; (c) renovation of clean rooms and replacement of equipment to facilitate decontamination; (d) installation of new ventilation systems; and (e) provision of incineration equipment. DOD gave high priority to training of personnel in biosafety and biosecurity and the need for upgraded biosafety cabinets.

During my first visit to biological research laboratories in Obolensk in 1998 I was taken aback by experimental rodents that had escaped from their cages and were running loose on the floor of the working areas. Two years later, however, a visit to the same laboratories offered a stark contrast. The cleanliness of the facilities was truly impressive. And during the visit the animals remained in their cages where they belonged. The ISTC was working as planned.

At the research center Vector in Koltsovo, the security upgrades during the early 2000s were also extensive and striking. High, impenetrable fences were erected around the facility where research on variola—a smallpox strain— was in progress. Camera monitoring of all approaching visitors became routine, and security forces banned visitors from photographing the approaches to the building.

The institutes that became engaged in programs sponsored by various U.S. partners included (a) research institutes devoted to studies of infections by bacteria that housed large collections of pathogens, (b) research institutes concerned primarily with viruses that also stored many types of pathogens, and (c) plant disease research centers, with large crop collections. Initially, a half-dozen institutes were involved both in enhancement of biosecurity and in the conduct of collaborative research projects. Within several years the number of participating Russian institutes targeted for upgrading of personnel, facilities, and research activities had doubled. In time, the number had increased to several dozen. Related crosscutting activities of broad interest included improvement of guidelines for conducting research with dangerous pathogens, translations and distribution of Western biosafety documents, and establishment of biosafety committees at the institute level.[7]

IMPACTS OF BIOSECURITY PROGRAMS

Reflecting the sizable financial resources embodied in partner projects and in regular projects, a number of impacts in strengthening the capabilities of the biosecurity infrastructure in Russia can be attributed, at least in part, to the ISTC's role. These outcomes have improved national and local capabilities to prevent the theft or diversion of dangerous materials as well as increased productivity and efficiency of the facilities. Many defense-oriented researchers have taken on civilian research tasks. Also, should dangerous pathogens be released by hostile

individuals or groups, Russia has in place strengthened systems to help minimize the adverse consequences from such incidents, as well as from naturally
occurring outbreaks of diseases. The types of programmatic impacts that have
been recorded by the center as of special importance include the following:

- Upgrades of internal and external communication systems of institutes,
  including Internet connectivity, computerization of library resources, and
  training of information specialists. Beginning in 2006, for example, more
  than thirty biomedical organizations in Russia and other Soviet states obtained free access to leading international journals published by Elsevier.
- Improvement of infrastructures within a number of Russian biomedical
  institutes so that they could produce medical preparations in accordance
  with international standards. In a procedure related to the upgrading, hundreds of specialists were trained to work at new levels of hygiene and biosafety that met international standards.
- In Pushchino, modernization of an aging facility that became the only site
  in Russia to be certified as a center for preclinical research and then became an important component of the technopark in the city.
- Establishment of a center for carrying out research on new drugs for treatment of tuberculosis in accordance with requirements of the World Health
  Organization. The center is located at the Sechenov Moscow Medical
  Academy.[8]

In another far-reaching effort, in the late 2000s the Russian government
adopted a Targeted Drug Program to support a coordinated approach for research by a number of institutes in several directions. The ISTC again played a
facilitative role in bringing together potential funders, scientific experts, and
leaders of interested organizations, as follows:

- A consortium of research institutes, Orkhimed, became a leader within
  Russia for development of new drugs; it soon actively supported government and academic organizations.
- In the field of tuberculosis, a consortium was formed for consolidation and
  intensification of research and development on new diagnostic, prophylac-
  tic, and therapy measures for addressing tuberculosis.
- In cooperation with European scientists, a consortium for cooperation in
  development of drugs for treating viral diseases was established.
- The Center of New Medical Technologies (TEMPO) was organized.

- A consortium of research institutes carrying out research in the field of probiotics became an important coordination organization.[9]

Another area wherein ISTC has played an important role was the promotion and coordination of projects financed through partner and regular projects for establishment of platforms that help achieve international standards. Particular objectives include compliance with Good Laboratory Practices, Good Manufacturing Practices, and Good Clinical Practices. This effort has been quite significant, in view of the stringent requirements in the United States and European countries in determining how much weight should be given to experiments and clinical trials conducted abroad for ensuring the safety of pharmaceuticals. To this end, the ISTC promoted a number of approaches, such as upgrading facilities; improving flow of documentation; auditing, training, and monitoring personnel; and forming new intergovernmental networks of officials and specialists.

A testimonial in 2007 by the director of a leading Russian research center as to the importance of these efforts is as follows: "We no longer need external funding to sustain our research and production programs. However, we highly value continued contacts with Western colleagues, which were established through ISTC projects. They have been particularly helpful to us in ensuring that we could meet international standards in our production of antiviral drugs."[10]

Another area of project activity for which the ISTC can take significant credit is upgrading of vivariums. The center has been instrumental in improving such facilities in Moscow, Obolensk, Koltsovo, Pushchino, Lyubchany, Kazan, St. Petersburg, Chernogolovka, and Serpukhov. Also, the reconstructed and upgraded rodent-breeding facility in Pushchino, which now meets Charles River guidelines, has been certified by the Association for Assessment and Accreditation of Laboratory Animal Care, International. By 2009 the annual breeding capacity had reached three hundred thousand rodents.[11]

MAINTAINING FACILITY UPGRADES

One of the greatest challenges that the ISTC has faced is the long-term viability of improved procedures and activities that it has helped put in place. This issue is particularly vexing within the Russian scientific community. Institute directors had not been accustomed to assuming personal responsibility for international obligations agreed to by others without allocation of adequate funding. Such activities have been considered peripheral to core concerns of generating publishable research results and supporting near-term revenue-providing activities by extending services to paying customers.

Further complicating effective sustainability, Western approaches have given priority to up-to-date equipment and to design of unique facilities. In the Soviet Union, the government emphasized training procedures and benchtop practices to help overcome deficiencies in the laboratories, with less attention to the adequacy of the facilities. For example, plague research was frequently carried out on open benchtops, rather than in biosafety cabinets, by workers wearing antiplague protective gear. In short, Russia inherited guidelines and legal frameworks that are not compatible with modern approaches. Clearly, broader commitments to international standards are essential in order to move forward.

Often, equipment and laboratory practices transferred from the West may not be sustainable without continued external funding. Utility costs are of particular concern. Also, diagnostic methods that depend on imported test kits may be safe and efficient but may not be affordable during economic belt-tightening. The absence of reagents sometimes means that equipment designed to rely on particular reagents is not used. Imported security lighting may function only until the bulbs burn out. Costs of operating and maintaining imported laboratory approaches may be untenable. Scientists trained to use disposable inoculating loops may find themselves without training or equipment to use other types safely.

Thus, in many instances a hybrid approach to biosafety is desirable, integrating elements from both local and international approaches. Particular emphasis should be given to local sourcing of as much equipment and materials as possible.

In short, sustainability at times requires abandonment of cookie-cutter approaches that replicate practices in particular foreign laboratories. Such methods may be the safest and most reliable course in the near term. But the metric for success should not be whether a certain practice mirrors that of a particular foreign laboratory, but whether it is in fact safe, authoritative, and sustainable.[12]

Against this background, the ISTC record has been impressive. According to a well-respected Russian research manager, "U.S. programs carried out through the ISTC have provided critical support for thousands of Russian scientists who otherwise would have left the research system of the country, and particularly young scientists."[13]

A daunting problem that remains is the protection of intellectual property developed throughout Russia. Informal approaches, such as the following, which was reported by a leading Russian laboratory manager in 2004, have often been the only option: "In Russia, copyright protection virtually does not work. In rare instances when researchers receive a worthwhile reward for a new drug, it is not a result of a legal mandate or requirement. It is the result of a personal agreement (not legally documented in any way) with the manager (owner) of the manufacturing company or as the result of the inventor's leverage to control the production flow (in particular when the inventor can terminate the production at his own volition)."[14]

However, as Russia endeavors to become a more significant player on the world's biotechnology stage, these approaches must give way to more intensive efforts to adopt or adapt well-developed Western models.

INTERPRETING EXPERIENCES

Regardless of the fate of ISTC's presence in Russia, individual participants and funding organizations can report many lessons learned during the past seventeen years in the development and implementation of bioengagement projects through the center. Given the legacy of mistrust that characterized the Cold War—particularly with regard to intentions in the biological field—and the increasing concern over the likelihood of bioterrorist activities, Western engagement with Russia's biology institutions will remain an important objective of Western nonproliferation policy. Also the scientific benefits to be derived globally from Russian efforts in the biology research laboratories of the country will be of continuing interest. Against this background, the following conclusions in a number of areas should be kept at the forefront of bioengagement strategies:

- *Assessing the scientific importance of publications*: Engagement provides opportunities to "ground-truth" reports and articles prepared by colleagues. Witnessing colleagues in action provides useful insights as to the care taken in preparing publications.
- *Transparency*: Understanding the intentions and capabilities of colleagues in dealing with dual-use technologies is essential in estimating the likelihood that such technologies might be devoted to malevolent purposes. There is no alternative to transparency as the basis for building confidence

concerning the purpose of experiments of colleagues who are handling dangerous pathogens.

- *Multiyear efforts*: Cooperative efforts require continued interactions over a number of years to obtain meaningful joint findings and to establish a good basis for sustainable partnerships.
- *Constraints on pathogen strain exchanges*: Export controls will invariably intersect with desires to exchange strains across national borders. While such exchanges might be possible in some cases, difficulties for the scientists will increase as governments are encouraged to enforce and to tighten their export control regulations.
- *False alarms*: There will be unsubstantiated signals over the occurrence of significant disease outbreaks, uncertainties as to the causes of the outbreaks, and differing opinions as to the best approaches in controlling the outbreaks.
- *Laboratory accidents*: Despite biosafety precautions, the likelihood is high that from time to time accidents will threaten the health of laboratory workers.
- *Continuing roles of international organizations*: The World Health Organization, the Organization for Animal Care, the Food and Agriculture Organization, and other international and regional organizations will become increasingly involved in developing international standards and reporting requirements. Most nations will commit to complying with their requirements. It is important that scientists understand their responsibilities in compliance and that organizations undertake their regulatory responsibilities without unnecessarily impeding science.

In all of these areas, the ISTC has practical experience in enhancing the importance of international collaboration. It has documented its activities in considerable detail. Let us not leave this documentation on storage shelves but put it to use by new entrants into the field and new participants in international projects.

CHAPTER TEN

The Aerospace File

Missile specialists make weapons to deter, not to commit, aggression. They view signs of weakness in the nation's missile potential as threatening Russia and its security.
—Survey of scientists at Russian missile enterprises, 1995

Nineteen aeronautics proposals by fifteen Russian institutions have been recently approved and now are open for funding by interested parties.
—ISTC announcement, November 2009

MANY STORIES WERE CIRCULATING in Russia during the early days of the ISTC about the export of rocket and missile components from large Russian enterprises to states in the Middle East and South Asia, where some local officials had questionable security agendas. Analyzing the known and unknown activities of recipients of military hardware produced in Russia was a high-priority agenda item during diplomatic discussions involving Western and Russian officials, as legacies of the Cold War dominated many interactions in Moscow and other capitals. The following story was but one of dozens of reports that raised eyebrows in a never-ending saga over the irresponsibility of the Russian government in not cracking down on dangerous export practices of enterprises and research institutions.

A young Palestinian-Jordanian hustler and middleman managed to pass easily in and out of the secret Russian military institutes, signing deals for a wide array of missile goods, technology, and services. His biggest triumph came in 1995, with the purchase of gyroscopes and missile guidance components removed from ballistic missiles on SSN-18 submarines, under an arms control treaty. He took ten gyroscopes as samples back to Baghdad, and he had about eight hundred more packed up and delivered to Sheremetyevo airport, a major international airport in Moscow. The gyroscopes were flown out of Russia on two Royal Jordanian flights to Amman. From there, at least half of the gyroscopes made their way to Baghdad.[1]

An example of equally troublesome trade deals engineered by the military-industrial complex in Russia during the 1990s was as follows:

Indian missiles use technologies included in motors of Russian SA-2 missiles. The current Indian shopping list for dual-use technologies that will support their rocket development program (and that should be of interest to Russian suppliers) includes aluminum alloys with protective coatings, ceramic chip capacitors, FM signal generators, gas-field effect transistors, bare semiconductor chips, function generators, oscilloscopes, gear-head DC motors with slewing ring bearings, and torque motors.[2]

Against such a troublesome background, this chapter briefly reviews a few ISTC projects that have supported redirection of scientists at Russian aerospace institutions. As to be expected, some of these research centers have continued their work on aircraft, rocket, and space technologies of interest to the Russian defense sector as well. At the same time, however, at many aerospace industrial institutions hundreds of researchers have sought with some success permanent niches in contributing products for civilian aircraft and related support systems.

In fulfilling obligations associated with acceptance of ISTC support, a number of Russian aerospace institutes have become quite transparent. The international civilian research community has increasingly accepted these technology centers as important components of the global industrial aerospace network. While development of dual-use technologies cannot be avoided in this field, the ISTC parties have repeatedly concluded that institution transparency involving collaborating specialists from the West, which has accompanied support of projects, outweighed the projects' contributions to improving Russian military capabilities. Such contributions are an inevitable development in advancing aerospace capabilities, with or without ISTC support.

The ISTC focused its initial support at Russian aeronautics institutes, since they were well prepared to develop early proposals. Even before establishment of the center, the institutes had opened some of their previously locked doors to international visitors, as they tried to attract paying customers for their technological wherewithal. Clearly, security concerns were less of a hindrance in

moving forward with specific projects at these easily accessible aeronautical research institutions than in considering potential projects in the country's closed
areas where most missile and rocket activities were located.

The number of ISTC aerospace projects has been modest in comparison with
the number of nuclear and biological projects. Still, the center has played a
significant role in enabling Western scientists to capitalize on achievements of
Russian specialists who had been pioneers in aviation and in the exploration of
outer space.

As plans began taking shape for investigations of Mars, for example, the ISTC
served as an important mechanism in facilitating linkages between Russian and
Western space research centers. The focus on collaboration involving space
medicine technologies has been particularly popular among some ISTC parties.
International plans developed with assistance of the center complemented the
more extensive cooperation that was under way in the development and flight
of the International Space Station, which predated the establishment of the center by more than a decade.

A large number of Russian institutes and research centers have participated
in ISTC aerospace projects. As of 2011 the center had supported more than one
hundred regular and partner projects involving more than eighty Russian institutions. Financial contributions from the West and Japan totaled about $29.5
million. In addition, international partners from the private sector contributed
substantial resources to a number of projects. Some of these partners are identified later in this chapter.[3]

EARLY PROJECTS SUPPORTED BY THE ISTC

One of the first projects financed by the ISTC in 1994 followed a surprising approach. A mathematics institute of the Russian Academy of Sciences, located
in Yekaterinburg, had for many years supported the Soviet effort in designing
components for cruise missiles. The scientists developed a variety of mathematical models that would help guide the low-flying missiles over rolling terrain.
The guidance system was programmed to take into account and to monitor the
distances from the missile to the earth's surface on the horizon, continuously
adjusting the flight path to maintain predetermined altitudes.

Learning about the formation of the ISTC, the scientists from the Urals con-
sulted with colleagues at a geophysics institute in Moscow. They came up with
a novel scheme. If modeling of the earth's terrain could be used in designing the

guidance system and supporting software for a cruise missile system, couldn't the mathematical underpinnings also be helpful in providing a framework for ecological investigations and for planning responses to earthquakes and other types of natural disasters that erupted on the earth's surface? The mathematicians and the geophysicists worked together for three years to improve terrain modeling. At the end of the project, several well-respected Russian seismologists informed me that they were very pleased about the insights they had obtained from their colleagues, who understood important aspects of transforming mathematical theory into practical applications involving disturbances on the earth's surface.

In short order, many other scientists associated with the defense sector came up with a host of ideas as to how they could use their skills for peaceful endeavors. But a constant criticism that quickly arose once the ISTC began supporting projects in the aerospace arena was the assertion that projects were providing technology for improving Russian weapons systems. Three projects that raised early uneasiness were the following:

- Testing a Feed System for Nuclear Propulsion Technology for Exploration of Mars
- Low-Cost Hemispherical Resonators for Small Commercial Aircraft
- New Methods of Laminar Flow Control and Turbulent Drag in Aircraft

After experts analyzed the proposals in Western capitals, the ISTC parties supported all three research projects. During the ISTC's lifetime, far more controversial projects were put on the table for special scrutiny, as the ISTC parties became particularly sensitive to any appearance that the center was becoming a support institution for bolstering Russian military research and development efforts. Some proposals were put aside for security as well as other reasons. At the same time, the parties approved a number of dual-use projects in cases where they considered redirection of weapons scientists more important than the likelihood of leakage of newly acquired know-how into the Russian defense complex.[4]

UNRESTRAINED INTEREST OF THE AERONAUTICS FACILITIES

Given the various types of proliferation threats that could involve aircraft as transport or weapons delivery vehicles, it is not surprising that the ISTC approved a number of project applications from several of Russia's prominent aeronautics institutions. This initial emphasis on institutions directly linked to aeronautics—rather than those devoted to missile, rocket, or space technologies—eased some of the concerns of the Russian security authorities. The aeronautics institutes did not disappoint their Western counterparts, as Russian specialists were well attuned to the ways of doing business in the West. The institutions that received the largest levels of support over the ISTC's lifetime and some areas of institutional specialization include the following:

- Central Aerohydrodynamics Institute (Zhukovsky). Control systems and aircraft safety, aeroacoustics and green solutions to noise problems, service life and damage tolerance, and aerodynamic modeling and testing.
- Khristianovich Institute of Theoretical and Applied Mechanics (Novosibirsk). Mathematical modeling focused on aerogas dynamics, physico-chemical mechanics, and mechanics of deformation and destruction of solid components.
- Baranov Central Institute for Aviation Motors (Moscow). Gas dynamics and heat physics, ground and altitude testing of advanced aviation engines, scram jet studies, compressor acoustic performance, and certification testing.
- Moscow Aviation Institute. University training, space technology and rocket science, electronics and energy, and cybernetics and instrumentation.
- Gromov Flight Research Institute (Zhukovsky). Propulsion, avionics and system integration, flight mechanics, and ground/flight test instrumentation.[5]

The Central Aerohydrodynamics Institute, commonly referred to as TsAGI, is located just a few miles to the east of Moscow. While the other institutions mentioned above all received support from the ISTC, TsAGI activities dominated the aerospace portfolio of the center, particularly in the early years.

This institute had long been a birthplace of Soviet aviation technologies. For decades the institute had carried out many classified research programs in some of the most advanced wind tunnels and related experimental devices in the world. But in 1992 the portion of the institute's budget that came from military sources had slumped to almost zero. This low level of defense involvement contrasted sharply with the 50 percent budget support by the defense sector only several years earlier.

Some facilities at TsAGI became obsolete as the budget declined. However, others remained highly functional and offered a variety of opportunities for the conduct of research on projects of international interest.

Dozens of customers were already coming to TsAGI from abroad when the ISTC began soliciting proposals. In particular, foreign aircraft manufacturers were paying modest fees to use the wind tunnels and other facilities.

However, for a number of years the institute unsuccessfully promoted many new types of major innovations that seemed relevant to future advances in a variety of fields of both civilian and military interest. These efforts were often components of large defense conversion programs. They included, for example, design of (a) large seaplanes, (b) test stands for simulating truck operations in desert areas, and (c) highly automated greenhouses. Even though some of these new concepts had market appeal, highly qualified competitive institutions in other countries had already captured the limited markets in most areas.

Other traditional services remained of great interest to TsAGI and its customers. They included airframe tests, flight simulator experiments, creation of flight control systems, and improved data acquisition and processing systems. At the same time, as American and European organizations were vying for international market shares, many of the experimental facilities at TsAGI were no longer on the forefront of international capabilities. Still the price for using the institute's facilities and expertise was right, and concerns over undesirable proliferation of some technologies encouraged Western governments to promote use of the facilities and underemployed specialists, which would add to the transparency of the institute.

For several years during the 1990s a redirection activity at TsAGI became a very profitable business—the production of material for parquet floors, heralded as a defense conversion program. The institute's high-temperature ovens provided an excellent facility for this profitable business that attracted the interests of both large construction companies and wealthy residents in the Moscow area. But after a few years of the institute's success, Western companies had advanced their competing technologies considerably and began to take over the Russian markets.

Throughout the lifetime of the ISTC, specialists at TsAGI who received support from a variety of the center's projects became an important bridge between ISTC and the rebounding aviation industry of Russia more broadly. The institute's experiences in many ways reflected the trends in moving from military-related programs to programs of broad civilian interest. Given its location close to Moscow, the institute became a popular venue for international conferences on aviation issues. As to still broader international outreach, the institute was a pioneer in establishing a representation office near Washington, D.C., TsAGI International, Ltd. For a number of years, this office played a useful role in advertising the strengths of the institute.

The ISTC has been a good starting point for some Western companies searching for better technological approaches for aircraft design and operation. The center has used its good offices to promote a number of technologies spread throughout Russia as follows:

- Flight physics: aerodynamics, aeroelasticity, and aeroacoustics; computational fluid dynamics; measurement techniques; and instrumentation
- Flight dynamics: system architecture and avionics; on-board mission planning and guidance; control techniques; flight and ground tests; qualification, certification, and post-test analysis
- Alternative fuels; supersonic/hypersonic aircraft propulsion; and scramjet and multimode ramjet
- Helicopters, including new rotorcraft configurations
- Structures and materials, including high-performance steels, alloys, titanium, and composites
- Design of advanced cockpits, including onboard software and cabin systems
- Micro- and nanotechnologies, industrial processes, integrated design and manufacturing[6]

Three categories of activities summarize the broad set of interests of the ISTC parties in drawing on the capabilities of Russian aeronautics experts. Within each category, a project is identified together with the funding provided by the center.

Category 1. Enhancement of flight performance, economy, and efficiency: Experimental investigation of transition of supersonic boundary layers relevant to high-speed air transportation. Turbulent Laminar Flow, Institute of Theoretical and Applied Mechanics, Novosibirsk, $400,000, 1996.
Category 2. Improvement of safety and operational capacity: Optimization of characteristics of low-cost hemispherical resonator for small commercial

navigation systems. Resonator Gyroscope, MEDICON, Miass, Chelyabinsk Region, $125,000, 1998.

Category 3. Decrease of environmental impact: Development of methods for conducting research on atmospheric contamination and conditions of formation and composition of airplanes' condensation trails. Airplanes' Condensation Trails, Gromov Flight Research Institute, Zhukovsky, Moscow Region, $310,000, 2006.[7]

Finally, three projects that the ISTC Secretariat has highlighted as being of particular importance are the following:

1. Construction of an Experimental Installation for Research on Unstable Processes and Means for Increasing Efficiency of Compressors. Carried out by the Central Institute for Aviation Motors in cooperation with the SNECMA Corporation (France) and the Rolls-Royce Corporation (United Kingdom). The objective of the project was to create a test stand and to conduct studies on that stand of unsteady gas dynamic processes for different types of compressors. The research activities addressed the following issues:

   • Gas-dynamic interactions of blade rows
   • Influences of unsteady processes on gas dynamics
   • Unsteady aerodynamics and air-elasticity of compressor elements
   • Influence of blade forms on flow in compressors

   Swedish experts have given rave reviews to this project, which in their view has opened important new research opportunities to help address problems of vibration fatigue and also to reduce acoustic noise. These problems are of considerable interest both to scientists and to industry in Europe.

2. Investigation of Aircraft Vortex Wake Evolution and Flight Safety. Carried out by TsAGI, in cooperation with Boeing, Airbus Industrie, Aerospatial, British Aerospace, DLR-German Aerospace, DASA-Daimler Benz Aerospace, ONERA-SERT (France), and Japan Aircraft Development Corporation. The objective of the project was to help determine safe separation distances between successive aircraft using the same runways for takeoff or landing. An important component of the project was designed to study specific conditions, namely, Wake Turbulence Problems at the Frankfurt am Main Airport Final Approach Area. In brief, the project involved

creation of a stochastic vortex wake model to simulate different approach patterns and safe separation distances. It considered ways to create visualization systems for vortex wake monitoring at airports and to assess the feasibility of using existing ground-based anemometers for vortex wake monitoring near the runways.

3. Development of New Methods of Laminar Flow Control and Turbulent Drag Reduction. TsAGI, in cooperation with Airbus Industrie and ONERA. The four objectives of the project include:

- Investigate subsonic swept wing designs in order to maximize laminar flows
- Assess laminar flow control and turbulent drag reduction through local boundary layer heating
- Acquire data concerning influence of clouds and dust on laminar-turbulent transition during two-phase flow
- Analyze reduction of boundary layer receptivity caused by acoustic and vibration disturbances[8]

ECONOMIC DECLINE IN THE MISSILE AND ROCKET SECTORS

As discussed in chapter 5, the conditions in the closed regions of Russia that housed missile and other advanced aerospace technologies in some ways mirrored the economic decline in the nuclear cities. In isolated areas of the country, the economic collapse was much more serious than in the more urbanized regions of the country. Relatively remote clusters of tens of thousands of enterprise workers were losing many jobs as orders for new vehicles and supporting equipment began to dry up—and no options existed for other types of employment. The enterprises and institutes did not have the level of support in Moscow that Minatom extended to the nuclear institutions under its jurisdiction; and to the international community, the plight at the missile centers in the early 1990s was less visible than the much-publicized setbacks in the nuclear cities.

The missile research centers, nevertheless, attempted to keep up with the rapid advances in other countries in improving existing technologies and developing new approaches. One technique was to recruit a few outstanding young scientists. However, these new entrants to the field stirred rumblings of dissatisfaction among the specialists who had long careers in improving rocket science.

In a 1995 survey of 240 hard-core missile and rocket technologists at three rocket and missile centers, veteran scientists reacted negatively to early practices of hiring unqualified young, but inexpensive, new recruits. They commented, for example, "We are hiring recent graduates with poor engineering training. Some are well-connected easy riders. They are children of higher ups. Many receive jobs unrelated to their professions. We have almost no inflow of specialists trained in core occupations."[9]

On a broader basis, the attitudes and the productivity at the centers were on the decline. While the ISTC was aware of the deteriorating conditions and the related outreach efforts of the institutions to shady institutions that were not appropriate international partners, the center had difficulty making good contacts with the core elements of the missile sector. All the while, the United States and other Western countries were initiating bilateral efforts to interact with missile research centers and with rocket enterprises, as well as with research institutes. They were enlisting Russian specialists, for example, for jobs to help monitor activities related to the international commitments of the Russian government to reduce the number of its launch vehicles.

Survey results concerning personnel issues at three centers included the following finding: "The older scientists know a lot, but some have left for private business. The younger ones have to start from scratch. There is a dearth of new ideas and over-reliance on earlier research projects. We largely work for some upstarts overseas. Operations are unstable, and there is no one to carry out routine work. There is a sudden increase in the number of bosses with no responsibilities. The government does not care."[10]

Against this background, the ISTC had considerable difficulty engaging Russian missile-oriented and rocket-oriented institutions in specific project activities. Surprisingly, neither the Russian government nor the ISTC parties criticized this limited success in outreach to an important segment of the Russian weapons community that was in deep financial difficulties. Perhaps all recognized that security concerns complicated cooperative projects involving missile and rocket scientists. Even today these institutions have remained in the center of the closed defense sector. Further, they have had their own agendas for engaging in commercial activities. They probably have seen little advantage in becoming involved in ISTC activities that required revelation of considerable information and access to sensitive facilities by teams of foreign auditors.

In short, the key institutes found less-complicated ways of increasing their incomes in difficult days than working through the center. Of course, engagement by the Western scientific community would have increased transparency and perhaps uncovered some technologies that would have been important to Western nonproliferation efforts. But of what benefit would that have been to the Russian innovators other than short-term incomes?

Two exceptions to this closed outlook of the military industrial complex were significant, however. First, as discussed in chapter 8, the ISTC had a robust working relationship with CERN. Russian rocket scientists had considerable expertise of interest to the basic physics community. Specifically, the rocket development firm Mashinostroitel in Perm in the early 2000s joined a strong Russian team consisting primarily of physics research institutions in designing and constructing operating rings for complex detectors for the ATLAS/LHG experiments. These experiments were carried out in a particle collider in Geneva.

A second exception was a broad-ranging conference in Perm that the ISTC organized in 2003. Highlighting the conference, several local institutions, which had been involved in designing important missile components, demonstrated their strong linkages with Gazprom and with the regional government in their marketing of newly designed equipment to improve gas pipeline transmissions. They were manufacturing important components to strengthen the gas transmission infrastructure in large segments of the country.

Unfortunately, the number of international attendees at this large conference, which the ISTC organized explicitly to acquaint foreign visitors with opportunities to benefit from Russian innovation activities, was very small. Indeed, I was the sole American in attendance. While considerable publicity was given to the anticipated events at the conference, there was little interest by Western parties of the ISTC in following up the leads that the conference highlighted.

EXPLORATION OF SPACE

During the 1990s the ISTC supported a number of projects related to space exploration as opportunities arose. Of particular early interest were the technological requirements for the International Space Station. However, during the mid-1990s only limited effort was expended by the center to develop strategic directions for its space-related project portfolio. The secretariat simply responded to ad hoc ideas of interested institutions.

During 1998–99, however, the secretariat made an effort to develop a framework for projects with a clear emphasis on manned space flight. The ISTC based this effort on a project titled Preliminary Project for Exploring Mars. The scope subsequently expanded within the concept of a second project titled Development of Key Technical Means for Manned Planetary Missions. The following issues then began to provide a framework for developing a robust program:

- Architecture of the manned Mars expedition
- Variants of the in-space propulsion system
- Power plant options for on-surface operation on Mars
- Transportation schemes on the basis of reusable, environmentally safe propulsion systems
- Conceptual design of land planetary module
- Creation of medical-biological onboard facilities to support long-term human activities in space
- Safety equipment for onboard and on-planet protection (protection from radiation and meteorites)
- Robotic and measuring equipment for study of space and on-planet phenomena[11]

Six Russian institutes carried out projects to develop and to begin implementation of the framework: the Keldysh Research Center, Energia Enterprise (Russian Aerospace Committee), Institute of Space Research (Russian Academy of Sciences), Krasnaya Zvezda enterprise (Rosatom), research institute NIKIET (Rosatom), and Institute of Medical Biological Problems (Russian Academy of Sciences).

The impressive array of collaborating institutions from abroad included the following: NASA, Boeing, CNES (Paris), Universities Space Research Association, and ESA (the Netherlands). Many books were prepared and distributed pursuant to activities involving these organizations.

Several particularly significant events occurred during 2003 and 2004. First, in 2003, the ISTC and the International Academy of Astronautics organized an international conference in Moscow to set forth visions of the future that would stimulate cooperation concerning space exploration. Leading officials and experts from the United States, Europe, Russia, and other countries participated. They gave special attention to the exploration of Mars. Conference presentations addressed the development of future long-distance manned space missions and reviewed experience accumulated by humans in space—in particular within the framework of moon exploration, the MIR program, and the International Space Station. Among the highlighted topics were the following:

- Human effects of long-term space flights, remediation of these effects, and life support systems
- On-board power generating systems (solar, electrochemical, nuclear) and propulsion systems using new fuels
- Engineering issues including spacecraft and re-entry vehicle architecture, design, and robotics
- Risk assessments and approaches to minimize meteorite and radiation hazards[12]

At the conclusion of the conference, the participants agreed on the need for creation of an international contact experts group and for regular conferences every two years.

The meetings of the contact experts group, held in various countries, have been quite productive. The gatherings have been well attended. In short, the ISTC has played an important coordination and facilitative role in this field.[13]

Finally, reflecting the ISTC's wide reach within Russia and abroad, a project titled Engineering of High Performance Techniques of Oxygen Production and Respiratory Gases for Space Systems and Public Health involved scientists who did not play central roles in space-related activities but who wanted to contribute their expertise. They were drawn primarily from the Institute for Experimental Physics, in Sarov, and the Institute for Biomedical Problems in Extreme Conditions, in Moscow. Reflecting the broad interest in this activity, eight international working group meetings were held in Europe and in Russia over a period of three years. The project results, which improved instruments and demonstrated measurement methodologies, were considered very valuable by all concerned for supporting activities in environments fraught with potential accidents, including possibilities for interruption of oxygen flow.[14]

In summary, the ISTC's aerospace coordination efforts have been modest in comparison with the parallel efforts of interested governments to work together, and particularly joint efforts of the Russian and U.S. governments concerning the International Space Station. Nevertheless, the ISTC has filled an important niche in bringing to the table key Russian scientists to enhance the work of the core teams that will carry out space missions. Many Russian specialists who have participated in ISTC-sponsored activities have repeatedly expressed appreciation for the opportunity to contribute to the overall international effort.

Space research projects have focused on the following areas: astronomy, extraterrestrial exploration, manned space station, space vehicle and support equipment, spacecraft trajectories and mechanics, and unmanned spacecraft. Among the Russian institutions that have not been previously mentioned but that have played important roles in developing and carrying out space projects have been the Lavochkin Association, the Chemical Automatics Engineering Design Corporation, and the Central Research Institute of Machine Building. The international sponsors of partner projects have been EADS Space Transportation (France), EADS Space Transportation (Germany), and the European Office of Aerospace Research and Development (United States).[15]

IMPACTS OF ISTC ACTIVITIES

The contribution of the ISTC to advancing science in the field of aeronautics has been significant. While expenditures have been limited, the center's projects have provided important support for key Russian specialists at critical economic times. The interest of aviation institutions from around the world in Russian activities supported by the ISTC underscores the importance of the highly targeted activities of the center.

The lack of deep involvement of a wide range of Russian missile-oriented institutions in ISTC activities is noticeable. The threat of leakages of sensitive technologies to countries with governments having questionable security discipline throughout the world has always been of concern. While the ISTC could not have prevented the proliferation of dangerous technologies, it should have been able to shine a bright light on developments that would have been of considerable interest to all of the ISTC parties, including some of the agencies of the Russian government itself.

Already in 1993, for example, the Institute of Graphite—a key participant in the Soviet effort to develop rocket technology—reached out to the ISTC Preparatory Committee and invited us to visit their facility. We walked through the buildings—which were extensive but seemed almost dead—with few lights even turned on. Unfortunately, neither we nor our immediate successors in the ISTC Secretariat followed up on that visit, and the institute struggled to survive the worst of economic times with the help of Indian firms that were later accused of violating international limitations on transfers of sensitive technologies.

The Institute of Graphite reportedly became a conduit for transfer of technology to Iran, eventually resulting in the imposition of U.S. sanctions on the institute in 1998. Finally, a decade after our initial visit, the sanctions were lifted as the institute became a responsible partner in promoting trade with organizations abroad. Had we been more alert, perhaps we would have been effective in limiting proliferation of technologies that may have contributed to arms races in other countries.[16]

Finally, with regard to manned exploration of space, the convening power of the ISTC has been impressive. Thus, in measuring the success of the ISTC, factors that are not reflected in the level of financial expenditures are important. While the center's financial contributions in this area may seem insignificant, its facilitative contributions have been substantial.

CHAPTER ELEVEN

Measuring Success

Simple measurements to evaluate success of some programs may not be applicable. The ISTC must often rely on the collective sense of the parties, scientists and secretariat staff to determine program impact.
   —Conclusion of two-year ISTC review, 2000

Institutes with ISTC support use as their metric the number of international grants they receive—the more the better. Our metric is the number of international grants that they need to get back on their feet—the fewer the better.
   —Senior official of Department of State, 2005

THE INTERNATIONAL NONPROLIFERATION COMMUNITY has widely recognized the importance of redirecting underemployed Russian weapons scientists to civilian careers during a time of economic turmoil throughout the country. Each redirected weapons scientist who has changed his or her career has become a small plus sign on a huge screen depicting multifaceted responses to the challenges of reducing incentives for proliferation of weapons of mass destruction. The ISTC can take credit for many pluses that increasingly blacken the screen, although neither the individual importance nor the aggregated significance of the black impressions—in the near term or in the long term—can be easily quantified.

ISTC projects have undoubtedly helped in preventing rogue governments, hostile organizations, and disillusioned individuals from illicitly gaining access to dangerous technical know-how, rooted in Russia and in other new states that emerged from the Soviet Union. However, even the most sophisticated analyses cannot put price tags on the worth to dissidents of such know-how. Nor can the benefits to the international community of prevention of leakage of weapons expertise be estimated with a high degree of confidence.

In addition to specialized brain power, adversaries need access to facilities, materials, equipment, blueprints, supplies, and test areas, as well as access to shadowy security environments, where they can prepare and mount devastating attacks. Gaining such access would probably involve complicity by renegade insiders, who are most likely scientists. These specialists are needed to plan and guide theft operations and then to ensure that the pilfered materials will be assembled and work as planned. Measuring the likelihood of such complicity by turncoats seems impossible.

SEARCHING FOR APPROPRIATE METRICS

Nevertheless, qualitative and, to the extent possible, quantitative assessments of impacts of ISTC activities are important. Assessments should be carried out within the context of overall progress in reducing the likelihood of proliferation of weapons of mass destruction. A number of overlapping programs are designed to safeguard the world from the dangers of nuclear, chemical, or biological attacks and from the devastation of terrorist attacks using sophisticated weaponry, or even relatively simple weaponry. Progress in improving safety and security cannot easily be attributed to any single program. Usually a number of well-designed and well-implemented programs should be able to claim a share of the credit for success.

Beginning in the early days of the ISTC, a wide range of metrics, explicitly or indirectly related to international security, played an important role in program planning and in operations of the center. They raised important flags concerning the feasibility of deterring destructive incidents—both red and green flags—during the funding decisions of the ISTC parties. Also, they guided the frequent assessments of the effectiveness of the center's programs.

From the outset, the governing board and the staff of the ISTC discussed many indicators of the levels of risk associated with the diffusion of expertise within and beyond the former Soviet Union that could then be misused. Against this background, the funding parties quickly embraced two metrics when selecting projects for support. They were (a) the number and capabilities of former weapons scientists involved in a proposed project and (b) the scientific merit of the project.

Also, the parties were usually aware of the national defense role of Russian institutions supporting proposals and the scientific significance of the institutions. The parties could factor these considerations into judgments as to priorities among proposed projects. Therefore, it was no surprise when the Institute for Experimental Physics in Sarov—the birthplace of Russia's nuclear weapons—soon became the recipient of the largest number of ISTC project awards. Proposals from the institute consistently scored high marks in the two key areas—first, weapons expertise of the participants in the proposed projects and, second, the scientific importance of the proposed research tasks and soundness of the methodologies that were to be followed. The third consideration also carried considerable weight, namely the traditional role of the institute in contributing to national security objectives.

From a broad perspective, the ISTC focused on potentially dangerous "trees" of intellectual capabilities (the research institutes). They were located within the "forests" of overall risks (the most dangerous proliferation scenarios). The contours of the global landscape covered by these forests and the significance of the Russian trees have consistently been in the background of decisions concerning approval of projects by officials in Washington, Brussels, Tokyo, Ottawa, and other capitals. Of course, security aspects have been carefully reviewed by the Russian government as it decided which project proposals should be sent forward for consideration by the ISTC.

This chapter presents several perspectives on metrics relevant to the objectives of the ISTC, beginning with the importance of head counts of the weapons scientists involved in projects. More broadly, I present metrics that prestigious groups have used to clarify public understanding of the roads to effective containment of dangerous weapons and their components. Impacts of biology-related programs, which are among the most difficult programs to assess, let alone to measure impacts, receive special attention. Returning to a focus on specific ISTC achievements, I offer a personal assessment of the center's overall performance using crude metrics. At times, a back-of-the-envelope approach is useful in stimulating debate that leads to more elaborate approaches.

The discussion then turns to an ambitious metrics program developed by an international team that was assembled to recommend approaches for assessing the impacts of ISTC activities—with particular emphasis on sustainable redirection of weapons scientists. At the beginning of the 2000s the team worked out a methodology for assessing the strengths of Russia's science infrastructure that could support alternative careers for disenfranchised weapons scientists. The approach now seems somewhat academic and distant from on-the-ground realities at the time, and implementation of the recommendations of the team was limited. Nevertheless, the effort provided a checklist of issues that should have been given more serious consideration during the first decade of the ISTC's operations and that will continue to have relevance for future support of scientists in Russia and elsewhere.

Finally, during 2011 the governing board mounted an effort to review achievements during and following implementation of clusters of projects supported by the center. Review teams used important criteria for assessing scientific achievements and economic impacts, with particular attention to identifying technologies for further development and applications. The first cluster included seventeen oil and gas projects and is discussed later in this chapter. It was followed by assessments of other clusters.[1]

This potpourri of indicators of impacts reflects the immaturity of quantitative methodologies for understanding many dimensions of proliferation concerns. The diverse, and at times overlapping, interests of individuals, institutions, and governments in metrics do not neatly fit into jigsaw-puzzle mosaics. But ISTC leaders have frequently discussed the topic throughout the lifetime of the center. Hopefully, the metrics considered by policy officials in Russia and elsewhere will continue to improve and lead to better understanding of the payoffs from various approaches in coping with global security risks and demonstrating the payoffs from scientific cooperation.

Program evaluation is frequently linked with program metrics. Budget officials who allocate resources among programs are often more comfortable when justifying their decisions if they have quantitative or qualitative indicators of success, however primitive. The alternative is reliance on testimonials of program managers and interested observers as to the importance and effectiveness of programs—a weak surrogate for structured evaluation.

Within governments, budget-related assessments of program progress are usually annual undertakings. Developing the basis for national allocations of resources for the ISTC has not been an exception. However, while different types of measures for assessing achievement of program objectives can be very useful, care is needed not to assume that such measures reflect the impacts of programs with a great deal of precision or that achieving program objectives can be equated to attainment of security goals.

Indicators that are measurable are not necessarily good evidence of success—particularly in terms of enhanced security and sustainability of programs. Some useful indicators of success are measurable. But usually the most important assessments of near-term and long-term security impacts are structured, collective judgments of well-informed specialists. At the same time, reducing hostile intent, building confidence in reliability of partners, and gaining political commitments to limit proliferation of expertise are critical aspects of engagement programs and almost always defy approaches to precise measurement.

COUNTING THE NUMBER OF REDIRECTED SCIENTISTS

As previously noted, a favorite metric of government officials for evaluating the success of activities of the center has been the number of former weapons scientists who have been engaged in projects. Initially, this metric was particularly important to demonstrate rapid progress. It provided an easily understood indication of the interests of the Russian government and of many highly skilled scientists throughout the country in embracing the redirection approach of the center. Prestigious scientists from some of the most sensitive facilities in Russia patiently stood in line for grant financing to support development of their ideas, demonstrating official and personal buy-ins to the ISTC experiment.

In time, however, this numerical metric began to lose some of its significance. Funding of research activities from multiple sources became more common. It was increasingly difficult to attribute career changes to ISTC activities, given the different funding streams. Also, as funding priorities shifted between fields of scientific interest, many uncertainties arose whether career changes would be permanent.

Nevertheless, this indicator withstood frequent criticism as to its appropriateness as the primary measurement of program impacts. Of particular concern has been the part-time employment on ISTC projects of some weapons scientists who worked on defense projects at the same time. When the ISTC projects are completed, they may return to their defense-related activities. This circulation defeats the purposes of the center, claim the skeptics.

But ISTC officials have consistently believed that part-time involvement and short-term career changes have been better than no involvement. Some of these part-time stints have probably encouraged participants to eventually give up their defense-oriented career tracks as they gained satisfaction from civilian-oriented tasks. Others undoubtedly returned to their defense-related careers, having received financial benefits that helped keep them satisfied during the dark economic days of the country.

During visits to Russian research centers in recent years, I have witnessed how modest investments in the careers of scientists by the ISTC are paying off.

Learning that a laboratory employing five or ten former weapons scientists has reoriented activities to civilian tasks has made and will continue to make long-remembered impressions on skeptical visitors, particularly as a young component of the civilian staff within a laboratory grows. Also, the transformation of secret hideaways, where even the researchers had not always known how their findings would be used, to meeting grounds for dozens of Russian and highly regarded foreign scientists wrestling with global problems of common concern has been impressive.

BROAD-RANGING SCORE CARDS

Using very broad metrics, in 2008 a prestigious Washington-based and congressionally endorsed bipartisan organization, Partnership for a Secure America, issued its report card on the efforts of the United States to prevent terrorists from gaining access to weapons of mass destruction. The concern was the possible theft of intact weapons or, more likely, the theft of components of weapons that are assembled into complete weapons. The possibility that this would take place within the borders of the United States triggered the inquiry.

The report card set forth below was distressingly pessimistic. If we could not prevent proliferation onto our own soil, how could we effectively assist in preventing the spread of such dangerous weapons in distant lands? The ISTC has been interested in the scenarios that were considered in preparation of the report card, which inevitably would involve participation by highly skilled scientists. Clearly, the purpose of the report card was to stir political support for security programs, and it did. But the absence of a good evidentiary basis for the scoring, beyond the broad judgments of well-known political and scientific figures, raised questions. The scoring was as follows:

1: Prevention of Nuclear Terrorism: Overall Grade: C
   - Nonproliferation programs: C+
   - Detection/interdiction of weapons and materials: B
   - Integration of government programs: D
   - Long-term sustainment of programs: D
2: Prevention of Chemical Terrorism: Overall Grade: B−
   - Recognition and prevention of threat: C−
   - Detection, resilience, and mitigation programs: B

- Protection of industrial and transportation facilities: C+
- Elimination and demilitarization of chemical weapons: B

3: Prevention of Biological Terrorism: Overall Grade C–

- Denial of access to biological agents: B
- Detection of covert bio-terror preparations: C–
- Interdiction by law enforcement: B–
- Confidence-building to distinguish bio-defense and threats: D+
- Resilience: new vaccines and drugs: C+
- Good public health preparedness and response: B[2]

These scores served their intended purpose, namely, gaining increased attention to proliferation threats by important officials within the U.S. government and among significant elements of the American public. It was not difficult for the committee to agree that terrorism is a dangerous problem. However, the metrics greatly oversimplified a set of complex problems that deserved more detailed consideration and clear criteria for scoring.

As repeatedly underlined in this book, one of the most important, and also most elusive, aspects of proliferation is the human dimension, which was not explicitly considered in detail by the international community prior to the establishment of the ISTC. Now, many experts advocate a global lockdown of dangerous materials, and intuition suggests that such a goal is very appropriate. At the same time, even the most stringent lockdown of brain power that would be feasible on a global, regional, or national basis—which, of course, would be directly related to the task of the ISTC—would have some characteristics of a huge sieve. Thus, transparency is an essential goal in deterring surreptitious behavior of individuals; and the openness that is integral to international scientific cooperation should receive equal billing with locking down material.

Turning to another effort to document progress toward nonproliferation, for many years the U.S. Congress has used a scorecard to measure the success of the Cooperative Threat Reduction (CTR) program of the Department of Defense (DOD), with particular emphasis on activities in Russia (i.e., the Lugar Scorecard). It has been clear in Washington that systematically destroying portions of Russia's capabilities to launch long-range attacks would enhance U.S. security. At the same time, Russia has been eager to unburden itself of the costs of maintaining unnecessary military capabilities. Therefore, the approach to establishing meaningful metrics has been relatively simple—counting destroyed items—although the execution of destruction programs for such an approach has not been easy.

The U.S. and Russian governments have set targets for reductions within various categories of weapons systems, targets that are to be reached by 2012. For example, by that date, 9,222 nuclear warheads are to be deactivated, 1,078 ICBMs should be destroyed, and 645 ICBM silos should be eliminated. Surely, such reductions in the weapons arsenals will contribute to a more secure world. Given such targets, the Pentagon then keeps close tabs on the destruction timetables; and DOD reports to Congress each year the percentage of the job that has been completed in each category of weaponry.

In some categories, 100 percent of the 2012 targets was reached early. By 2010, for example, 906 nuclear air-to-surface missiles were destroyed, 1,255 bombers were eliminated, and security had been upgraded at all 24 nuclear weapons storage sites. In most of the other areas of interest, considerable progress toward reaching the 2012 goals has been made. In 2011 only several submarines carrying nuclear weapons were still scheduled to be destroyed, submarine-launched ICBMs were nearing complete elimination, and destruction of land-based launchers was fast approaching the 2012 target.[3]

This scorecard represents a relatively easy and understandable application of security metrics. Destruction of physical objects is certainly quantifiable.

However, in some programs, development of new infrastructures to address security weaknesses is the primary objective. A good example is prevention of bioterrorism, which is discussed below, wherein the development of the regulatory, physical, research, and education infrastructures are keys to preventing and responding to hostile actions. However, they defy meaningful quantitative measurements.

BIOTERRORISM: MEASURING INTENT, CAPABILITIES, VULNERABILITIES, AND CONSEQUENCES

The threat of bioterrorism attacks springs largely from malevolent intent of disgruntled individuals who have capabilities to do harm. These individuals may be mobilized within foreign or local groups, or they may be individual dissidents. Capabilities of such individuals have been a long-term focus of the ISTC. But understanding the drivers of intent has always been an elusive aspect of the threat.

Essential capabilities needed by bioterrorists include scientific expertise, access to pathogens, and entry to facilities where pathogens can be prepared for release. Conspirators may have the expertise themselves; or they may be associated with insiders, other local specialists, or foreign coconspirators who supplement the expertise of the planners of attacks. The facilities may be self-constructed or may be facilities belonging to others. They may be portable or permanent. All these requirements suggest focal points for actions to disrupt plots, but the significance of prevention activities around each of the many focal points cannot be easily measured.

Turning to the reduction of the consequences of a release of pathogens, responses should focus both on near-term effects (e.g., disease outbreaks, contamination, psychological impacts) and long-term effects (e.g., lack of confidence in government security, diversion of civilian resources to cope with unanticipated consequences, loss of agricultural productivity, overregulation of scientists). Steps to minimize such consequences should in some cases be identifiable if not measurable. Clearly the types of consequences and difficulties of measurement vary from scenario to scenario.

In recent years DOD has been a leader in developing bioterrorism metrics. In 2007 the department advocated the following measures of success of the CTR biological program: number of analytical laboratories constructed to support disease surveillance activities, number of Internet connections to link surveillance networks together and to tie them into relevant data bases, and number of cooperative research projects undertaken that would help improve transparency of previously opaque activities. But the department subsequently considered these metrics to be inadequate for characterizing threat reduction.[4]

In 2010 DOD adopted the following second-generation categories of metrics concerning bioterrorism, with "measures of efficiency" specified for each category:

- Consolidate collections of especially dangerous pathogens in a minimum number of secure facilities.
- Enhance partner country's capability to prevent sale, theft, diversion, or release of biological weapons–related materials and expertise.
- Increase partner country's capability to detect, diagnose, and report endemic and epidemic outbreaks.

- Ensure enhanced capabilities are designed to be sustainable.
- Facilitate international engagement of partner country's scientific and technical personnel in research areas of mutual interest.
- Eliminate biological weapons–related infrastructures and technologies.

These metrics took into account the changing nature of the CTR program. The new directions emphasize building capacity both for containing dangerous agents and for conducting surveillance to deter, detect, report, and respond to emerging natural biological outbreaks and to illegal trafficking threats.[5] DOD is continuing its efforts to have metrics that are meaningful, understandable, and useful. Such metrics are directly applicable to many programs that the ISTC has facilitated.

Commenting on the metrics for the CTR program, the National Academies have underscored the importance of linking measurements of achieving program objectives to reduction of threat or risk. Also, in assessing the success of programs that strengthen capacity of other countries to enhance security (such as improved systems for detecting outbreaks of diseases), two approaches have been suggested. First, expert observations by independent evaluators of routine operations can be carried out. Second, more ambitious field exercises to test the full scope of enhanced capabilities can be mounted, with the level of effort tailored to the scope of the program, its resources, and its relative importance.[6]

The foregoing focus of DOD has been quite divorced from the programming interests of the ISTC. This is unfortunate since important components of the CTR program in Russia were implemented through the center. More generally, the metrics of DOD and other organizations in the United States and Europe involved in preventing proliferation seemed to be of little interest to officials of the parties that provided guidance for the center.

Since the center has operated on the basis of projects selected by individual parties for financial support using funds available to each party, the clustering of activities within specific strategic frameworks with metrics for judging success has not been developed. The ISTC Secretariat has had no choice but to use expert judgments on a case-by-case basis in judging the merits of proposed projects. The relative significance of science projects that have been at the head of the approval line in comparison with other potential projects either waiting in line or simply incubating in the heads of talented Russian scientists has seldom been addressed.

MEASURING EARLY ISTC SUCCESS

Prior to and following the establishment of the ISTC, I became increasingly familiar with the types of metrics that seemed appropriate in measuring curtailment of the spread of know-how. However, I was not prepared to stretch my limited knowledge of measures of effectiveness to encompass ISTC activities in a detailed manner when I returned to Moscow for a brief visit in 1995.

At that time U.S. officials working on national security issues in the White House asked me to prepare an evaluation of the progress of the ISTC. The center was attracting considerable attention, both in government circles in Washington, Brussels, Tokyo, and Moscow and in the press. The generally positive reports from around the globe about this new experiment stood out as bright lights amid many distressing stories of continued economic chaos in Russia and uncertainties as to the safekeeping of the Russian weapons arsenals. Positive press reports of effective utilization of approaches for security that were new in Russia, although well tested in the West, slowly but surely became more frequent.

One year earlier, in 1994, I had terminated my affiliation with the ISTC. But fortunately, I had planned to travel to Moscow during the week following my receipt of the request for a quick assessment. Thus, I could again examine activities at a close distance. In particular, there would be opportunities to consult with the staff of the center, with participants in projects financed through the center, and with several ISTC watchers who had found a new task—the development of metrics—for their nongovernment policy centers in Moscow.

Upon arrival in Moscow, I asked a well-informed Russian colleague also to prepare a report card on the ISTC. He enthusiastically accepted this task. We could then compare our assessments and discuss similarities and differences in our findings. Our evaluations focused on the following questions:

- Had important Russian specialists of proliferation concern become engaged in ISTC projects?
- Were the financial and technical rewards of working on ISTC projects sufficient to offset financial enticements that might be offered by unreliable organizations that were interested in obtaining weapons know-how from the project participants?
- Did the projects encourage weapons specialists to switch their careers to peaceful endeavors?
- Were the projects contributing to the transition within Russia to a market-

based economy through changes in management approaches, changes in financial approaches, and/or efforts to commercialize research products?

- Were the projects contributing to a revitalized civilian science base of the country?
- Did the projects effectively link weapons and civilian specialists in common peaceful endeavors?
- Did the projects bring weapons scientists into the mainstream of international civilian science?
- Were the projects encouraging openness in formerly closed facilities?
- Was the ISTC effectively coordinating Western and Japanese efforts directed to common objectives?
- Did the center respond to Russia's defense conversion priorities?
- Were the administrative procedures of the ISTC effective and efficient?
- Were the center's financial operations efficient and fiscally sound?

In all categories, the ISTC seemed to be performing well even though it had only been operational for about one year. Using the Russian system of scoring 5 for excellent and 1 for poor in each of the categories, I examined my results and then gave the ISTC an overall 4+. My Russian colleague carried out his assessment independently and came out with a 5−.

We were both very impressed by the high intensity of activity in the bustling corridors of the ISTC. The enthusiasm of the staff in effectively engaging the Russian scientific community was infectious. Also, the determination of the staff and project applicants to overcome administrative delays was refreshing in a city that was still entrapped in the Soviet legacy of multiple approvals for carrying out even the simplest task if there was not an appropriately signed document authorizing the particular task.

We both gave high marks to the speed and efficiency with which the center committed its initial fifty million dollars in a manner that would employ six thousand scientists and engineers. We were impressed with the broad range of experience of many of these project participants who had supported Soviet military efforts at some of the most sensitive facilities in the country. The management and financial accounting changes that had been implanted in the institutions that received ISTC projects were significant. For the first time, project managers in the research institutes below the levels of institute directors and deputy directors were given primary responsibility for ensuring that large projects were carried out in a way determined by the researchers themselves and that all funds associated with the projects were carefully guarded from diversions.

We strongly differed on one point. I felt that too many projects were devoted to supporting basic research, and therefore the center would have little impact on economic development that could create desperately needed jobs. My colleague argued that the ISTC had not been structured to accommodate technology commercialization activities and that basic research should indeed be the primary concern of the ISTC. As we have seen in earlier chapters, this debate has continued throughout the lifetime of the center.[7]

Almost a decade later I again turned my attention to reviewing progress of the ISTC. In 2004 I was invited to the celebration in Moscow of the tenth anniversary of the establishment of the institution. However, the commentaries of well-informed participants at this jubilee were so enthusiastic about the impacts of the ISTC that I decided to join in the euphoria and not try to look into the details of the activities of this international institution, which had surely found a niche in the midst of the security structure of Russia. Wasn't it obvious from the commendations offered by important science and security leaders in many countries that the ISTC had become and would continue to be a success story? And all the while, I had mistakenly thought that the lifetime of the center would not extend beyond a decade. But ten years had already gone by.

Then when I returned to Moscow in 2009 for celebration of the fifteenth anniversary, I realized that neither I nor other ISTC alumni had given adequate attention to the changing environment in Russia. We had not adjusted our measures of success to adequately take into account evolving political, economic, and security conditions. Nor did we pay attention to the views of the Russian government as to payoffs for Russia from the center. It was no wonder that we were not prepared for the events that led to the withdrawal of Russia from the ISTC Protocol and Agreement.

SUSTAINABILITY METRICS

Three important interrelated concepts that could have provided platforms for qualitative assessments of program activities from the earliest days of the ISTC, but that were not adequately recognized by the center until the 2000s, were as follows:

- International partnerships that were developed during implementation of specific projects should in time facilitate graduation of institutions from the need for ISTC support. To this end, institutions should have plans for an exodus from dependence on the center.
- Viable national systems sponsored by the Russian government for developing and supporting science and technology infrastructures were of great importance. Redirected scientists needed assurance of permanent employment in respectable jobs in Russia. Activities to assist in this process should have been given priority.
- Individual institutes needed to strive for self-sustainability, without the need for international assistance. Partnerships were critically important, but the concept of external assistance should have quickly faded from the scene.

Belatedly, in 2002 a commercially oriented participant in ISTC efforts to develop metrics offered the following advice: "More realistic expectations of the ISTC parties are needed in order to establish both short-term and long-term objectives concerning commercialization, balanced partnerships, and self-sustainability of Russian institutes. Russian industry-science partnerships for innovation need to be considered in the light of current institutional frameworks which often depend on traditional models of behavior, e.g. dependence on central government finances and outdated regulatory frameworks, such as complex and ambiguous intellectual property laws."[8]

Returning to 2000, the ISTC engaged an international group of experts to review activities within all of its programs, giving particular attention to long-term sustainability in carrying on research activities initiated with the center's support. These specialists analyzed past approaches and suggested future directions within a broad framework of national economic and social development. They gave particular attention to the benefits for Russian institutions of international outreach. They then proposed a wide array of metrics to guide efforts during the following decade.

Summarized below are some of the highlights of their report concerning the need for and character of recommended measurements of the success of the array of ISTC programs. A few comments are offered on the suggestions in the report.[9]

The approach emphasized seven pillars that would lead to success of programs to redirect weapons scientists to sustainable civilian careers that were previously discussed in chapter 3. The focus was on establishing a viable science support base for the new economies of the states that emerged from the Soviet Union, particularly Russia. An important argument was that unless redirected scientists had career alternatives over the long run, the ISTC's efforts to find immediate job opportunities for underemployed weapons scientists would not be successful for very long.

The analyses gave only limited attention to the priorities for near-term redirection payoffs, based on risk-reduction considerations. Which experiences of nuclear scientists were of greatest immediate concern? Should aerospace engineers who had skills commonly available throughout the world be at the top of the risk lists? How significant is expertise in manufacturing dangerous chemicals that have both industrial and military uses?

The report argued that successful long-term job placement would have the greatest security impact if targeted on fields wherein risk-reduction opportunities were the most attractive. Thus, the report should have given consideration to establishing priorities within the various classes of weapons scientists. But this task was left to others.

The seven pillars of success are as follows:

- *Internationally open and networked.* Knowledge sharing and transparency for confidence building are critically important.
- *Emphasis on research excellence that contributes to new knowledge.* Selectivity is the key to world-class research that can become sustainable.
- *Economic value that attracts an inflow of financial resources.* Involvement of corporate partners is important for improving competitiveness.
- *Multisourced funding from national budgets, foundations, international programs, and industry.* Independence requires financing options.
- *Attraction of young talent that brings entrepreneurial spirit to the task.* A constant influx of new generations of scientists is a key to sustainability.
- *National purpose that encompasses national priorities.* Objectives must include, but should go beyond, nonproliferation activities, which may not receive high national priority.
- *Societal value that reflects concerns of individual citizens.* The quality of life depends on many scientific applications, including clean water, energy efficiency, health promotion, and environmental preservation. But adaptation of military technologies is not always the best approach in these fields.[10]

The report underscored that several crosscutting support systems are also critical to achieve nonproliferation goals and sustainable economic development. They include educational excellence, political stability, and rule of law. While ISTC activities obviously were intertwined with such concerns, the role that the center was to play in these areas was not set forth.

In sum, the seven pillars and three support systems covered such a broad swath of criteria that their usefulness in selecting program activities that deserved priority was questionable. In particular, the pillars did not have a sharp enough focus on core concerns in promoting nonproliferation objectives in the near term, such as, "Were the scientists who received support associated with institutes that had well-known security vulnerabilities?" Yet the center was established to emphasize this aspect.[11]

To set the stage for recommending metrics, the aforementioned report linked each of the ISTC programs—whether large or small—with one or more of the seven pillars described above. The nine programs that existed at the time were as follows:

- Science Projects
- Partner Projects
- Travel Support
- Workshops
- Technical Databases
- Business Management Training
- Valorization Support
- Patent Support
- Communications Support

All of these programs were identified as being relevant to three pillars: engagement of *Young Talent*, contributions to *National Purpose*, and contributions to *Societal Values*. In the view of the authors of the report, the programs for Travel Support, Workshops, and Communications Support contributed to *International Openness*. Science Projects were clearly designed to enhance *Research Excellence*. The programs for Business Management Training, Valorization Support, and Patent Support were designed to add *Economic Value*. Finally, Partner Projects and Technical Databases helped expand *Multisourced Funding*, according to the report.[12]

With this crosscutting matrix of pillars and programs as a framework, the following metrics are a sampling of the many that the outsiders suggested:[13]

1. *Basic metrics for near-term assessments of activities*: number of former weapons scientists engaged, number of trips to visit collaborators, number of resident scientists from abroad, number of workshops attended and contracts generated, extent of other international travel, new partners and new funding sources, entrepreneurial role models that were adopted, technology transfer lessons that were implemented, and number of requests to sponsor joint activities

2. *Metrics for near-term return on ISTC investments*, an intermediate goal: publications in international journals, successes in obtaining competitive international grants, attraction of young talent, spin-off companies established, support by multiple funding sources, recognition awards, patents obtained, licenses obtained, transformation of nonfunding partners to funding partners

3. *Metrics for sustainable nonproliferation activities*, the ultimate goal: technologies commercialized, sustainable partnerships formed, self-sustaining research programs established, licenses obtained, transition from dependence on funds-in from partners to outsourcing components of new value chains, cost sharing of projects with foreign partners, workshops carried out at an international level of excellence, compatibility of institution's communications capabilities with partner capabilities, retention of young talent, linkages with emerging industries, steady budget growth, lack of intellectual property bottlenecks, transition from technology push to market pull, and global competitiveness

As the report documenting the foregoing issues came to completion, the ISTC was already going through a transition to new approaches to address perennial problems. Several programs were being terminated or revised (e.g., valorization program); others were being promoted (e.g., partner program); and still others were continuing to be mainstays of the ISTC (e.g., science projects and workshops). In short, the detailed analyses set forth in the report were interesting and theoretically very promising. However, they were not easily embraced by an organization that was in high gear and just becoming accustomed to new approaches—some that worked and others that did not.

SUCCESS AND DISAPPOINTMENT

Turning to a specific example of measurable sustainable results, in the early 2000s I became a strong advocate of the communications program of the ISTC. This program helped institutions become internationally open and networked, a pillar that ranked high in measuring impacts of ISTC activities. I began working with a significant Moscow research institute that was seeking new partners within Russia, and particularly industrial partners. But the institute had only sporadic access to the Internet through a radio frequency connection, even though it was located in the center of the city. Consequently it had great difficulties in maintaining good communications with its current or potential industrial clients.

With a little prodding, ISTC became interested in the activities of the institute—particularly those devoted to research that was targeted on adding value to minerals so that processed metals could be exported. The center provided a grant of $127,000 for linking the institute to the fiber-optic backbone transiting the city through tunnels of the metro. The institute then proceeded to make arrangements for a new fiber optic cable of a length of seven kilometers through the tunnels to the main computer of the Russian Academy of Sciences, where it linked to nodes throughout the entire world. As a byproduct of the project, six nearby institutes were invited to tie into the new connection to the fiber-optic line. Within six months, seven previously isolated urban institutes had become linked to the global Internet systems—an impressive metric.

Far less impressive metrics were recorded in ISTC's efforts to promote new electronic and biotech inventions that would become profit-earning innovations. ISTC's technology commercialization program was a primary focus of the report discussed above. But many observers considered the center as a very weak mechanism to stimulate high-tech developments within Russia. While a number of small enterprises benefited from ISTC support for their efforts to produce marketable goods, the contributions of these firms to economic growth of the country were barely discernible in any snapshot of the economy. Comments on the ISTC commercialization program by several ISTC project managers in 2002 were as follows:

- "When I find success that involves a Russian commercialization scenario, we often have nothing on record. They do it themselves as they believe that getting us involved in the process will just bog them down."

- "There have been about 200 records of invention/patent applications that ISTC has supported and forwarded to the parties; but they have yielded only three U.S. patents, one license, and no royalties. Also, 67 patent applications have been sent to the European Union—53 in Russia and 2 in Eurasia, with no patents issued. Parties have few incentives to actively pursue commercialization."
- "Russian colleagues treat a patent as an award for technical competence— like some type of honor—rather than applying for a patent in order to protect a technological process that is ready to go to market."[14]

In summary, ISTC's search for useful metrics to help assess its impacts on nonproliferation through creation of sustainable career alternatives that reduced the incentives for illicit activities was commendable. However, as discussed in chapter 6, reliance on technology-push approaches for commercialization of technologies was not very effective, with or without metrics. Fortunately, the partner program that brought both large and small Western firms into the picture, firms that emphasized market-driven technology projects, was a far better approach in achieving both market impact and sustainability.

LONG-TERM IMPACTS OF SELECTED PROGRAMS

As the ISTC approached the closure of its center in Moscow, the governing board decided to review the outcomes of a large number of projects as noted earlier in this chapter. The projects were compiled according to the fields of activity, beginning with a review of oil and gas projects. The seventeen projects of interest involved development of technologies for cleaning bore holes, monitoring pipelines, improving mechanisms of oil recovery, producing biodiesel fuel, and designing power plants based on fuel cells, for example. The focus was on the following metrics:

- Accomplishment of major tasks
- Contributions to relevant scientific fields
- Impacts
- Dissemination of results
- Establishment of collaboration networks with institutes in Russia and other states of the region
- Partnerships with foreign institutions

The preliminary conclusions of the ISTC Governing Board were as follows:

- Project managers and their teams were organizationally competent, innovative, and dedicated to successful completion of their projects.
- A sampling of the projects revealed that some managers were able to find interested parties to continue developing and commercializing results.
- Foreign partners should have been more involved in the projects before, during, and after implementation.
- Protection of intellectual property rights should have been better planned.
- Dissemination of nonproprietary results in international journals and at conferences should be increased.
- A mechanism to help bring project results to interested parties is needed.[15]

The results of the review to date have been very impressive. However, greater attention should be given to the linkages with nonproliferation, which presumably are reflected in the backgrounds of the participating scientists and engineers in the projects.

CHAPTER TWELVE

Replicating ISTC Experiences While Avoiding Pitfalls

The Science and Technology Center in Ukraine has been a model of how nations work together for the common good. For 15 years, it has pursued peaceful science by researchers who had been responsible for weapons of mass destruction.

—Former Chairman of the Science and Technology Center in Ukraine Governing Board, 2010

Lessons learned by the ISTC and the STCU could be adapted to shape appropriate new projects beyond the G8 countries that contribute to global nonproliferation efforts.

—Working Group of the G8 Global Partnership, 2009

AS THE DOORS OF THE ISTC headquarters in Moscow slowly began to close in 2011, a handful of officials from member governments were searching for ways to preserve the center's legacy. They correctly assumed that lessons learned from transforming a radically new idea about curtailing proliferation into a successful program over seventeen years, with most efforts carried out in Russia, should be of broad international interest in the years ahead. These officials had a large array of allies in this effort—namely, the tens of thousands of scientists who had positive memories of their participation in ISTC-supported programs.

A prominent Russian scientist, who had been immersed in ISTC activities during the entire lifetime of the organization and who condemned the Russian decision to withdraw from the ISTC, persuasively highlighted important on-the-ground impacts of the center as follows:

- During the difficult 1990s, the center's financial support for economically struggling scientists with defense-oriented skills successfully limited brain drain to countries of proliferation concern.
- The ISTC contributed significantly to the integration of Russian scientists into the international science community.
- The center brought young leaders into the foreground.
- The center began to transform results of research projects into useful outputs.
- The ISTC strengthened academic links between scientists in Russia and scientists in adjacent states.[1]

His views resonated strongly with many scientific colleagues who were convinced that the legacy of the ISTC's activities in Russia should remain on center stage as other countries developed and expanded nonproliferation programs. Now is the time to spread the experience from the center's successes in Russia. We should not wait until the center has disappeared from the scene, they have argued.

The tenth anniversary celebration of the ISTC in Moscow in 2004 was punctuated with many success stories, and the enthusiasm for the ISTC continued unabated until the fifteenth anniversary jubilee. Then the ISTC encountered turbulent waters in Russia. At the same time, the enthusiasm of the member states other than Russia where projects were sited reached a high pitch.

Since the doors of the Moscow center will not close immediately, there is time for collective reflections on the experiences in Russia. Unfortunately, the parties to the ISTC Agreement may not spend much of their limited energy and funds on capturing what has been learned. They will be far more interested in moving in new directions elsewhere. But consideration of lessons learned at the Moscow science center deserves a place on international agendas in other areas of the world, as well as contributing to the development and implementation of future programs in Russia.

THE FOCUS ON SCIENTISTS

The concept of a small, special-purpose international organization was not new when the ISTC was born. Large international organizations, particularly the United Nations and its specialized agencies, have spawned a number of such organizations over the past decades. But usually the newcomers have been closely linked to the parent organizations. For example, UNESCO created the successful International Oceanographic Commission (IOC), but UNESCO has held the IOC on a relatively short leash through the budget process and review procedures.

Two independent organizations that were exceptions to such linked arrangements also emerged during the 1990s. The Organization for Prohibition of Chemical Weapons stands alone, but it has only a few issues similar to the challenges faced by the ISTC. Second, the International Thermonuclear Experimental Reactor organization, which is devoted to research on fusion in the decades-long search for new energy sources, has been an interest of many Russian physicists who have been deeply involved in ISTC projects. However, the energy organization is still in its formative stage and is somewhat distant from most of the security concerns that have surrounded the ISTC.

The ISTC has been unique in one significant respect. It provides financial support on a project-by-project basis for a specific class of individuals who have been important participants in sensitive research activities. The contents of the new projects have been important. But the overriding aspect that has determined the recipients of project awards has been the technical capability—both for weapons and for civilian activities—of the key scientists who commit to redirection from defense-oriented careers to civilian endeavors. The proposed projects identify all participants in advance, name by name and specialty by specialty. No other international organization has been so sharply focused on the backgrounds of so many participants, and particularly their defense-related backgrounds as well as their specific roles in proposed projects.

Demonstrating how highly skilled weapons scientists and engineers can be encouraged to enter new civilian-oriented professional environments has been at the top of the list of significant contributions of the ISTC to the international community. The cluster of considerations that have facilitated these transitions should be extracted from the center's experience. Many have been discussed throughout this book. Money, of course, is important, particularly in the short term. However, opportunities for long-term professional achievements that command different types of rewards and engender great respect from society should not be neglected. The experience can be summarized as "high-tech specialists redirected to civilian-oriented projects within a diplomatically agreed management framework."[2]

Many of the redirected specialists had provided important inputs for the military enterprise in the Soviet Union. They then became important strengths of the science and technology infrastructures inherited by the successor states to the USSR. As the guardians of many types of dual-use technologies that are now permeating the entire globe, the specialists had comprised and will continue to comprise a highly visible human dimension of international security— in their home countries and abroad.

MANY LESSONS FROM THE ISTC EXPERIENCE IN RUSSIA

ISTC documents record the successes of the center. Previous chapters have highlighted many replicable experiences. For example, the ISTC has repeatedly stressed the importance of sustainable partnerships, international peer review, and financial integrity of projects as these key aspects became widely accepted doctrine. In addition, the following lessons learned throughout the years of carrying out programs in Russia deserve attention, as replication of the center's approaches is considered.

(1) Importance of a solid legal basis for sensitive cooperative ventures

The diplomats deserve high praise for their patience and persistence in crafting the ISTC Agreement and the ISTC Statute in ways that anticipated almost every type of potential legal challenge of the center's activities by national authorities. Also, the technocrats from Washington, Brussels, Tokyo, and Moscow performed an excellent service in developing a clear and precise structure for project agreements. The project agreements define the relationships between the center and the organizations that carry out ISTC-financed projects, with little ambiguity. They are at the heart of the ISTC operations and serve as tutorials for project applicants who are entering a new world of international science.

Globally oriented scientists living in Western countries have become accustomed to collaborating with foreign colleagues with a minimum of controls over their activities. But even they have often admitted that given the special circumstances in interacting with Russian colleagues, a legal basis for meaningful collaboration is essential. Without duly authorized and documented approval for an engagement activity, cooperation can be very difficult as security personnel and other protectors of the homeland repeatedly raise questions as to the nature of international relationships.

(2) Insistence on full compliance of joint activities with national and international legislation in the field of nonproliferation

In general, the ISTC has done a good job in promoting compliance with many laws and regulations—national and international—that are linked to proliferation concerns. These laws and regulations have been evolving in many capitals throughout the lifetime of the center, and particularly in Moscow. Thus, uncertainties have at times blurred the allowable limits of transfers of sensitive technologies.

In general, the funding parties have the upper hand in determining the contents of project agreements, and therefore they can usually control the diffusion of Russian experiences. However, Russian interlocutors frequently point out, "While you provide the money for cooperation, we provide the brains, which are far more valuable." Nevertheless, the money argument has usually won such debates. In any event, the importance of mutually satisfactory donor-recipient arrangements that recognize the interests of both sides from the very outset cannot be overemphasized.

(3) Protection of intellectual property

From the beginning of negotiations to establish the ISTC, intellectual property issues have been on almost every discussion agenda. When the center began operations, a new system of patents was in its initial stage of development within Russia. Thus, some ISTC-related documents have lacked precise information on how intellectual property is to be handled within programs in Russia, and indeed throughout the region. At the same time, the issue often has raised more political than practical issues.

Of course, patents are often critical in providing confidence that creative work of researchers will be rewarded. However, as noted in previous chapters, meaningful international patents have only occasionally emerged from ISTC projects. The time and expense involved in obtaining such protection for results of the center's projects have usually been beyond the capabilities and interests of Russian scientists, and the center's efforts to ease the way have produced limited results. Nevertheless, the center has played an important role in helping many Russian scientists obtain a clear understanding of the role of patents and in encouraging them to be ready to seek patent protection whenever the anticipated payoffs exceed the costs.

Early in the lifetime of the ISTC, the Western parties rejected the traditional foreign assistance approach of granting all patent rights to collaborating institutions in assistance-recipient countries. It would have been a straightforward and simple course. However, the stakes appeared to be too large for such an approach. Looking ahead to other programs, all approaches to intellectual property rights (IPR)— owned by the donor, owned by the project team, or shared ownership—should be considered at the outset in developing relationships involving advanced technologies. Without savvy and sympathetic partners in the advanced countries, inventors from middle-income countries will continue to overestimate the novelty of and financial payoff from some discoveries, while not appreciating the value of other findings.

(4) Protection of business interests

As soon as foreign commercial organizations become involved in government-sponsored international programs, the local hosts for such activities become suspicious of motivations of the interlopers. While the ISTC has hailed most of its partner projects that engaged strong international companies as unqualified successes, Russian officials sometimes considered the tax-free advantages for international companies participating in partner projects as providing an unfair edge in competing with tax-burdened Russian companies.

(5) Commercialization of results of ISTC research projects

ISTC reports are punctuated with dozens of examples of ISTC-backed projects leading to commercial products that reward Russian innovators on a small scale. However, as frequently noted in this book, critics of the center often focus on the failure of the ISTC commercialization program to have *significant* impacts on the Russian economy. The emphasis on market-driven technology development, which has characterized partner projects, as contrasted to the technology-push approach of ISTC regular projects, has been widely recognized as an important dimension of the ISTC experiment.

(6) Disposition of obsolete scientific equipment

Obsolescence is an elusive term. A broad policy to discard old equipment in the quest for modernization—advocated at times by some supporters of the

ISTC—would have been a mistake. Russian scientists have demonstrated amazing abilities to carry out credible research on equipment that would have been discarded years earlier in the West. Unqualified advocacy of replacing old with new equipment can lead to unwise expenditures of scarce resources.

Many visitors to the nuclear research center at Dubna, for example, have criticized the continued use of out-of-date nuclear accelerators. Yet the research center in that city investigates many scientific phenomena of broad international interest. Relevant investigations were often leapfrogged in the West in the drive to obtain new technological devices for investigating more advanced concepts. Effective use of "available and easily maintained" scientific equipment is a policy that should be emphasized, particularly in countries such as Russia, which still suffers from inadequate financial support of the scientific infrastructure.

(7) Advantages of the unique multilateral approach

Thirty-nine governments surely speak with a loud voice. This chorus often overpowers the bureaucratic complexities associated with multilateral approaches, particularly when risky projects with uncertain payoffs are being considered. Fortunately, in the case of the ISTC, each funding party can decide for itself how its funding is to be used, regardless of the certainty or uncertainty of scientific rewards. Dissenting parties must formally object to block risky projects. Such interventions have occurred occasionally—primarily by Russia when it had concerns over security aspects of projects.

The uniqueness of the approach is the method of choosing projects for support within a common selection and implementation framework. Each funding party decides for itself which projects it will support—entirely or partially. This is unlike other international organizations wherein the project money in their core budgets that is provided by governments is pooled, and the participating governments then collectively decide how the funds in the pool are distributed.[3] Often international organizations have programs based on voluntary contributions of member states that in some ways parallel the ISTC approach. But major core programs that depend on pooled resources are usually also under way.

(8) Research grant funds provided directly to the research teams

In the early 1990s, the International Science Foundation supported by George Soros began providing grants in support of scientific activities directly to researchers in Russia, rather than routing the funds through the managers of the institutions where they were employed. The concern was that management would take large cuts of the funds for undisclosed uses, leaving the scientists with but a small portion of the new funds. The ISTC adopted the approach of direct funding to researchers to the distress of most institute directors who did not appreciate external involvement in their internal financial decisions. In time, most directors accepted the approach and found ways to cover overhead from other sources.

In a country plagued by corruption, limiting overhead payments to a modest level—in the case of the ISTC it was usually 10 percent—was a particularly wise decision. In the early 1990s in Russia, an overhead rate of 500 percent or greater was common. The ISTC supported an important precedent that was adopted by others as well. It limited corrupt practices of money diversion from scientists to extravagant expenditures of others who were accustomed to controlling all funds.

SCIENCE AND TECHNOLOGY CENTER IN UKRAINE

Originally, the ISTC negotiators in Moscow had planned for the center headquartered in Moscow to provide financial support to redirect weapons specialists in all interested states that emerged from the Soviet Union. Those of us in Moscow who were shaping the ISTC were quite surprised to learn in late 1992, however, that the U.S. government, joined by the Canadian and Swedish authorities, decided for political reasons that a separate center with an analogous goal should be established in Ukraine. U.S. government officials argued that subservience of Ukraine to Russia should become an artifact of the past and that Ukraine deserved its own place in the sun, whenever possible. However, Russian unhappiness with this approach has persisted for many years.

Despite the limited number of specialists in Ukraine of proliferation concern in comparison with underemployed weapons scientists in Russia, the diplomats who convened in Kiev conceived the Science and Technology Center in Ukraine (STCU) as a full-service organization with its approach patterned after the approach of the ISTC. The underlying international agreement and statute are quite similar to ISTC documents. Other management documents also drew heavily on ISTC experience.

The establishment of the STCU encountered many of the same problems that had emerged in Moscow. The initial political delay for gaining support throughout the Ukrainian government extended over many months. Once the STCU Agreement was formally adopted by Ukraine, the United States, Canada, and Sweden, further delays arose in Kiev, mirroring some of the problems encountered in Moscow. A suitable facility for the center was a problem. The Foreign Ministry was slow in according the promised diplomatic privileges to the STCU staff. And the tax inspectors were no more enthusiastic than their counterparts in Moscow about exemptions. Finally, in late 1995 the STCU Governing Board convened its first meeting in Kiev.

The initial financial commitments to the STCU from abroad were about fifteen million dollars. In comparison with commitments to the ISTC, which was to serve a much larger number of underemployed weapons scientists, the budget was substantial. While the STCU was not an identical twin of the ISTC, it was close to being a fraternal twin. The similarities in approaches will probably continue, even after closure of the Russian component of the ISTC. Many of the same officials from Europe and North America have responsibilities related to both centers, and a few international staff members have migrated between the two centers.

In time, Azerbaijan, Georgia, Moldova, and Uzbekistan joined Ukraine as members of the STCU.

The United States strongly advocated the controversial accession to the STCU in 1998 of Georgia, which was already a member of the ISTC. This political step to continue to wean Georgia away from the influence of Moscow stirred considerable resentment within the Russian government. Why should Georgia be a member of both organizations, queried the Russian Foreign Ministry? But neither the ISTC nor the STCU agreement precluded such dual membership; and serious politicization of the ISTC was under way. The disagreement over this decision was not forgotten by Russian officials and was probably a background factor in the Russian decision to withdraw from the ISTC Agreement.

By 2010 the STCU had received financial resources exceeding two hundred million dollars and had supported fourteen hundred projects. Has this been a good investment? Some important officials think so, as follows.

- "The U.S., Canada, and Sweden made a decision to allocate funds to retrain ex–weapons scientists. No flow-out of defense specialists from Ukraine took place." V. G. Baryakhtar, former STCU Governing Board member
- "International financial and administrative support for Ukraine's R&D network has been essential. One of the best examples of this support has been the STCU." Yaroslav Yatskiv, former STCU Governing Board member
- "Scientists from Ukraine, Azerbaijan, Georgia, Moldova, and Uzbekistan were confronted with isolation from the international scientific community. The STCU acted as a gateway to the world for these scientists." Zoran Stancic, former STCU Governing Board chairman[4]

Positive attitudes toward specific activities included the following:

- "The U.S. Department of Health and Human Services is financing the work of a team of 18 Ukrainian scientists to create a model Geo-Information System for epidemiological surveillance for tuberculosis in the western Ukrainian region of Lviv." Description of new partner project, STCU
- "Since we were introduced to the STCU in 1997, the synergy between Ukrainian scientists and Canadian researchers enabled us to create a truly international company that, despite its small size, can compete at par with larger companies in our industry." Vice president for marketing and business development, Tesseral Technologies, Inc., Calgary, Canada
- "Within an STCU targeted-initiative project, ten Ukrainian scientists developed a novel technology for the production of macroscopic samples of a new nano-structural material based on 1.1 GPa pressure-oriented single-walled carbon nano-tubes." Description of a U.S.-EU-Ukrainian project[5]

From the beginning, I had considered the establishment of the STCU as a mistake—a move by Western governments that would seriously politicize the ISTC at a time when the neutrality of science was a strong argument for establishing and retaining the center in Moscow. Also, I considered that the exclusion of Ukraine from the ISTC would result in a weakening of the Moscow center, which would then be constrained in reaching out to the second most powerful country that emerged in the wake of the former Soviet Union. The cross-border professional ties among important weapons scientists and their institutions in Russia and Ukraine had always been strong. Finally, large-scale science-related problems that ignored borders would not be adequately addressed. Examples included the aftermath of the Chernobyl accident and heavy pollution along the coast of the Black Sea.

But in 2010, when Russia was preparing for its departure from the ISTC, I wondered whether I had been wrong in not advocating a backup plan, should Russia lose interest in the ISTC. Now some officials argue that the ISTC, without Russian membership, should be merged with the STCU. But there are no signs that such a merger will take place, given the desire of the other ISTC members to have their own organization separate from the STCU.

In any event, the Kiev center has become an important player in helping to capture and retain the best of the ISTC experience. STCU will be among the leading organizations that will continue to address the brain drain and related challenges facing the new independent states of the region and other nations throughout the world.

INTEREST IN REDIRECTION OF NORTH KOREAN NUCLEAR SCIENTISTS

"Tell me more." This was the reaction of a senior U.S. official who was leading U.S.–North Korean negotiations when I set forth for him in 1996 my proposition that an ISTC-type approach might be useful in redirecting high-tech North Korean scientists from work on weapons to peaceful endeavors. (I refer to the Democratic People's Republic of Korea as North Korea and the Republic of Korea as South Korea.) I proceeded to make the following points.

First, a program to engage North Korean scientists and engineers in international collaborative activities would introduce a new dimension of openness into that country. If North Korean specialists were involved in peaceful endeavors, they would have less time to devote to dangerous activities. Their country, as well as the participants in the program, would benefit.

Second, since the standard of living in North Korea is low, the costs of providing salaries to attract high-quality specialists to civilian projects should not be a major hurdle, as long as the North Korean government endorsed the idea. However, based on previous approaches to the North Korean government concerning other types of engagement activities, a substantial—but not prohibitive—overhead charge would probably be required by the cash-starved country. Of course, given the total subservience of the workforce, and particularly the military workforce, to the government, the individual scientists would not challenge in any way the positions of the government concerning money or any other issue.

Further, as is well known, the future of North Korea is of vital regional importance to South Korea and to Japan. These two countries would more than likely eagerly participate in such an arrangement that would provide unprecedented transparency into attitudes and activities in North Korea. Perhaps even China would want to participate. Russia would probably be interested, given its long involvement in security matters in North Korea, including training of some of the leaders of the country.

With a cautious nod, my acquaintance said, "You are right. But it is all a matter of time. Our relations with North Korea need to be sufficiently well developed to introduce such a concept."

Since that time, South Korean officials involved in the ISTC have on several occasions discussed in the corridors of the center the possibility of North Korean participation in specially designed ISTC projects. Topics of interest such as geology and oceanography have been suggested. But this optimism of a few South Korean officials has always been overridden by military-related developments on the ground.

In an ambitious, although somewhat unrealistic, effort to entice North Korean interest in redirection of members of its military forces in 2008, several American nongovernmental organizations began designing ISTC-type projects for consideration in Pyongyang. Four U.S. private foundations offered their support. Extensive discussions were held in Washington as to how North Korea might be encouraged to engage in serious consideration of a proposal for redirection of weapons scientists. Unfortunately, North Korean officials were absent during these discussions, reflecting the unlikelihood that such steps would be taken in the near term.

Almost all ideas set forward by the Americans were for redirection of North Korean nuclear scientists. At the top of the list of projects were dismantlement of the Yongbyon nuclear facility and reorientation of nuclear talent to development and construction of a light water nuclear reactor. Several nonnuclear projects were belatedly added to the menu. Many of the engagement mechanisms placed on the list had been employed successfully by the ISTC as well as other Western organizations: for example, workshops, training courses, Internet access, discussions of legal frameworks, and demonstrations of cost-based accounting procedures. On at least one occasion, the South Korean press carried a story that indicated interest to the north in security engagement activities under the headline "Pyongyang Signals Its Willingness to Accept the Nunn-Lugar Cooperative Threat Reduction Program."[6] But most of the redirection activity was based on wishful thinking in the West with no buy-in for, or perhaps even awareness of, the activities by appropriate officials in Pyongyang.

Since that time, the relationships of North Korea with its neighbors and with the United States have continued to be acrimonious. While the redirection concept remains attractive to some observers, the likelihood of a turnaround in accepting Western involvement in nuclear security developments seems low. Nevertheless, we should not forget the ideas of the past, as Washington searches for even the slightest opening to reverse the dangerous situation on the Korean Peninsula.

REDIRECTION OF WEAPONS SCIENTISTS IN IRAQ

Introduction of the ISTC concept for redirecting former weapons scientists was easier in Iraq. The U.S. government succeeded, at least to a limited degree, in attracting former military-oriented scientists familiar with technologies used in weapons of mass destruction to work on civilian projects. In October 2003, a Department of State spokesman trumpeted the effort. "Over the next two years, the Iraqi International Center for Science and Industry will work closely with the Iraqi government to identify, develop, and fund activities in support of Iraqi reconstruction. Of fundamental importance is the need to provide meaningful civilian employment for Iraqis, who have experience related to weapons of mass destruction."

The effort involved training and research activities for hundreds of former weaponeers. One favorite topic was desalination of water, although significant breakthroughs were not recorded. The overall funding levels were modest—only two to three million dollars annually, provided almost entirely by the U.S. government.

Three years later the center closed and was replaced by several limited bilateral engagement projects managed by the Department of State and other interested U.S. government agencies. These programs were continuing in 2011.

SPREADING THE LEGACY MORE BROADLY

For many years, ISTC advocates have discussed diffusion of ISTC-type programs to still other countries. Encouraging the reorientation of military talent to civilian programs in Serbia and Bosnia was raised in the early 2000s. Then modest redirection efforts were introduced in Libya. In Pakistan, biologists are being encouraged to work in the public health sector in a transparent manner, thereby helping to ensure that pathogen collections are not illicitly diverted to military use. Even in China, there are occasional discussions of reducing military weapons arsenals so that dual-use expertise can be refocused on critical technological developments to serve civilian sectors.

In short, the dual-use issue is at the center of proliferation concerns of the future. Redirection of military-oriented high-tech talent is an important step— both in reducing the threat of proliferation of weaponry and also in contributing to economic development. Regretfully, there have not been adequate opportunities to adequately document the impacts of the center's effort in Russia. But in time the spade work that has been carried out will be reflected in the activities of the highly talented members of Russia's workforce who remember their experiences with the ISTC.

As appropriately stated by the leaders of the G8 countries in their call for expanded efforts to encourage responsible science:

> Preventing the illicit use of sensitive knowledge in the chemical, biological, radiological, and nuclear areas is one of the most difficult nonproliferation challenges to address as we are dealing with a wide variety of scientists, engineers, and technicians. In some cases they may not consider their expertise and current activities as potentially vulnerable to misuse by others for whom their "proliferation critical" knowledge could represent a route to develop a weapons capability. They should be made aware that their legitimate work could have dual-use applications and be diverted for malicious purposes.[7]

A PERSONAL ODYSSEY IN KAZAKHSTAN

In 2008 the Kazakhstan government established the International Experts Council on Science and Technology under the purview of the prime minister. I was selected to serve as chairman. Then in 2011, that government selected me also to serve as the chairman of the International Science and Commercialization Board under the purview of the Ministry of Education and Science and the World Bank. In both capacities I have had numerous opportunities to bring to bear in Central Asia the lessons learned during my time as executive director of the ISTC in Moscow.

Commercialization of technologies, good laboratory practices, design of research projects, and transparency in the process of distributing research funds, for example, are all topics that the ISTC has addressed over and over in Russia; and they are now on the stage in Kazakhstan. While Kazakhstan is a member of the ISTC, the center's activities in the country have been focused on a dozen institutions, whereas my new challenges spread much more broadly throughout the country. Thus, one component of the ISTC legacy is spreading lessons learned in Russia to program challenges elsewhere through hundreds of scientists who have participated as managers and researchers in the ISTC experiment and now travel abroad.

In short, I and many other alumni of the Moscow science center have had the opportunity to transfer our experiences in Russia to other countries as international interest in redirection of weapons scientists and international collaboration in dealing with dual-use technologies expands. Each country has its own idiosyncrasies and challenges. However, the theme of responsible science should be a common theme that needs to be reinforced at every possible intersection of science and security. And responsible science has become a signature activity at the Moscow science center.

A NEW APPROACH IN THE MIDDLE EAST

As this book goes to press, the United Nations is in the process of organizing a summit meeting in Helsinki in 2012 to consider the establishment of a zone in the Middle East that would be free of weapons of mass destruction. This new initiative may open opportunities for the ISTC experience to be brought to the forefront of international negotiations to cope with the tinder boxes that permeate the region. Security cooperation among scientists may offer a very useful entry point in attempting to constrain the further development of weapons or acquisition from abroad of dangerous technologies that are deployed in the region.

Many skeptics doubt that the countries of the region will reach agreement on limiting their military options. They see a region that is already punctuated with nuclear weapons, while biological and chemical capabilities are not under adequate control. But responsible science—as pioneered at the Moscow science center—may be an important theme in making the region safer for the world. The stakes could not be higher.

CHAPTER THIRTEEN

The Way Forward

Every new nuclear armed state will add to the risks of accidents or
miscalculations as well as deliberate use of these weapons and may
encourage more states to acquire nuclear weapons to avoid being left
behind.
  —International Commission on Nuclear Nonproliferation and
  Disarmament, 2009

The world has changed. Lines are now blurred: lines between nations,
regions, and peoples; lines between disciplines, tools and applications
of chemistry, physics, and biology; lines between use of technologies for
good or for evil.
  —U.S. National Academy of Sciences, 2010

IN 2010, REFLECTING ON the successes of the ISTC, the former director of a
leading Russian nuclear research center bitterly condemned Russia's impending
withdrawal from the ISTC Agreement with the following assertion: "All Russian stakeholder agencies united in fighting against the ISTC. They were scared
of the ISTC's successful corruption-free system of allocations of research funds,
without kickbacks. What if the country's leaders suddenly realized that the
same experience could be applied to other research projects? How would they
then participate in the growing sales of Audis and Mercedes in the impoverished country?"[1]

Meanwhile, the possibility of dangerous consequences of misbehavior in
laboratories in other countries raises new concerns as technical capabilities
spread rapidly throughout a world torn by political and military disputes. The
globalization of weapons-relevant technologies calls for continuing development of effective means for preventing misuse of dual-use expertise and for

thwarting the assembly of primitive tools of terrorism. But it is a long and often opaque road from (a) policy statements by G8 governments urging nonproliferation and counter-terrorism efforts to (b) effective on-the-ground programs that constrain malevolent activities and enhance international security.

NEVER-ENDING STRUGGLE WITH PROLIFERATION

During the past two decades important institutions—from government agencies in Washington, Ottawa, Brussels, and Tokyo to international organizations headquartered in New York, Geneva, and Vienna—have given high priority to safeguarding dangerous material. They have underscored the following themes:

- Destroy excess nuclear warheads, missiles, and launchers.
- Dismantle facilities that produce components for weapons of mass destruction.
- Lock down highly enriched uranium.
- Collect abandoned radioactive sources.
- Neutralize highly toxic chemicals.
- Consolidate and protect especially dangerous pathogens.
- Control exports of dangerous technologies.

The significance of these actions is clear. The United States and its allies have devoted tens of billions of dollars to such efforts at home and abroad in recent years. These approaches will undoubtedly continue for the indefinite future.

Let us hope, however, that officials who strongly support the safeguarding of such tangible items give comparable attention to constraining scientific innovation that creates the weapons of the world. *Restraining the illicit activities of scientists who can provide the technologies for weapons is of no less importance than controlling the weapons components themselves.* If nonproliferation efforts are to be effective, then the creators of weapons deserve as much attention as the protectors of the finished products.

In short, a sharp focus on the expertise dimension of nonproliferation has been ready for prime time since the 1990s, and the ISTC has been on center stage until today. Finding room on the crowded stage of diplomacy for expanding the concept of responsible science is not easy. Still, the Moscow science center has managed to establish a critical niche in responding to a core proliferation problem, namely, the problem of hostile intent by technically skilled discontents with access to dangerous technologies.

At the governmental level, policymakers must ensure that bureaucracies do not tolerate, deliberately or by neglect, illicit development or acquisition of technologies for destructive purposes. At the laboratory level, scientists must understand their responsibilities for preventing such activities and the possible personal consequences for failure to do so. Without the support of government officials and scientific experts, discontents will have great difficulty using advanced technologies to cause massive damage to society.

In short, the ISTC has shined a bright light on the uncertain foundation of the road to peaceful coexistence in the high-tech world of tomorrow. Never before in history have the world's scientists navigated along such a treacherous pathway of technological innovation—along a trajectory with many possibilities for huge positive or equally large negative impacts on the global community. The Moscow science center has illuminated the critical role of scientific know-how in determining the future of civilization. Most important, the center has repeatedly demonstrated that very modest investments can encourage scientists of many backgrounds to play leading roles in steering the planet toward prosperity and peace, which trump greed and violence.

The ISTC has been only a pilot effort for a broader and more sustained international movement that is now needed to help prevent irresponsible behavior by dissatisfied or misguided scientists and by their patrons. The center has influenced nonproliferation policies of Russia and other states of the region. It has supported day-to-day activities of tens of thousands of scientists embarked on civilian careers. Similar efforts to constrain inappropriate research, development, and outreach activities should involve scientists from other countries as well in demonstrating the importance of a unified effort to promote responsible science across all continents. The ISTC's work has put on display a replicable prototype for moving in the right direction.

It may seem strange that the government in Moscow decided to withdraw from the ISTC Agreement in the wake of many success stories. But Russia is in no mood to be considered as simply a recipient of foreign aid, with status only slightly above that accorded to the weaker states on its periphery that are also members of the center. Russia is moving down the road to economic achievements in many fields and is proud of its scientific potential.

The other ISTC parties repeatedly acknowledged that Russia had evolved both economically and financially and that nonproliferation challenges had changed. They invited Russia to participate in a process that would transform the ISTC into a new organization based on these factors. However, a report of the governing board in this regard did not elicit a response from the Russian government. It was simply too late. The withdrawal decision had already been made.

At the same time, however, some Russian officials still long for continuation of well-tested approaches that the ISTC effectively demonstrated. Of particular interest are (a) programs that have encouraged international technology-oriented firms to pay attention to business opportunities in Russia and (b) programs that have strengthened the country's ties with scientific leaders throughout the world. Russian institutions, as the major beneficiaries of ISTC programs, have a responsibility to be pathfinders in the search for other mechanisms to achieve these and related objectives for Russia and for countries where Russia's interests are strong and the country's influence is growing.

RESONANCE OF ISTC PROJECTS

Buried in the nearly twenty-eight hundred ISTC project portfolios are guideposts for addressing innumerable technical, managerial, technology transfer, export control, and educational hurdles in the quest for a safer world. Results of individual projects may not seem of broad significance in and of themselves, but the aggregated impacts of the many projects that have been successful at the laboratory, national, and international levels will be felt for years into the future. Of special importance, many of the once-isolated laboratories in Russia have become important nodes of global networks of scientific peers. But these connections need continued nurturing.

As expected, financial support was undoubtedly the greatest initial attraction for most Russian scientists who entered into arrangements with the ISTC. However, the institutional and personal benefits of participation in the center's activities often extended beyond simply access to new revenue sources for underemployed and underpaid researchers. At a time when science had lost considerable respect within Russia, being a recipient of an ISTC project was important international recognition of the significance of high-quality research.

Then, too, an identifiable and important international audience awaited progress reports from the newly engaged Russian researchers. Someone of significance was truly interested in the laboratory achievements of each scientist. Throughout the world, the quest for such peer recognition in searching for the unknown has long been in the DNA of successful scientists.

Over the years, ISTC-funded projects in Russia have captured the attention

of important international colleagues who have been impressed by the achievements in searching for valuable new products and services. Among the projects
with results linked directly to concerns of the public are the following:

- Small Laser-Converter for Use in Dentistry
- Airborne Lasers for Detecting Pipeline Leaks
- New High-Molecular Weight Compounds for Long-Term Immobilization
  of Soils Contaminated with Radioactive Particles
- Artificial Neural Networks for Stereo-Displays of Financial Data
- Ion Milling of Resonator Gyroscopes for Oil Drilling
- Assessments of Contamination of the Sea from Radioactive Waste Disposal
- Plasma Reactor for Neutralization of Pesticides and Herbicides
- Demountable Couplings for Pipelines Using Titanium-Nickelide
- Live Oral Vaccine to Prevent Measles[2]

In 2011 Jun Sugimoto of Japan, chairman of the Scientific Advisory Committee (SAC) of the ISTC, set forth the view of nine members of the committee from
seven countries on the strengths of the center:

> The cumulative potential of the parties cooperating with the Russian Fed-
> eration through the ISTC represents more than 50 percent of the world's re-
> searchers and about 71 percent of the world's research and development ex-
> penditures, according to the latest UNESCO statistics. The ISTC Secretariat in
> Moscow, the only executive branch of a scientific international organization
> located in the capital of the Russian Federation, has accumulated through
> the years an excellent knowledge of the Russian science and technology po-
> tential and is well equipped for promoting cooperation between all parties
> through regular projects, partnerships, seminars, and other types of activi-
> ties. The need for international cooperation is still very much present in
> areas such as nuclear safety, global security, global disease surveillance and
> reduction, prevention and mitigation of risks. Exploiting the ISTC tools for
> reaching common goals related to these issues still made sense in 2011.[3]

UNFINISHED BUSINESS IN RUSSIA

Does it really matter to Western and Asian countries whether Russian civilian research rapidly moves forward? After all, Russia's contributions to international science, measured in terms of percentage of worldwide scientific

publications authored by Russian scientists, have been on the decline. Its profit-generating international patents and licenses have been few, and only a handful of recent Russian innovations have stirred economic interest abroad.

The country, to an extraordinary extent, relies on foreign technologies, often in preference to its own proven technologies. At the same time, large numbers of potential scientific leaders have deserted their laboratories for commercial offices that have little relevance to science. Many other experienced scientists spend less and less time at the bench. Notwithstanding the grand plans of the government to become an international technology powerhouse, it is questionable whether Russian research will soon make substantial inroads into the pattern of scientific decline that has been prevalent in recent years. A candid critique of the state of Russian science, prepared under the auspices of the U.S. Embassy in Moscow in 2010, was as follows:

> Experts believe that Russia wasted two decades by neglecting science and education. Many talented people have left and will never return, and entrenched institutional interests resist genuine internationalization and competition. Enormous investments in a few institutions and planned projects contrast unacceptably with low incomes of research personnel at Russian research and development institutions. Many scientists and engineers are troubled by the current philosophy of the government with respect to the research and development enterprise and ruthlessly criticize the need for initiating grandiose "innovation" projects, which are perceived as a colossal waste of sparse resources.[4]

By 2008, the Russian government had finally recognized the consequences of its declining competitive position, which was already far behind dozens of other countries also striving to establish economies based on advanced technologies—including, for example, Brazil, Finland, Israel, Singapore, Korea, and China. The government once again decided to try to close the gap. Its strategy for breaking into the ranks of the world's technology leaders has had five key components: (a) establishment of the firm Rusnano, with promises of an initial investment in nanotechnology by the government and interested businesses from home and abroad of ten billion dollars in order to earn thirty billion dollars annually through exports of nano-based products by 2015; (b) creation of the Skolkovo innovation center—Russia's new Silicon Valley, as discussed in chapter 6; (c) upgrading of twenty-nine leading universities to the status of national research universities and designation of knowledge hubs at seventy-six universities, with generous government financing of research, targeted on improving the transfer of technologies developed within universities to industry; (d) dozens of five-million-dollar megagrants to entice scientists from abroad as well as from Russia to lead efforts to establish new laboratories in Russian universities; and (e) anticipated accession to the World Trade Organization, which could level the playing field for international trade and enhance Russia's competitive position.

But even if movement to reach all targets embodied in these objectives is fully up to expectations, Russia will need many years to move up the ladder as one of the world's leading powers in the design and marketing of high-tech civilian products. An innovation culture—driven not only by money but more importantly by entrepreneurship, risk taking, personal satisfaction, and societal respect—is essential. And it will not emerge overnight.

Despite the harsh realities that currently characterize the capabilities and functioning of Russia's science infrastructure, it is in the interest of the international community that Russia's civilian science capacity moves forward on many fronts and indeed begins to thrive in some areas. Clearly military research and development will continue and will play an important role within Russian industry. But several arguments for encouraging international interest in Russian civilian science are as follows:

- Sustainable redirection of former weapons scientists in Russia is not yet complete, despite the claims of the government that the era of redirection is over. The potential weapons skills of many underemployed scientists may lie dormant and become rusty, but they have not deteriorated to the point of becoming unattractive to terrorists and renegade states. At the same time, newly emerging postdoctoral scientists are working in dual-use environments where money—whether clean or dirty—plays a strong role as a reward for achievements. These scientists continue to need motivation to confine their interests to peaceful objectives, including adequately equipped and properly managed laboratories where they can satisfy their peaceful ambitions.
- Enhancement of the traditions of scientific objectivity and contributions of technology to economic advancement can help ensure stability in a state that is still seeking its future course within an imperfect market economy. Russia will always devote significant resources to scientific research in the belief that at least some benefits will surely reach the population

and temper political rumblings. Science can become one of the few rudders that keep the country on course as it attempts to navigate through the struggles for economic rewards in a society where mistrust of government and of newly minted oligarchs is rampant.

- A disciplined cadre of nuclear, biological, and chemical researchers, gainfully employed in key industries, is essential to secure dangerous technologies. They can offer approaches that will reduce the likelihood of pipeline explosions, underground mining disasters, disease pandemics, or even another Chernobyl-scale catastrophe that reverberates throughout the world.

- Not to be neglected is the argument that other industrialized countries will benefit directly from Russian research. Some activities such as geological surveys, environmental studies, and investigations in polar regions have obvious benefits to researchers who have few opportunities to work in the environments encompassed within Russia. In many other areas, we regularly witness positive outcomes, not only because Russian laboratories are functioning at a high technical level, but also because well-qualified Russian researchers become international scientists working part-time in better equipped laboratories abroad where they can more easily move the frontiers of science forward.

The principal exception to the many pessimistic assessments of the potential of Russian science is the nation's success in space exploration. Momentum, which built up during the time of the USSR, continues to push researchers in Russia into opening the vast caverns of the distant unknown. Many Russian scientists working in other fields complain that too large a share of the government's research budget is devoted to space exploration. However, the general public will surely continue to take pride in Russia's role as a leader in space exploration.

Clearly, the Russian research system needs a continuing infusion of youthful expertise if the country is to become a wellspring of scientific discoveries of international significance. At the same time, Russia should be concerned about the transfer of Russian dual-use technologies abroad. The many unpredictable neighbors in the Middle East, close to the southern border of Russia, are reason enough to provide civilian employment alternatives for Russia's restless high-tech specialists who are eager to use their skills.

The newly emerging generation of scientists needs more hands-on training in laboratories as well as better preparation in economics, marketing, and management techniques. While most Russian research institutions may not thrive as sources of modern technologies in the near future, their specialists can play crucial roles in helping Russian enterprises and agencies select and effectively use Western technologies that are available. In short, the Russian government must address the size and shape of the research base of activities in the context of the economic, social, and environmental needs in the years ahead and not in the comfort zone of nostalgia of decades past.

Yes, Russia surely needs a strong high-tech research and applications base, and the international community needs a well-fed rather than a hungry Russian industrial bear that depends on the country's own laboratories for sustenance. But the nourishment provided to these laboratories by the ISTC will soon disappear, and new supplements are now essential.

NEW MECHANISMS FOR INTERNATIONAL COOPERATION

What approach should the Russian and other governments advocate to fill the void that will be left when the ISTC ceases operations in Russia? Is yet another international organization dedicated to promoting international scientific cooperation needed? Should the international community establish an ISTC 2.0 that simply modifies past approaches to recognize the interests of Russia while adding a few new components such as (a) providing scientific support for international organizations involved in nonproliferation activities, while also (b) mobilizing international experts to respond to nuclear disasters such as the incident at Fukushima, Japan?

I suggest two approaches that can serve the mutual interests of both the Russian government and many partner governments. Each approach can build on the ISTC experience.

First, many governments undoubtedly will continue to cooperate with Russia bilaterally in reducing the likelihood of proliferation and in taking advantage of the country's scientific strengths. As discussed in chapter 7, many bilateral programs have long been in place. Some of these efforts will increase in importance in the years ahead. Given the apparent mutual interests of Russia and its international partners in bilateral activities, an intergovernmental information and coordination center in Moscow could help improve the effectiveness of the separate, but related, efforts.

A modest center could be located within one of the Western embassies in

Moscow. Interested governments could second experienced science coordinators to the center, thereby ensuring diplomatic privileges and immunities for the staff. The new center could focus on measures to improve synchronization of bilateral approaches, with funding decisions concerning programs remaining in the hands of the political and financial offices of the respective governments.

The second approach, perhaps orchestrated by a secretariat located in close proximity to the coordination center, would have a more wide-ranging scope of activities than the ISTC but a smaller budget, with few large projects that exceed fifty thousand dollars. It would be a Center for Responsible Science, with funding of selected international activities its primary tool. The mission could include workshops, training programs, and demonstration projects directed to nonproliferation and the strengthening of the scientific infrastructure of Russia and other participating countries. It could also cover travel costs of scientific exchanges of special interest.

To be effective, this Center for Responsible Science would require (a) a champion within the Russian government, such as the minister of education and science, (b) provision of funds by Russia to match international contributions, and (c) a new international agreement for carrying out activities in Russia and in partner countries as appropriate. Unlike the ISTC Agreement, a new agreement could give Russia status and funding responsibilities equal to those of the other major parties to the agreement. Russian scientists would have reciprocal access to facilities in other countries that are involved in joint efforts, comparable to the foreign access to facilities in Russia needed to carry out cooperative projects. While the programs would be relatively small, they would focus on important issues, and particularly those that touch on difficult aspects of dual use, export control, and global science. A reasonable overall budget would be twenty million dollars annually, with one half provided by the Russian government, including both cash contributions to the center and direct payments to Russian participants in cooperative activities.

Why should this Center for Responsible Science be located in Moscow rather than in another country? With its huge land mass, extensive natural resources, and lengthy maritime routes, Russia is involved in almost every type of global issue on the international agenda. We know too that the country will retain a large weapons arsenal, related technological infrastructure, and widespread dual-use expertise. Russia's engagement in achieving global security and prosperity through science is a very good fit with Russian interests at home and abroad and offers transparency important to the West. When international activities are orchestrated from other countries, the likelihood of active Russian participation drops dramatically.

ISTC'S FUTURE ACTIVITIES IN EURASIA

Beyond Russia, leaders of other states that gained independence with the collapse of the USSR and have become ISTC members, except for Belarus, appear united in their desires to retain the center in its current form without participation by Russia. They would like to continue to use the ISTC mechanism for establishing and pursuing joint efforts without taking a back seat to Russia's interests. At least one of the countries—Kazakhstan—has expressed a strong interest in providing the new headquarters for the center, building on the branch office of the ISTC that has been functioning in Almaty for many years. The government has identified appropriate facilities for the ISTC Secretariat in Almaty. In June 2011, the other members of the center welcomed this demonstration of interest. By the end of the year, the government of Kazakhstan had repeated the offer to host the ISTC headquarters. The ISTC leadership then supported a budget for preparatory work on the relocation proposed but had not taken a position on this offer. Some senior Russian scientists who wanted a new type of affiliation with the center argued for relocating the secretariat to Kiev, perhaps side by side with the Science and Technology Center for Ukraine.

The new countries beyond Russia are adjusting to the scope of their commitments as partners in proliferation prevention. At the same time, they struggle daily against economic problems within their own borders, and the countries are still categorized as assistance-eligible within the international development field. This status often circumvents the need for the international benefactors to pay taxes and customs duties, as host countries quickly extend appropriate tax exemptions. Also, when supported by international assistance programs, the host institutions often have preferential rights to intellectual property that emerges from collaborative activities. There seems to be little doubt that the countries of the region that will remain ISTC members will continue to welcome the center's activities in their countries and will provide support for future projects to the extent that they have matching resources.

A POSTSCRIPT ON RUSSIA'S FUTURE

Several aspects of Russia's technological future are clear and go to the heart of the ISTC mission. Russia will retain a sizeable nuclear military establishment to deter adversaries and gain recognition at the tables of power throughout the world. The stockpiles of nuclear weapons and materials throughout the country will remain for many decades. Their safe and reliable storage of some nuclear materials will continue to raise concerns around the world. Russia's ongoing pursuit of space exploration will make use of systems with dual-use capabilities. Russian chemists and biologists will continue to carry out research that, if misdirected, could be of great concern.

The ISTC has provided a rallying point for those Russian specialists who have wanted to contribute to positive development of their country and avoid unsavory international entanglements. The center has mobilized a variety of government officials from many countries who believe that investing in the future of these specialists was and still is an investment in the future of collective security and a safer world. In short, the ISTC has been the birthplace of approaches that have helped lay the groundwork for important international peace and security efforts.

Many international collaborators in ISTC projects in Russia hold out hope that the admirable goals of the center can be pursued in Russia through other channels. The center has been far from perfect, sometimes neglecting interests of key Russian scientists or responding too slowly to windows of opportunity that closed quickly. It too often has built false expectations as to its funding capabilities, particularly with its promises to support sustainability efforts of a few key research centers. And it could not counter the widespread perception that the return on investment in its commercialization activities was very low. Despite such shortcomings, the uniqueness of the center has made a significant difference in enhancing security and promoting science in Russia and globally.

The officials who will manage future related efforts should look back at the lessons that were learned during the ISTC experiment. They can benefit from the approaches that were developed, adopted, and sometimes rejected. They will soon understand why the ISTC was able to successfully promote responsible science—the core concept that will determine the future of the world.

NOBEL PEACE PRIZE FOR THE ISTC?

According to an authoritative report circulating in Moscow during 2010, the ISTC was one of several hundred organizations and individuals that were nominated for the Nobel Peace Prize in 2009. But important payoffs from ISTC activities have yet to be realized. Most research outcomes require incubation periods until they enter the mainstreams of society. Also, governments only slowly accept changes in their policies involving sensitive technical areas, such as those that the ISTC has explored. The ISTC experiments of the past will surely inform the solutions of many problems of the future.

The alumni of the center's programs will carry their experiences down many avenues in ways that will make the world a more hospitable planet. By 2015, metrics will surely be devised to improve measurements of the impacts of nonproliferation programs and payoffs from high-tech research. Assessment of achievements of the ISTC should then make the center a strong contender for the international prize for peace.

EPILOGUE

Tsar Vyslav rejoiced greatly to see his two sons. To Tsarevitch Dimitri, who had brought him the firebird, he gave half of his Tsardom, and Tsarevitch Vasilii was to wed the Tsarevna, Helen the Beautiful.
—"Tsarevitch Ivan, the Firebird, and the Gray Wolf"

NOBEL PEACE PRIZE OR NOT, government officials around the world have recognized the unique role that the ISTC has played in restraining flocks of nuclear firebirds from flights into dangerous nesting areas.

The Russian government has decreed that the country's involvement in the activities of the ISTC is no longer necessary. The other member states will continue to embrace the work of the center, and hopefully Russia will preserve and broaden the many positive imprints of the center throughout the country. These impacts have demonstrated time and again that Anton Chekov foresaw the global trajectories of learning many decades ago when he prophetically stated, "There is no national science. What is national is no longer science."[1]

The ISTC has truly made a difference for Russian science. More than thirty thousand former weapons scientists and thousands of civilian partners with dual-use skills have participated in projects supported by the center. The proliferation threat has receded dramatically. And Russian scientists have time and time again demonstrated that Chekov's prophecy is spot on.

Fifteen years ago my earlier book titled *Moscow DMZ: The Story of the International Effort to Convert Russian Weapons Science to Peaceful Purposes* provided a suitable summary of the intent of this companion book as follows:

> *Moscow DMZ* has been a first attempt to capture and evaluate the performance data from the ISTC experiment. Now, the challenge is to package the conclusions in appropriate security, political, and economic envelopes. The objective must be to help policymakers use the best of the ISTC experiences in addressing the future problems of cooperation with the countries that emerged from the former Soviet Union, in supporting conversion at many

levels in Russia, in countering the proliferation of weapons of mass destruction and their delivery systems, and in improving approaches to fostering economic development throughout the world.[2]

This book provides a starting point to achievement of these goals. I invite colleagues from around the world to join the search for new tools of science to respond to the never-ending challenges of increased international security and economic prosperity on all continents.

For those of you who have made your way to this final page, I would welcome your suggestions as to how the international community can design a second experiment that builds on the achievements of ISTC 1.0. You can reach me at campubs@msn.com.

Agreement Establishing an International Science and Technology Center

The European Atomic Energy Community and European Economic Community, acting as one party, and the United States of America, Japan and the Russian Federation:

Reaffirming the need to prevent the proliferation of technologies and expertise related to weapons of mass destruction—nuclear, chemical, and biological weapons;

Taking note of the present critical period in the states of the Commonwealth of Independent States (hereinafter referred to as "CIS") and Georgia, a period that includes the transition to a market economy, the developing process of disarmament, and the conversion of industrial-technical potential from military to peaceful endeavors;

Recognizing, in this context, the need to create an International Science and Technology Center that would minimize incentives to engage in activities that could result in such proliferation, by supporting and assisting the activities for peaceful purposes of weapons scientists and engineers in the Russian Federation and, if interested, in other states of the CIS and Georgia;

Recognizing the need to contribute, through the Center's projects and activities, to the transition of the states of the CIS and Georgia to market-based economies and to support research and development for peaceful purposes;

Desiring that Center projects provide impetus and support to participating scientists and engineers in developing long-term career opportunities, which will strengthen the scientific research and development capacity of the states of the CIS and Georgia; and

Realizing that the success of the Center will require strong support from governments, foundations, academic and scientific institutions, and other inter-governmental and non-governmental organizations;

Have agreed as follows:

ARTICLE I

There is hereby established the International Science and Technology Center (hereinafter referred to as the "Center") as an inter-governmental organization. Each Party shall facilitate, in its territory, the activities of the Center. In order to achieve its objectives, the Center shall have, in accordance with the laws and regulations of the Parties, the legal capacity to contract, to acquire and dispose of immovable and movable property, and to institute and respond to legal proceedings.

ARTICLE II

A. The Center shall develop, approve, finance, and monitor science and technology projects for peaceful purposes, which are to be carried out primarily at institutions and facilities located in the Russian Federation and, if interested, in other states of the CIS and Georgia.

B. The objectives of the Center shall be:

 i. To give weapons scientists and engineers, particularly those who possess knowledge and skills related to weapons of mass destruction or missile delivery systems, in the Russian Federation and, if interested, in other states of the CIS and Georgia, opportunities to redirect their talents to peaceful activities; and

 ii. To contribute thereby through its projects and activities: to the solution of national or international technical problems; and to the wider goals of reinforcing the transition to market-based economies responsive to civil needs, of supporting basic and applied research and technology development, inter alia, in the fields of environmental protection, energy production, and nuclear safety, and of promoting the further integration of scientists of the states of the CIS and Georgia into the international scientific community.

ARTICLE III

In order to achieve its objectives, the Center is authorized to:

 i. Promote and support, by use of funds or otherwise, science and technology projects in accordance with Article II of this Agreement;

 ii. Monitor and audit Center projects in accordance with Article VIII of this Agreement;

 iii. Establish appropriate forms of cooperation with governments, inter-governmental organizations, non-governmental organizations (which shall, for the purposes of this Agreement, include the private sector), and programs;

 iv. Receive funds or donations from governments, inter-governmental organizations, and non-governmental organizations;

v.   Establish branch offices as appropriate in interested states of the CIS and Georgia; and

vi.   Engage in other activities as may be agreed upon by all the Parties.

ARTICLE IV

A.   The Center shall have a Governing Board and a Secretariat, consisting of an Executive Director, Deputy Executive Directors, and such other staff as may be necessary, in accordance with the Statute of the Center.

B.   The Governing Board shall be responsible for:

i.   Determining the Center's policy and its own rules of procedure;

ii.   Providing overall guidance and direction to the Secretariat;

iii.   Approving the Center's operating budget;

iv.   Governing the financial and other affairs of the Center, including approving procedures for the preparation of the Center's budget, drawing up of accounts and auditing thereof;

v.   Formulating general criteria and priorities for the approval of projects;

vi.   Approving projects in accordance with Article VI;

vii.   Adopting the Statute and other implementing arrangements as necessary; and

viii.   Other functions assigned to it by this Agreement or necessary for the implementation of this Agreement.

Decisions of the Governing Board shall be by consensus of all Parties on the Board, subject to the conditions and terms determined pursuant to Article V, except as provided otherwise in this Agreement.

C.   Each of the four Signatory Parties shall be represented by a single vote on the Governing Board. Each shall appoint no more than two representatives to the Governing Board within seven (7) days after entry into force of this Agreement.

D.   The Parties shall establish a Scientific Advisory Committee, made up of representatives to be nominated by the Parties, to give to the Board expert scientific and other necessary professional advice within forty-five (45) days of every project proposal's submission to the Center; to advise the Board on the fields of research to be encouraged; and to provide any other advice that may be required by the Board.

E.   The Governing Board shall adopt a Statute in implementation of this Agreement. The Statute shall establish:

i.   The structure of the Secretariat;

ii.   The process for selecting, developing, approving, financing, carrying out, and monitoring projects;

iii.   Procedures for the preparation of the Center's budget, drawing up of accounts, and auditing thereof;

iv. Appropriate guidelines on intellectual property rights resulting from Center projects and on the dissemination of project results;

v. Procedures governing the participation of governments, inter-governmental organizations, and non-governmental organizations in Center projects;

vi. Personnel policies; and

vii. Other arrangements necessary for the implementation of this Agreement.

ARTICLE V

The Governing Board shall have the discretion and exclusive power to expand its membership to include representatives appointed by Parties that accede to this Agreement, on such conditions and terms as the Board may determine. Parties not represented on the Governing Board and inter-governmental and non-governmental organizations may be invited to participate in Board deliberations, in a non-voting capacity.

ARTICLE VI

Each project submitted for approval by the Governing Board shall be accompanied by the written concurrence of the state or states in which the work is to be carried out. In addition to the prior agreement of that state or those states, the approval of projects shall require the consensus of Parties on the Governing Board, subject to the conditions and terms determined pursuant to Article V, other than such Parties that are states of the CIS and Georgia.

ARTICLE VII

A. Projects approved by the Governing Board may be financed or supported by the Center, or by governments, inter-governmental organizations, or non-governmental organizations, directly or through the Center. Such financing and support of approved projects shall be provided on terms and conditions specified by those providing it, which terms and conditions shall be consistent with this Agreement.

B. Representatives of the Parties on the Board and personnel of the Center Secretariat shall be ineligible for project grants and may not directly benefit from any project grant.

ARTICLE VIII

A. The Center shall have the right, within the Russian Federation and other interested states of the CIS and Georgia in which the work is to be carried out:

i.   To examine on-site Center project activities, materials, supplies, use of funds, and project-related services and use of funds, upon its notification or, in addition, as specified in a project agreement;

ii. To inspect or audit, upon its request, any records or other documentation in connection with Center project activities and use of funds, wherever such records or documentation are located, during the period in which the Center provides the financing, and for a period thereafter as determined in a project agreement.

The written concurrence required in Article VI shall include the agreement, of both the state or states of the CIS or Georgia in which the work is to be carried out and the recipient institution, to provide the Center with access necessary for auditing and monitoring the project, as required by this paragraph.

B. Any Party represented on the Governing Board shall also have the rights described in paragraph (A), coordinated through the Center, with regard to projects it finances in whole or in part, either directly or through the Center.

C. If it is determined that the terms and conditions of a project have not been respected, the Center or a financing government or organization may, having informed the Board of its reasons, terminate the project and take appropriate steps in accordance with the terms of the project agreement.

ARTICLE IX

A. The Headquarters of the Center shall be located in the Russian Federation.

B. By way of providing material support to the Center, the Government of the Russian Federation shall provide at its own expense a facility suitable for use by the Center, along with maintenance, utilities, and security for the facility.

C. In the Russian Federation, the Center shall have the status of a legal person and, in that capacity, shall be entitled to contract, to acquire and dispose of immovable and movable property, and to institute and respond to legal proceedings.

ARTICLE X

In the Russian Federation:

i.

a. In determining profits of the Center subject to taxation, funds received by the Center from its founders and sponsors—governments, intergovernmental organizations, and non-governmental organizations—and any interest arising from keeping those funds in banks in the Russian Federation, shall be excluded;

b. The Center, or any branch thereof, shall not be subject to any taxation on property that is subject to taxation under the tax laws of the Russian Federation;

c. Commodities, supplies, and other property provided or utilized in connection with the Center and its projects and activities may be imported, exported from, or used in the Russian Federation free from any tariffs, dues, customs duties, import taxes, and other similar taxes or charges imposed by the Russian Federation;

d. Personnel of the Center who are not Russian nationals shall be exempt from payment of the income tax in the Russian Federation for physical persons;

e. Funds received by legal entities, including Russian scientific organizations, in connection with the Center's projects and activities, shall be excluded in determining the profits of these organizations for the purpose of tax liability;

f. Funds received by persons, in particular scientists or specialists, in connection with the Center's projects or activities shall not be included in those persons' taxable income;

ii.

a. The Center, governments, inter-governmental organizations, and non-governmental organizations shall have the right to move funds related to the Center and its projects or activities, other than Russian currency, into or out of the Russian Federation without restriction. Each shall have the right to so move only amounts not exceeding the total amount it moved into the Russian Federation.

b. To finance the Center and its projects and activities, the Center shall be entitled, for itself and on behalf of the entities referred to in subparagraph (ii)(a), to sell foreign currency on the internal currency market of the Russian Federation.

iii. Personnel of non-Russian organizations taking part in any Center project or activity and who are not Russian nationals shall be exempt from the payment of any customs duties and charge upon personal or household goods imported into, exported from, or used in the Russian Federation for the personal use of such personnel or members of their families.

ARTICLE XI

A. The Parties shall closely cooperate in order to facilitate the settlement of legal proceedings and claims under this Article.

B. Unless otherwise agreed, the Government of the Russian Federation shall, in respect of legal proceedings and claims by Russian nationals or organizations, other than contractual claims, arising out of the acts or omissions of the Center or its personnel done in the performance of the Center's activities:

    i.   Not bring any legal proceedings against the Center and its personnel;

    ii. Assume responsibility for dealing with legal proceedings and claims brought by the aforementioned against the Center and its personnel;

    iii. Hold the Center and its personnel harmless in respect of legal proceedings and claims referred to in subparagraph (ii) above.

C. The provisions of this Article shall not prevent compensation or indemnity available under applicable international agreements or national law of any state.

D. Nothing in paragraph (B) shall be construed to prevent legal proceedings or claims against Russian nationals or permanent residents of the Russian Federation.

ARTICLE XII

A. Personnel of the Governments of the States or the European Communities that are Parties present in the Russian Federation in connection with the Center or its projects and activities shall be accorded, by the Government of the Russian Federation, status equivalent to that accorded to administrative and technical staff under the Vienna Convention on Diplomatic Relations of 18 April 1961.

B. Personnel of the Center shall be accorded, by the Government of the Russian Federation, the privileges and immunities usually accorded to officials of international organizations, namely:

    i.   Immunity from arrest, detention, and legal process, including criminal, civil, and administrative jurisdiction, in respect of words spoken or written and all acts performed by them in their official capacity;

    ii. Exemption from any income, social security, or other taxation, duties or other charges, except those that are normally incorporated in the price of goods or paid for services rendered;

    iii. Immunity from social security provisions;

    iv. Immunity from immigration restrictions and from alien registration;

    v.   Right to import their furniture and effects, at the time of first taking up their post, free of any Russian tariffs, dues, customs duties, import taxes, and other similar taxes or charges.

C. Any Party may notify the Executive Director of any person, other than those in paragraphs (A) and (D), who will be in the Russian Federation in connection with the Center's projects and activities. A Party making such a notification shall inform such persons of their duty to respect the laws and regulations of the Russian Federation. The Executive Director shall notify the Government of the Russian Federation, which shall accord to such persons the benefits in subparagraph (B)(ii)–(v) and a status adequate for carrying out the project or activity.

D. Representatives of the Parties on the Governing Board, the Executive Director, and the Deputy Executive Directors shall be accorded by the Government of the Russian Federation, in addition to the privileges and immunities listed in paragraphs (A) and (B) of this Article, the privileges, immunities, exemptions, and facilities generally accorded to the representatives of members and executive heads of international organizations in accordance with international law.

E. Nothing in this Article shall require the Government of the Russian Federation to provide the privileges and immunities provided in paragraphs (A), (B), and (D) of this Article to its nationals or its permanent residents.

F. Without prejudice to the privileges, immunities, and other benefits provided above, it is the duty of all persons enjoying privileges, immunities, and benefits under this Article to respect the laws and regulations of the Russian Federation.

G. Nothing in this Agreement shall be construed to derogate from privileges, immunities, and other benefits granted to personnel described in paragraphs (A) to (D) under other agreements.

ARTICLE XIII

Any state desiring to become Party to this Agreement shall notify the Governing Board through the Executive Director. The Governing Board shall provide such a state with certified copies of this Agreement through the Executive Director. Upon approval by the Governing Board, that state shall be permitted to accede to this Agreement. This Agreement shall enter into force for the state on the thirtieth (30th) day after the date on which its instrument of accession is deposited. In the event that a state or states of the CIS and Georgia accede to this Agreement, that state or those states shall comply with the obligations undertaken by the Government of the Russian Federation in Articles VIII, IX(C), and X–XII.

ARTICLE XIV

Although nothing in this Agreement limits the rights of the Parties to pursue projects without resort to the Center, the Parties shall make their best efforts to use the Center when pursuing projects of character and objectives appropriate to the Center.

ARTICLE XV

A. This Agreement shall be subject to review by the Parties two years after entry into force. This review shall take into account the financial commitments and payments of the Parties.

B. This Agreement may be amended by written agreement of all the Parties.

C. Any Party may withdraw from this Agreement six months after written notification to the other Parties.

ARTICLE XVI

Any question or dispute relating to the application or interpretation of this Agreement shall be the subject of consultation between the Parties.

ARTICLE XVII

With a view to financing projects as soon as possible, the four Signatories shall establish necessary interim procedures until the adoption of the Statute by the Governing Board. These shall include, in particular, the appointment of an Executive Director and necessary staff and the establishment of procedures for the submission, review, and approval of projects.

ARTICLE XVIII

A. This Agreement shall be open for signature by the European Atomic Energy Community and European Economic Community, acting as one party, the United States of America, Japan and the Russian Federation.
B. Each signatory shall notify the others through diplomatic channels that it has completed all internal procedures necessary to be bound by this Agreement.
C. This Agreement shall enter into force upon the thirtieth (30th) day after the date of the last notification described in paragraph (B).

IN WITNESS WHEREOF the undersigned, being duly authorized thereto, have signed this Agreement.

Done at Moscow on 27 November 1992, in the Danish, Dutch, English, French, German, Greek, Italian, Japanese, Portuguese, Russian and Spanish languages each text being equally authentic.

#   #   #

Protocol on the Provisional Application of the Agreement Establishing an International Science and Technology Center

The United States of America, Japan, the Russian Federation, and the European Atomic Energy Community and the European Community, acting as one party, hereinafter referred to as the "Signatory Parties," recognizing the importance of the Agreement Establishing an International Science and Technology Center, signed in Moscow on November 27, 1992, hereinafter referred to as the "Agreement,"

HAVE AGREED AS FOLLOWS:

ARTICLE I

1. The Agreement shall be provisionally applied in accordance with its terms by the Signatory Parties from the date of the last notification of the Signatory Parties of the completion of internal procedures necessary for entry into force of this Protocol.
2. The Agreement shall be applied provisionally until its entry into force in accordance with article XVIII thereof.

ARTICLE II

The Agreement shall be subject to review by the parties two years after the beginning of the provisional application of the Agreement notwithstanding the provisions of Article XV(A) of the Agreement.

ARTICLE III

Any of the parties may withdraw from this Protocol six months from the date on which written notification is provided to the other parties.

ARTICLE IV

1. Any state desiring to become a party to the Agreement in accordance with Article XIII thereof, after fulfilling the conditions set forth in that Article, and after completing its internal procedures that will be necessary for accession to the Agreement, shall notify the Signatory Parties of its intention to provisionally apply the Agreement in accordance with this Protocol.
2. The provisional application by that state shall begin from the date of notification referred to in Paragraph (1) of this Article.

Done in Moscow on December 27, 1993, in the English and Russian languages, each text being equally authentic.

For:

The United States of America, Japan, The Russian Federation, and The European Atomic Energy Community and the European Community (with four appropriate signatures).

# # #

President Dmitry Medvedev's Decree No. 534, August 11, 2010

"On the Withdrawal of the Russian Federation from the Nov. 27, 1992, Agreement on the Establishment of the International Science and Technology Center and from the Dec. 27, 1992, Protocol on the Temporary Application of the Agreement on ISTC"

1. The President accepts the proposal of the Government of Russia on the Russian Federation's withdrawal from the Agreement from Nov. 27, 1992, on establishment of the ISTC and from the Protocol on Temporary Application of the ISTC Agreement with the goal to cease participation of the Russian Federation in the implementation of the above international acts in accordance with their conditions, including financial obligations and payments by the Russian Federation.

2. The state corporation Rosatom, together with the other federal organs of executive power and organizations, should conduct the work related to withdrawal of the Russian Federation from the Agreement and Protocol.

3. The Ministry of Foreign Affairs, with participation of Rosatom, is to notify each party of the Agreement and Protocol through diplomatic channels on the decision.

4. Consider the Agreement and Protocol to cease to be in force six months after the day that written notification is provided to the other parties.

President Dmitry Medvedev

# # #

Diplomatic Note on Russian Withdrawal from the ISTC Agreement and Protocol

To: Executive Director ISTC
Moscow # 13 July 2011

The Ministry of Foreign Affairs of the Russian Federation extends its respect to the Executive Director of the International Science and Technology Center (hereinafter—ISTC) and has the honor to report on the following, referring to the Agreement Establishing the International Science and Technology Center of 27 November 1992 (hereinafter—the Agreement) and to the Protocol of 27 December 1993 on the Provisional Application of the Agreement, establishing the International Science and Technology Center (hereinafter—the Protocol).

The Russian Party hereby informs you of its intention to terminate the provisional application of the Agreement and to withdraw from the Protocol. These actions will be taken in compliance with the provisions of both the Agreement and the Protocol upon completion of the last ISTC-funded project currently under implementation in Russia, to take place by mid-2015. Termination of the provisional application of the Agreement by the Russian Federation and its withdrawal from the Protocol will be exercised with the observation of mutual rights and obligations, arising from the Agreement and the Protocol.

The Ministry avails itself of this opportunity to renew to the ISTC Executive Director the assurance of its highest consideration.

Stamp

# # #

ISTC Project Funding and Beneficiary Scientists, 1994–2011

Project Funding by Source

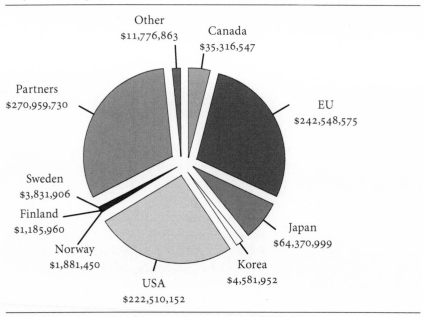

Other
$11,776,863

Canada
$35,316,547

Partners
$270,959,730

EU
$242,548,575

Sweden
$3,831,906

Finland
$1,185,960

Norway
$1,881,450

Japan
$64,370,999

Korea
$4,581,952

USA
$222,510,152

Information provided by ISTC Secretariat, January 2012

Partner Project Funding by Source

Party	Type of Partner Company	No. of Projects	Partner Funding ($)
United States	TOTAL	533	212,719,557
	G	500	206,616,595
	NG	33	6,102,962
Japan	TOTAL	64	7,501,167
	G	16	2,154,953
	NG	48	5,346,214
European Union	TOTAL	132	48,257,871
	G	73	37,012,902
	NG	59	11,244,969
Korea	TOTAL	10	1,904,929
	G	6	1,580,000
	NG	4	324,929
Canada	TOTAL	5	576,206
	G	1	20,000
	NG	4	556,206
TOTAL:	TOTAL	741	270,959,730
	G	596	247,384,450
	NG	148	23,575,280

Note: G = government partner; NG = nongovernment partner
Information provided by ISTC Secretariat, January 2012

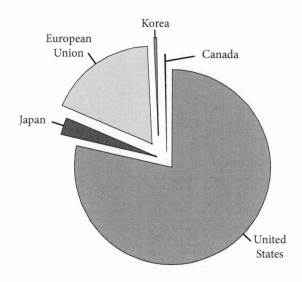

Project Funding by Beneficiary per Country

Country	No. of Funded Projects	Allocated Funds ($)
Armenia	168	40,759,810
Belarus	99	25,318,422
Georgia	143	29,270,473
Kazakhstan	184	66,244,917
Kyrgyzstan	86	22,215,795
Russia	2,034	665,646,146
Tajikistan	36	9,444,275
Ukraine	1	64,296
TOTAL:	2,751	858,964,133

Information provided by ISTC Secretariat, January 2012

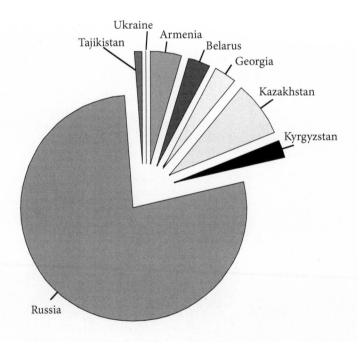

Project Funding by Technology Area

Technology Area	No. of Funded Projects	Allocated Funds ($)
Agriculture	87	33,335,844
Biotechnology	309	117,610,958
Chemistry	200	53,786,313
Environment	437	135,366,567
Fission Reactors	272	93,625,903
Fusion	51	15,520,755
Information and Communications	107	28,536,916
Instrumentation	135	37,306,860
Manufacturing Technology	75	21,376,419
Materials	214	69,133,994
Medicine	232	83,895,569
Nonnuclear Energy	63	21,990,981
Other	18	2,798,135
Other Basic Sciences	29	6,479,930
Physics	418	108,541,805
Space, Aircraft, and Surface Transportation	104	29,657,184
TOTAL:	2,751	858,964,133

Information provided by ISTC Secretariat, January 2012

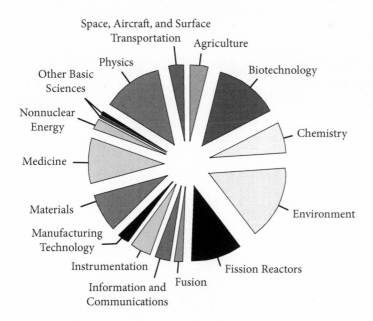

Grants paid by ISTC to Beneficiary Scientists in 2011 and Total—by Country

Country	Number of Scientists	Grant Payments ($)
Armenia	3,307	26,280,956
Belarus	1,816	13,990,919
Georgia	2,392	19,210,696
Kazakhstan	4,591	34,427,098
Kyrgyzstan	1,308	8,643,534
Russia	60,575	422,587,458
Tajikistan	542	4,301,898
TOTAL:	74,531	529,442,559

Information provided by ISTC Secretariat, January 2012

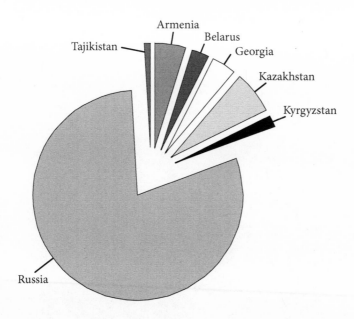

Trend in Funding for ISTC Projects in Russia

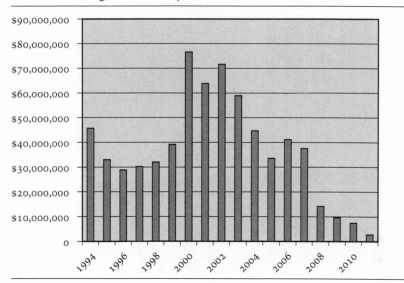

Information provided by ISTC Secretariat, January 2012

Allocation of ISTC Project Funds by Topic (as of April 1, 2011)

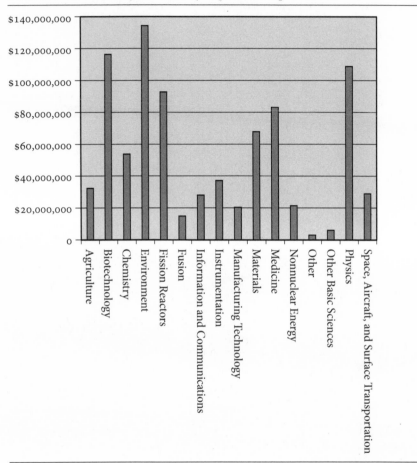

Information provided by ISTC Secretariat, May 2011

NOTES

CHAPTER ONE. A Unique Experiment for Security and Prosperity

1. Glenn E. Schweitzer, *Moscow DMZ: The Story of the International Effort to Convert Russian Weapons Science to Peaceful Purposes* (Armonk, N.Y.: M. E. Sharpe, 1996), 17.

2. Ibid., 35.

3. Ibid., 69.

4. Global Security, www.globalsecurity.org/wmd/world/Syria/cw.htm, accessed Nov. 2011.

5. Sergey Strokan and Elena Chernenko, "Soviet Physics Set Forth in IAEA Report," *Kommersant*, Nov. 10, 2011, 8 (in Russian). Additional information provided by ISTC Secretariat, Nov. 2011.

6. Schweitzer, *Moscow DMZ*, 64.

7. In 2007 the ISTC Secretariat developed an impressive new vision for the center that was never formally adopted by the ISTC Governing Board.

8. Comments at an informal meeting in Washington, D.C., with Minister of Education and Science Andrey Fursenko, June 2010.

9. An informal World Bank assessment of science and technology capabilities, weaknesses, and priority needs is reported in a working manuscript titled "From Knowledge to Wealth: Transforming Russian Science and Technology for a Modern Knowledge Economy," Mar. 1, 2002. This assessment, together with supporting documentation, was prepared by the World Bank office in Moscow under the leadership of Alfred Watkins, Sylvie Bossoutrot, and Ljudmilla Poznanskaya.

10. "From Knowledge to Wealth."

CHAPTER TWO. Off to a Fast Start

1. *ISTC Annual Report, 1994* (Moscow: ISTC), 5. Annual reports are available at www .istc.ru.

2. *ISTC Annual Report, 1997*, 6.

3. Glenn E. Schweitzer, *Moscow DMZ: The Story of the International Effort to Convert Russian Weapons Science to Peaceful Purposes* (Armonk, N.Y.: M. E. Sharpe, 2006),

275. The comments in the text expand on the brief discussion of the issues in this reference.

4. The section that follows is based on ISTC annual reports for 1994–2000.

5. *ISTC Annual Report, 1994*, 9.

6. *ISTC Annual Report, 1998*, 13.

7. Information provided by the ISTC Secretariat, March 2011.

8. *ISTC Annual Report, 1998*, 9–11.

9. *ISTC Annual Report, 2000*, 14.

10. Ronald F. Lehman, "Statement by the Chairman of the ISTC Governing Board," *ISTC Annual Report, 2001*, 4.

11. *ISTC Annual Report, 1996*, 13.

12. National Research Council, *An Assessment of the International Science and Technology Center* (Washington, D.C.: National Academy Press, 1996), 1.

13. Ibid, 15.

14. Ibid, 13.

15. Ibid, 19–23.

16. General Accountability Office, *State Department Oversight of Science Centers Program* (Washington, D.C.: GAO, May 2001).

17. Ibid.

18. Roger Cashmere, research director, CERN, *ISTC Annual Report, 1999*, 14.

CHAPTER THREE. An Era of Euphoria

1. *ISTC Annual Report, 2006* (Moscow: ISTC), 9.

2. The leaders of the American Chamber of Commerce in Moscow provided an important perspective on these trends in discussions with the author, Mar. 2003.

3. Andrey Fursenko, comments at a meeting in Moscow involving leaders of the Russian government and the Russian Academy of Sciences, draft transcript, Apr. 24, 2003.

4. Ibid.

5. ISTC, "Instructions for Proposal Preparation," Mar. 2007.

6. IC2 Institute, University of Texas at Austin, "ISTC 2020: Toward Global Security and Sustainability," draft report, Mar. 19, 2003, 85.

7. *ISTC Annual Report, 2008*, 8.

8. ISTC, Partner Brochure, 2004, 5.

9. Ibid, 4.

10. IC2 Institute, "ISTC 2012," 95.

11. ISTC, "More than Money," informal memo prepared by ISTC Secretariat, July 12, 2002.

12. ISTC, "Plugging into the Power of Russia and CIS Innovation," 2008, 3–6.

13. Comments by science policy expert who had participated in ISTC activities, Moscow, Oct. 2011.

14. Data provided by ISTC Secretariat, Apr. 2011.

15. *ISTC Annual Report, 2006*, 9.

16. ISTC, *Summary Report on the Main Results of the International Science and Technology Center during the Period 1994–2010* (Moscow: ISTC, Nov. 2009), 5.

17. *ISTC Annual Report, 2007*, 8–16.

18. ISTC, *Summary Report*, 5.

19. Peter J. Idenburg, *Sustainability of ISTC Party Funded Projects* (Brussels: European Commission, Directorate-General for Research, 2004), 3.

20. IC2 Institute, "ISTC 2020."

21. Idenburg, *Sustainability of ISTC Party Funded Projects*, 4.

22. ISTC, Vision Statement/Strategic Plan, May 14, 2007.

23. Ibid.

*

CHAPTER FOUR. Unraveling of the Moscow Science Center

1. *ISTC Annual Report, 2007* (Moscow: ISTC), 26.

2. ISTC, "Progress Report on Implementation of Existing Sustainability Plans," June 2011.

3. Ibid.

4. PowerPoint presentation by ISTC Secretariat, Apr. 2011.

5. PowerPoint presentation #1 by ISTC Secretariat, May 2010.

6. Ibid.

7. Ibid.

8. Ibid.

9. PowerPoint presentation #2 by ISTC Secretariat, May 2010.

10. Ibid.

11. PowerPoint presentation by ISTC Secretariat, Apr. 2011.

12. Ibid.

13. Ibid.

14. Information provided by ISTC Secretariat, June 2011.

15. "Over 300 Gather to Celebrate ISTC's 15 Years," ISTC e-Newsletter, issue 007, Jan. 2010.

16. Presidential Decree no. 534, Aug. 11, 2010. Reported by *RIA Novosti*, Aug. 16, 2010.

17. Article 3 of ISTC Provisional Protocol and Article 15 of ISTC Agreement.

18. Conversation with a participant in the meeting of the G8 Global Partnership in

Berlin during the summer of 2006 when officials of the Russian Ministry of Foreign Affairs announced that redirection of Russian scientists was a concern of the past and was no longer relevant.

19. Text of statement provided by ISTC Secretariat, June 2010.

20. Comments by Russian colleague involved in Russian decision making, May 2010.

21. Comments by Russian colleague who participated in meeting, Apr. 15, 2010.

22. ISTC Secretariat, June 26, 2011.

23. Ibid.

24. Ibid.

25. Ibid.

26. Ibid.

27. Public statement of the minister of finance, provided by the U.S. Embassy in Moscow, Feb. 21, 2010.

28. Letters available at ISTC Secretariat, Nov. 2009.

29. Dmitry Medvedev's Video Blog, http://blog. Kremlin.ru/theme/28?page=3 (accessed Aug. 25, 2010).

30. G8, "Renewed Commitment for Freedom and Democracy," May 26–27, 2009, G8 Summit, Deauville, France.

31. Email comment by senior official of U.S. National Security Council staff circulated widely in Washington, D.C., Sept. 2010.

32. Richard Lugar, Madrid speech, released by Lugar's office, Nov. 8, 2010.

33. Options developed by ISTC Secretariat, Apr. 2011.

CHAPTER FIVE. The World Market for High-Tech Expertise

1. UNESCO Regional Office for Science and Technology for Europe, *Brain Drain in Russia: Problems, Perspectives, and Ways of Regulation* (Venice: UNESCO, Nov. 1994), 51.

2. Ibid.

3. Daniel Clery, "Publications and Expats Warn of Russia's Dangerous Decline," *Science* 327, no. 5966 (Feb. 5, 2010): 631.

4. National Research Council, *An Assessment of the International Science and Technology Center* (Washington, D.C.: National Academy Press, 1996), 9.

5. Glenn E. Schweitzer, *Moscow DMZ: The Story of the International Effort to Convert Russian Weapons Science to Peaceful Purposes* (Armonk, N.Y.: M. E. Sharpe, 1996), 103.

6. Ibid.

7. For discussions of the plight of scientists during the early 1990s, see, for example, Irina Malakha, "Brain Drain in Russia: Scale, Directions, and Structural Features," Institute of International Economic and Political Studies, Moscow, unpublished manuscript,

1999; Elena Nekipelova, Leonid Gokhberg, and Levan Mindeli, *Emigration of Scientists: Problems and Real Estimations* (Moscow: Center for Science Research and Statistics, 1994; Irina Dezhina, "Adjustment of Russian Science and Brain Drain," Moscow Institute for the Economy in Transition, unpublished manuscript, 1997; and UNESCO, *Brain Drain in Russia*.

8. National Academy of Sciences, National Academy of Engineering, and Institute of Medicine, *Reorientation of the Research Capability of the Former Soviet Union: A Report to the Assistant to the President for Science and Technology* (Washington, D.C.: National Academy Press, 1992).

9. National Academy of Sciences, National Academy of Engineering, and Institute of Medicine, *Sustaining Excellence in Science and Engineering in the Former Soviet Union: Report of a Conference on February 9, 1993* (Washington, D.C.: National Academy Press, 1993).

10. National Research Council, *Assessment of the International Science*, 8.

11. Data provided by colleagues at the Higher School of Economics, Moscow, Apr. 2011.

12. Ibid, 9.

13. Dezhina, "Adjustment of Russian Science."

14. Ibid.

15. Nekipelova, Gokhberg, and Mindeli, *Emigration of Scientists*, 17.

16. Malakha, "Brain Drain in Russia."

17. Glenn E. Schweitzer, *Scientists, Engineers, and Track-Two Diplomacy: A Half Century of U.S.-Russian Inter-Academy Cooperation*, National Research Council (Washington, D.C.: National Academies Press, 2004), 67.

18. Valentin Tikhonov, *Russia's Nuclear and Missile Complex: The Human Factor and Proliferation* (Washington, D.C.: Carnegie Endowment for International Peace, 2001), 77–124.

19. Ibid, 110.

20. Ibid.

21. Deborah Yarsike Ball and Theodore P. Gerber, "Will Russian Scientists Go Rogue? A Survey on the Threat and the Impact of Western Assistance," PONARS Policy Memo 357, Lawrence Livermore National Laboratory, Nov. 2004.

22. Ibid.

23. Ibid.

24. Ibid.

25. ibid.

26. William J. Broad, "In Russia, Secret Labs Struggle to Survive," *New York Times*, Jan. 14, 1992, C1.

27. Dezhina, "Adjustment of Russian Science."

28. Unpublished results of survey in closed cities by leading Russian sociologists, Moscow, Oct. 1996.

29. James A. Baker, *The Politics of Diplomacy: Revolution, War, and Peace, 1989–1992* (New York: G. P. Putnam, 1995), 615.

30. Clery, "Publications and Expats Warn."

CHAPTER SIX. The Long Road to a Silicon Valley in Russia

1. "Proverbs and Quotations," http://www.proverbmountain.blogspot.com/ (accessed Nov. 10, 2011).

2. Arkady Dvorkovich, "Keynote Address: From Silicon Valley to Skolkovo," U.S.-Russia Business Council, 18th annual meeting, *Russia Business Watch* 18, no. 2 (Winter 2010–11): 10.

3. In October 2010 the U.S. National Science Foundation (NSF) began developing an alternative approach to the internationally accepted practice of collecting global data on funds spent on innovation. Historically the data had included the entire research and development budgets of the member countries of the Organization for Economic Cooperation and Development. NSF had become an advocate for defining innovation as limited to expenditures that led to *successful* introduction into the marketplace of new processes or products. The funds spent on activities that were not directly related to such implementation along with funds spent on unsuccessful implementation should not be included in comparing expenditures on innovation, according to NSF.

4. Vladimir Putin, address to Russian Federation's Federal Assembly, Apr. 18, 2002.

5. Glenn E. Schweitzer, *Swords into Market Shares: Technology, Economics, and Security in the New Russia* (Washington, D.C.: Joseph Henry Press, 2000), 33.

6. Ibid., xii–xiii.

7. Ibid.

8. Ministry of Education and Science of the Russian Federation, "National Innovation System and State Innovation Policy of the Russian Federation, Background Report for OECD Country Review of the Russian Innovation Policy" (Moscow: Ministry of Education and Science of the Russian Federation, 2009), 102.

9. Mikhail Ugryumov, "Modernization and Innovation, Russian Academy of Sciences," presentation at National Academy of Sciences, Washington, D.C., Oct. 7, 2010.

10. Ian Sample, "Nobel Prize for Physics Goes to Manchester University Scientists," *Guardian*, Oct. 5, 2010, 1.

11. Russian deputy minister of finance, statement at the meeting of the U.S.-Russia Business Council, San Francisco, Oct. 2010.

12. See, for example, Thomas D. Nastas, "The GoForward Plan for Scaling Up Innovation," Innovative Venture Inc., 2007, obtained from author, Apr. 2011.

13. For a positive assessment of developments see untitled report by Andrey V. Sharov, Ministry of Economic Development, Moscow, Feb. 12, 2011.

14. See, for example, Maria Douglass, "Towards an ISTC Valorization Strategy" (Moscow: ISTC, 2001); Maria Douglass and Peter Falyn, "Small Technology Spinoffs of the WMD Complex," *Johnson's Russia List*, no. 10 (July 12, 2002).

15. World Bank unpublished memorandum, provided by Moscow office of the World Bank in July 2003, 4–5.

16. Ibid., 32.

17. Leonid Gokhberg and Tatiana Kuznetosova, "Russian Federation," *UNESCO Science Report, 2010* (Paris: UNESCO, Nov. 10, 2010), 215.

18. Ibid.

19. Ibid.

20. This section is based in large measure on the following sources: Ministry of Education and Science, Federal Service for State Statistics, and Higher School of Economics, *Science and Technology: Innovation, Information Society, Pocket Data Book* (Moscow, 2010); and Irina Dezhina, "The Present State of Science, Technology, and Innovation Policy in Russia," presentation at American Association for the Advancement of Sciences, Washington, D.C., Aug. 15, 2010.

21. Dezhina, "Present State of Science."

22. Ibid.

23. "Victor Zvagelskiy, Leading Duma Member," Report by Elena Lokteva, Russia today.com, Sept. 23, 2010.

24. Margaret O'Mara, "Don't Try This at Home: You Can't Build a Silicon Valley Just Anywhere," *Foreign Policy*, Sept./Oct. 2010, 149.

25. "Skolkovo Foundation and MIT to Collaborate on Developing the Skolkovo Institute of Science and Technology," Oct. 26, 2011, http://web.mit.edu/newsoffice/2011/skolkovo-agreement-1026.html (accessed Nov. 15, 2011).

26. Olga Razumovskya, "Skolkovo Innovation Hub Is Braving the Waters," *Moscow Times*, June 16, 2011, 7.

27. Mikhail D. Usubyan, "Skolkovo Update," Conference on Doing Business in Russia sponsored by Eurasia Center, Washington, D.C., Dec. 5, 2011.

28. Ministry of Education and Science et al., *Science and Technology*.

29. Thomas L. Shillinglaw, "A U.S. Lawyer's Opinion of the Economic Impact of Technology and Corporate Law Developments in the USSR/Russia and China from the Mid-1970s to Today," *Demokratizatsiya, Journal of Post-Soviet Democratization* 17, no. 4 (Fall 2009): 309.

30. Leonid Gokhberg and Igor Agamirzyan, "From Stimulation of Innovation to Innovation-Based Growth," Conference on Transition towards Innovation-Based Growth, Higher School of Economics, Moscow, Apr. 8, 2011.

CHAPTER SEVEN. U.S.-Russia Bilateral Engagement Programs

1. Informational conversation at NASA Headquarters, June 2009.

2. See Glenn E. Schweitzer, *Experiments in Cooperation: Assessing U.S.-Russian Programs in Science and Technology* (New York: Twentieth Century Fund Press, 1997), appendix C.

3. 1993 National Defense Authorization Act, Public Law 102–484, Oct. 23, 1992, Title 14, Demilitarization of the Former Soviet Union.

4. 2011 Budget Estimate, Cooperative Threat Reduction Program, U.S. Department of Defense, Feb. 2010.

5. Conversation with Russian academician, Moscow, June 2007.

6. Report from DOE Office of U.S. Embassy, Moscow, Feb. 9, 2010.

7. 2009 Annual Report by DOE office of U.S. Embassy, Moscow, May 2010.

8. Ibid.

9. Glenn E. Schweitzer, *Swords into Market Shares: Technology, Economics, and Security in the New Russia* (Washington, D.C.: Joseph Henry Press, 2000), appendix D.

10. Government Accountability Office, "Nuclear Nonproliferation: DOE's Program to Assist Weapons Scientists in Russia and Other Countries Needs to Be Reassessed," GAO-08-189 (Washington, D.C.: GAO, Dec. 12, 2007.

11. For a discussion of the relationship between IPP and ISTC, see Sharon K. Weiner, *Our Own Worst Enemy? Institutional Interests and the Proliferation of Nuclear Weapons Expertise* (Cambridge, Mass.: MIT Press, 2011), 195–240.

12. This section is based on personal discussions with Russian officials and specialists from the early 1990s to the present and on observations in National Research Council, *Proliferation Concerns: Assessing U.S. Efforts to Help Contain Nuclear and Other Dangerous Materials and Technologies in the Former Soviet Union* (Washington, D.C.: National Academies Press, 1997).

13. See, for example, Gordon Prather, "Good-bye Gore-Chernomyrdin—and Good Riddance," WorldNetDaily.com, June 16, 2001, http://www.wnd.com/2001/06/9678/ (accessed Mar. 10, 2011).

14. Schweitzer, *Experiments in Cooperation*, 42–44. Interviews with key officials at more than a dozen U.S. departments and agencies indicated overwhelming support for the commission. Also, see Matthew Rojansky, *Indispensable Institutions: The Obama-Medvedev Commission and Five Decades of U.S.-Russia Dialogue*, report pre-

pared for Carnegie Endowment for International Peace, Washington, D.C., 2010, 15–23, 9–41.

15. Ibid.

16. Ibid.

17. Ibid.

18. Ibid.

19. The White House, "U.S.-Russia Bilateral Presidential Commission," Fact Sheet, July 6, 2009. See also U.S. Department of State, http://www.state.gov/p/eur/ci/rs/us russiabilat/index.htm (accessed Mar. 10, 2011).

20. National Research Council, *Partners on the Frontier: U.S.-Russian Cooperation in Science and Technology* (Washington, D.C.: National Academy Press, 1998), 15.

21. Ibid., 16.

22. Maija M. Kukla, "Prospective U.S.-Russia Collaboration in Science and Technology," informal report of U.S. embassy science fellow provided by the National Science Foundation, Moscow-Arlington, Va., 2010.

CHAPTER EIGHT. The Nuclear File

1. See an important commentary in Gregory L. Schulte, "Stopping Proliferation before It Starts," *Foreign Affairs*, July/Aug. 2010, 85–95.

2. An excellent catalogue of steps that need to be taken as soon as possible to help ensure that nuclear weapons are not ever used again is contained in Gareth Evans and Yoriko Kawaguchi, *Eliminating Nuclear Threats: A Practical Agenda for Global Policymakers*, Report of the International Commission on Nuclear Non-proliferation and Disarmament (Canberra/Tokyo, Nov. 2009).

3. Kofi Annan as quoted in Matthew Bunn, "Securing the Bomb 2010," Project on Managing the Atom, Harvard University, Apr. 2010, 15.

4. Bunn, "Securing the Bomb 2010," 95.

5. "A Terrorist's To-Do List," *Issues in Science and Technology*, Winter 2010, 62.

6. For a popularized account of the program see "Opening the Closed Cities of the Soviet Union," Carnegie Corporation of New York, Winter 2010. While the report provides a generally accurate overview of the program, the role of NGOs was much less significant than indicated. Also, the community development emphasis of the program is discussed in Sharon K. Wiener, *Our Own Worst Enemy? Institutional Interests and the Proliferation of Nuclear Weapons Expertise* (Cambridge, Mass.: MIT Press, 2011), 241–90. This analysis points out flaws in the approach that was attempted.

7. Glenn E. Schweitzer, *Swords into Market Shares: Technology, Economics, and Security in the New Russia* (Washington, D.C.: Joseph Henry Press, 2000), 219.

8. "The Day after Tomorrow: ZATO's Status Will Affect Rosatom's New Strategy," information provided by colleagues at Sarov, Russia, Apr. 2, 2010.

9. *Rossiyskaya Gazeta* news service, reported in the *Washington Post*, Special Supplement on the Russian Economy, p. H2, Mar. 24, 2010.

10. W. Gudowski and L. V. Tocheny, "The 15-Year Experience in the Implementation of International Collaboration for Nuclear Science and Engineering," unpublished manuscript, ISTC, Moscow, 2010.

11. Information provided in a variety of internal ISTC documents, obtained June 2010.

12. Information provided by ISTC and supplemented with a visit to Chernobyl, Oct. 2010.

13. Discussion with officials of Gosatomnadzor, Yekaterinburg, June 2003.

14. Letter from Rolf Heuer to Adriaan Van Der Meer, May 20, 2010, ISTC, Moscow.

15. *Memorandum of Understanding between the International Science and Technology Center and the International Atomic Energy Agency*, Vienna, June 29, 2000.

16. "ISTC Targeted Initiative on 'Technical Support for an IAEA Advanced Safeguard and Verification Development Program,'" ISTC Report to Governing Board, July 13–14, 2010, Moscow.

CHAPTER NINE. The Biosecurity File

1. U.S. Army Chemical School, "Potential Military Chemical/Biological Agents and Compounds," Department of Defense, Jan. 2005, i–3.

2. National Research Council, *Biological Science and Biotechnology in Russia* (Washington, D.C.: National Academies Press, 2006), 73.

3. Information provided by the ISTC Secretariat, Moscow, Dec. 2010.

4. ibid.

5. National Academy of Sciences, *Controlling Dangerous Pathogens: A Blueprint for U.S.-Russian Cooperation* (Washington, D.C.: National Academy Press, 1997, 5.

6. Ibid.

7. L. Michael Weaver, "Biosafety and Biosecurity Activities of the International Science and Technology Center in the Republics of the Former Soviet Union: Accomplishments, Challenges, and Prospects," *Applied Biosafety* 15, no. 2 (2010).

8. Information provided by the ISTC Secretariat, Moscow, Jan. 2011.

9. Ibid.

10. Author interview at the Institute of Highly Pure Biopreparations, St. Petersburg, Russia, 2007.

11. Information provided by the ISTC Secretariat, Moscow, Jan. 2011.

12. Weaver, "Biosafety and Biosecurity Activities," 30.

13. National Research Council, *The Biological Threat Reduction Program of the Department of Defense* (Washington, D.C.: National Academies Press, 2007), 18.

14. National Research Council, *Biological Science and Biotechnology in Russia: Controlling Diseases and Enhancing Security* (Washington, D.C.: National Academies Press, 2004), 26.

CHAPTER TEN. The Aerospace File

1. David E. Hoffman, *The Dead Hand: The Untold Story of the Cold War Arms Race and Its Dangerous Legacy* (New York: Doubleday, 2009), 409.

2. Wisconsin Project on Nuclear Arms Control, "The Risk Report," University of Wisconsin, Jan.–Feb. 1995, 8–9.

3. T. Ryzhova and S. Frolov, eds., *Aerospace Research: ISTC-Funded Projects, 1994–2011*, vol. 2, *Space* (Moscow: ISTC, 2011), 6.

4. Glenn E. Schweitzer, *Moscow DMZ: The Story of the International Effort to Convert Russian Weapons Science into Peaceful Purposes* (Armonk, N.Y.: M. E. Sharpe, 1996), 125.

5. Waclaw Gudowski, Tatiana Ryzhova, and Sergey Frolov, eds., *Aerospace Research: ISTC-Funded Projects, 1994–2009*, vol. 1, *Aeronautics*, ISTC (Moscow: Torus Press, 2009), 7.

6. ISTC, *Aeronautics*, 4.

7. Unpublished drafts of ISTC reports, obtained Jan. 2011.

8. Informal correspondence with ISTC Secretariat, Feb., 2011.

9. Valentin Tikhonov, *Russia's Nuclear and Missile Complex: The Human Factor in Proliferation* (Washington, D.C.: Carnegie Endowment for International Peace, 2001), 122.

10. Ibid.

11. Correspondence with ISTC Secretariat, Jan. 2011.

12. Conference agenda provided by ISTC Secretariat, Jan. 2011.

13. Based in part on comments by Russian coordinator of contact group, June 2010.

14. ISTC Project Evaluation Form, project no. 1962, Nov. 1, 2002.

15. Ryzhova and Frolov, *Aerospace Research,* 2:8.

16. Iran Watch: Tracking Iran's Mass Destruction Weapon Capabilities, http://www.iranwatch.org/suppliers/records/niigrafit.html (accessed June 27, 2011).

CHAPTER ELEVEN. Measuring Success

1. Work was based on an operational guide prepared by ISTC Secretariat, Dec. 2011.

2. Partnership for a Secure America, "WMD Report Card, Evaluating U.S. Policies

to Prevent Nuclear, Chemical, and Biological Terrorism since 2005," Washington, D.C., 2008.

3. Richard G. Lugar website, "The Nunn-Lugar Scorecard," http://Lugar.senate.gov/nunnlugar/scorecard.html (accessed Oct. 12, 2010).

4. Discussion with officials of the Defense Threat Reduction Agency, Ft. Belvoir, Va., Oct. 2009.

5. Department of Defense, "Report on Metrics for the Cooperative Threat Reduction Program," Report to Congress (Armed Services Committees), Sept. 2010.

6. National Academy of Sciences, *Improving Metrics for the Department of Defense Cooperative Threat Reduction Program* (Washington, D.C.: National Academies Press, 2012), 1.

7. Glenn E. Schweitzer, *Moscow DMZ: The Story of the International Effort to Convert Russian Weapons Science to Peaceful Purposes* (Armonk, N.Y.: M. E. Sharpe, 1996), 193–94.

8. Jean-Pierre Contzen, EU member of the ISTC Scientific Advisory Committee, Oct. 2002, as quoted in IC2 Institute (University of Texas at Austin and International Collaborators from the EU, Japan, and Korea), *ISTC 2012: Toward Sustainable Global Security* (Moscow: ISTC, Oct. 2002), 40.

9. IC2 Institute, *ISTC 2012*. See entire report.

10. Ibid., 8.

11. See ISTC Secretariat, "A New Organization" (GOV-XXIX-011) and "Reorganizing the ISTC Secretariat and Implementing Change" (Moscow: ISTC, Jan. 2003.

12. IC2 Institute, *ISTC 2012*, 16.

13. Ibid., 18.

14. Ibid., 64, 79, 87.

15. Information provided by ISTC Secretariat, Dec. 2011.

CHAPTER TWELVE. Replicating ISTC Experiences While Avoiding Pitfalls

1. Yevgeny Avrorin, "DOE Moscow Office Weekly Report," no. 35," Oct. 11–15, 2010, 17.

2. Glenn E. Schweitzer, *Moscow DMZ: The Story of the International Effort to Convert Russian Weapons Science to Peaceful Purposes* (Armonk, N.Y.: M. E. Sharpe, 1996), 195–97.

3. These lessons learned are based in part on a presentation at the ISTC to invited guests in May 2010 by Adriaan Van Der Meer, executive director of the ISTC. They are also mentioned in various ISTC documents.

4. Science and Technology Center in Ukraine, *15 Year Anniversary*, (Kiev: STCU, 2010), 2, 8, 22.

5. Science and Technology Center in Ukraine, *Annual Report, 2009*, (Kiev: STCU, 2010), 25, 27, 31.

6. Shin Seok-ho, Kim Hyun-soo, and Lee Ki-hong, *Dong-a-Ilbo*, Seoul, Korea, Feb. 1, 2008, 2.

7. Global Partnership Working Group, "Recommendations for a Coordinated Approach in the Field of Global Weapons of Mass Destruction, Knowledge Proliferation, and Scientist Engagement," G8 Meeting, L'Aquila, Italy, 2009.

CHAPTER THIRTEEN. The Way Forward

1. Yevgeny Avrorin, "DOE Moscow Office Weekly Report," no. 35, Oct. 11–15, 2010, 17.

2. Informal document provided by ISTC Secretariat, Oct. 2007.

3. Jun Sugimoto, letter to academician Yuri Osipov, president of the Russian Academy of Sciences, May 2010.

4. Majia M. Kukla, "Prospective U.S.-Russia Collaboration in Science and Technology," U.S. Embassy Science Fellow, Moscow and National Science Foundation, 2010.

Epilogue

1. "Today in Science History," quotations from Anton Pavlovich Chekhov, http://www.todayinsci.com/C/Chekov_Anton/ChekovAnton-Quotations.htm (accessed Dec. 2011).

2. Glenn E. Schweitzer, *Moscow DMZ: The Story of the International Effort to Convert Russian Weapons Science to Peaceful Purposes* (Armonk, N.Y.: M. E. Sharpe, 1996), 212.

INDEX